MIDDLESBROUGH FOOTBALL CLUB
THE OFFICIAL YEARBOOK 2006/07

Editorial
Dave Allan, Graham Bell, Claire Foy

Sidan Press Team
Simon Rosen, Julian Hill-Wood, Marc Fiszman, Mark Peters, Karim Biria, Rob Cubbon,
Anette Lundebye, Marina Kravchenko, Gareth Peters, Janet Callcott, Trevor Scimes, John Fitzroy,
Jenny Middlemarch, Anders Rasmussen, Lim Wai-Lee, Emma Turner, Charles Grove, Tim Ryman

Photography
Getty Images

Copyright © 2006 Middlesbrough Football Club

Sidan Press, 63-64 Margaret St, London W1W 8SW
Tel: 020 7580 0200
Email: info@sidanpress.com

sidanpress.com

Copyright © 2006 Sidan Press Ltd

Club Directory

How to contact MFC

By telephone...
Main number (all departments): 0870 421 1986
MFC Corporate: 01642 757656
MFC Marketing: 01642 757658
Community Liaison: 01642 757655
Football in the Community: 01642 873804/5
Middlesbrough Football Community Centre:
01642 282128
Rockliffe Park Training HQ: 01325 722222

By email...
Customer service and complaints:
media.dept@mfc.co.uk
Media & Communications Department:
media.dept@mfc.co.uk
General enquiries: enquiries@mfc.co.uk
Disability: disability@mfc.co.uk
Conferencing & events: events@mfc.co.uk

By fax...
Main fax: 01642 757690
Ticket office fax: 01642 757693
Conferencing & events: 01642 757692

Boro Who's Who

Chairman
Steve Gibson
Chief Executive
Keith Lamb
Manager
Gareth Southgate

Department heads
Club Secretary: Karen Nelson
Accounts: Brian Brown
Administration: Yvonne Ferguson
Catering: Howard Porteous
Commercial: Graham Fordy
Finance: Alan Bage
Marketing: Judith Boal
Media & Communications: Dave Allan
Stadium Operations & Safety: Terry Tasker
Ticket Office: Jane Woods
Middlesbrough Football Community Project:
George Cooke

Supporters Clubs

Middlesbrough Official Supporters Club
Chairperson: Sue Gardener. Tel 01642 899412.
Email: susanm.gardener@ntlworld.com
Secretary: Geoff Richardson. Tel. 01642 801289.
Email: geoffrey.richardson1@ntlworld.com

Middlesbrough Supporters South
To join, send cheque for £15 (payable to MSS) to
Claire Smith, 121 Belgrave Road, Walthamstow,
London, E17 8QF. Email: missussmith@clara.co.uk

Yarm Reds
Andy Wilson. Tel. 07961 936 959. Website:
www.yarmreds.co.uk.

Derbyshire Reds
Secretary: Duncan Haywood. Tel. 01246 811244.
Email: janeduncan.haywood@btinternet.com

Sedgefield Supporters Club
Secretary: David Pratt. Tel. 07811 875105.

Middlesbrough Disabled Supporters Association
Chairman: Paddy Cronesberry. Tel. 01642 641620.

Middlesbrough FC
Riverside Stadium
Middlesbrough TS3 6RS

Website: **www.mfc.co.uk**

Contents

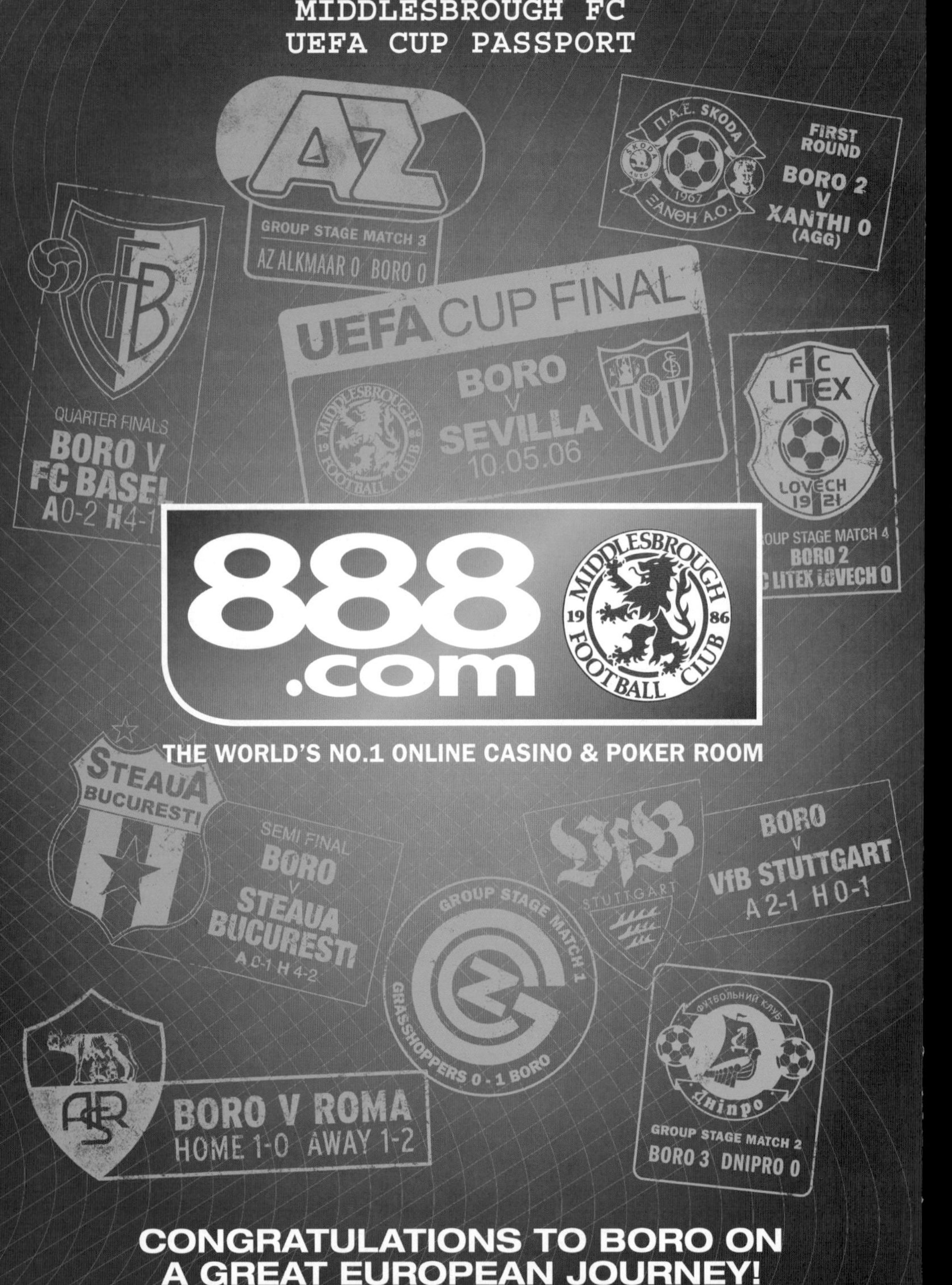

MIDDLESBROUGH FC
UEFA CUP PASSPORT

GROUP STAGE MATCH 3
AZ ALKMAAR 0 BORO 0

FIRST ROUND
BORO 2
V
XANTHI 0
(AGG)

UEFA CUP FINAL
BORO
V
SEVILLA
10.05.06

QUARTER FINALS
BORO V
FC BASEL
A 0-2 H 4-1

FC LITEX
LOVECH 19 21

GROUP STAGE MATCH 4
BORO 2
FC LITEK LOVECH 0

888.com
MIDDLESBROUGH FOOTBALL CLUB 1986

THE WORLD'S NO.1 ONLINE CASINO & POKER ROOM

STEAUA BUCURESTI

SEMI FINAL
BORO
V
STEAUA
BUCURESTI
A 0-1 H 4-2.

VfB STUTTGART

BORO
V
VfB STUTTGART
A 2-1 H 0-1

GROUP STAGE MATCH 1
GRASSHOPPERS 0 - 1 BORO

BORO V ROMA
HOME 1-0 AWAY 1-2

GROUP STAGE MATCH 2
BORO 3 DNIPRO 0

CONGRATULATIONS TO BORO ON
A GREAT EUROPEAN JOURNEY!

Ticket to the Limit

Are you making full use of your Boro season ticket? Here's exactly how you can utilise your Red or White Book during the 2006-07 season…

- Priority when purchasing tickets for cup games and away fixtures when demand is high and availability restricted.

- A guaranteed ticket price of just £5 for under-18s who attend any home cup-ties up to the quarter-final stage during 2006-07, subject to tickets being purchased by deadline. See mfc.co.uk and the local media for deadline details.

- Entry into a monthly draw to win superb Boro prizes, including matchday hospitality in the Riverside's executive suites. Details of monthly winners are announced at the end of each month on mfc.co.uk, in the matchday programme Redsquare, and on home matchdays on the electronic messageboard, concourse TV's and via PA announcements.

- 20% discount on our usual prices for Sunday lunch, celebration parties and wedding receptions. Call MFC Conferencing on 0870 421 1986 for further details.

- An opportunity to take advantage of exclusive price promotions at our MFC Retail stores – with up to 50% off most lines.

- Priority in purchasing the new Boro shirt, on production of appropriate voucher at the time of purchase.

- Free admission to Boro's second team games at the Riverside and Billingham Synthonia's Central Avenue ground.

- Guided tours of the Riverside for just £1 when you bring along an adult non-season ticket holder. Call 0870 421 1986 for further details.

- £7 discount on annual subscription to Redsquare.

- Exclusive Pontins holiday offers. Call 0870 604 5641 for further details.

- Plus, of course, the fantastic Boro Yearbook that you're reading right now!

Gareth Southgate

A message from Boro's new boss

This is the start of a new era for Middlesbrough FC. Like the supporters, I am extremely proud of all that Boro have achieved in recent years but my focus now has to be on the future and how we, as a club, can build on our hard work and continue to progress.

I am not going to make any unrealistic promises so early in my managerial career, but I can tell you that I am aware of the expectations Boro fans have and am every bit as ambitious as they are for success.

I am excited and enthusiastic about the challenge I am embarking on and I want Boro to play in a manner that reflects that. While I'm certainly not going to guarantee all-out attack at the expense of a sound defensive base, I am very conscious of the need to entertain the fans.

I am fully aware of what a fantastic opportunity this is for me so accepting the job was not a decision I had to consider for too long when Steve Gibson offered me the post. I have thoroughly enjoyed my playing career but opportunities like the one I now have do not come along too often in life.

My heart is with Middlesbrough and I would love nothing more than to bring success to this football club. I have already had five fantastic years here and I want the next five to be even better.

Our Carling Cup victory and two memorable years in Europe were wonderful experiences. Now the challenge is to build on that. But, as exciting as last season's cup runs were, my main priority will be to improve our league standing as our 14th place finish was not good enough.

We need to improve on that and I believe we can do that. The excellent set-up and structure that was already in place before my appointment gives us the best possible chance.

It has been a great bonus to me that I have been able to retain the excellent coaching team that has achieved so much in recent years, while the club's superb Academy and its production line of young players is clearly something most managers can only dream of.

The challenge now is for those young players who made such a good impact last season to go on to the next stage. They have dipped their toes in the water by experiencing first team football and doing very well, but now is not the time to think they have made it.

The coaching team is set up to ensure they get every possible help to enable them to fulfil their potential but ultimately it is up to them to decide just how far they want to go. Their attitude and conviction will determine whether they go on from here or fall by the way side.

I would ask all Boro fans for their backing this season. I want to make a positive start to my career as a manager and the supporters will be massively important to us. I need them with me from the start.

The following we had last year was a huge part in the cup runs we enjoyed. If we can make our home atmosphere like that week in and week out it could make the Riverside a place where opposition teams fear to come.

How to Read the Stats

This year's review is better than ever, packed with the sort of in-depth stats which really get you close to the action. If you'd like to know why a particular match turned out the way it did, how a player's form varied over the course of the season, or how Boro have fared against their biggest rivals, you'll find all the info inside.

To make sure you're getting the most out of the stats, we're including this section to highlight the information presented by some of the charts and tables.

Colours

Boro vs Opposition
There are lots of comparisons between Boro and our opponents throughout the book. Boro stats are shown in red; opponents are shown in grey:

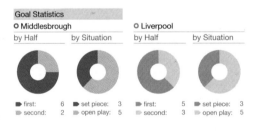

Goal Statistics

○ Middlesbrough — by Half — by Situation
○ Liverpool — by Half — by Situation

first:	6	set piece:	3
second:	2	open play:	5

first:	5	set piece:	3
second:	3	open play:	5

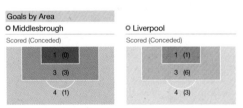

Goals by Area

○ Middlesbrough — Scored (Conceded)

1 (0)
3 (3)
4 (1)

○ Liverpool — Scored (Conceded)

1 (1)
3 (6)
4 (3)

Figure 1: Boro stats are in red; opposition stats are grey.

WDL, Scored, Conceded
When reviewing match results, wins, draws and losses are indicated by green, grey and orange blocks, respectively. For goals, green blocks indicate goals scored; orange blocks show goals conceded:

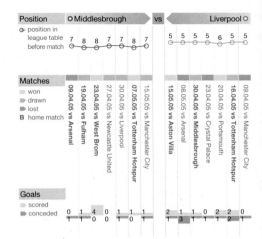

Position	○ Middlesbrough		vs		Liverpool ○

Figure 2: Wins, draws, losses and goals are clearly colour-coded.

Match Reports

The Match Report section contains reports, quotes, facts and stats from every Boro match of the 2005/06 season.

Stats Order (Home and Away)
The order of the stats varies depending on whether a match was home or away: for home matches, Boro stats are shown on the left, for away matches they're on the right:

Premiership Totals	○ Boro	Liverpool ○
Premiership Appearances	2,383	1,069
Team Appearances	1,003	889
Goals Scored	317	97
Assists	236	97
Clean Sheets (goalkeepers)	69	0
Yellow Cards	278	109
Red Cards	19	8
Full Internationals	12	11

Figure 3: For home matches, Boro stats appear on the left.

Premiership Totals	○ Tottenham	Boro ○
Premiership Appearances	710	2,013
Team Appearances	363	862
Goals Scored	113	275
Assists	68	221
Clean Sheets (goalkeepers)	31	70
Yellow Cards	53	246
Red Cards	1	15
Full Internationals	11	11

Figure 4: For away matches, Boro stats appear on the right.

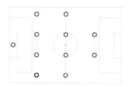

Figure 6: Major positions are shown in dark red; minor positions are shown in light red.

Form Coming into Fixture

Stats are from the previous seven league games. For the first few matches, these stats include games from the end of the previous season.

Team Statistics

Stats are for starters and playing subs. The "Premiership Totals" chart measures performance within the Premiership (with the exception of "Full Internationals").

Premiership Totals	○ Boro	Liverpool ○
Premiership Appearances	2,383	1,069
Team Appearances	1,003	889
Goals Scored	317	97
Assists	236	97
Clean Sheets (goalkeepers)	69	0
Yellow Cards	278	109
Red Cards	19	8
Full Internationals	12	11

Age/Height

Middlesbrough Age	Liverpool Age
▶ 29 yrs, 1 mo	▶ 26 yrs

Middlesbrough Height	Liverpool Height
▶ 6'	▶ 6'

Figure 5: Team statistics are for starters and playing subs.

Player Profiles

The Player Profile section provides season reviews and comprehensive stats for Boro's players. The section is organised by position, starting with goalkeepers.

Pitch Diagram

The diagram shows all positions the player played during 2005/06. The main position is denoted by a dark red circle; alternative positions are denoted by light red circles:

Player Performance

All stats show league performance, with the exception of the "Cup Games" table. The "League Performance" chart provides an excellent overview of the player's performance over the course of the season. At a glance, you can see when and how much he played, and how he contributed to the team's overall performance at different stages of the season. Note that outfield players receive a "clean sheet" when they played 75 or more minutes in a game where Boro didn't concede a goal.

Career History

Due to the difficulties involved in obtaining reliable stats for international clubs, the "Clubs" table is incomplete for players who have played for non-English clubs. The names of all clubs have been included for the reader's interest, but international stats have been left blank.

The Opposition

The Opposition section shows how Boro sizes up against the other 19 teams in the Premiership.

Points / Position

The points / position chart is a snapshot of the last 10 years' league performance of Boro and the opponent. For any season when the two teams met in the league, the results of their clashes are shown at the bottom of the chart.

Premiership Head-to-Head

Stats are only for the two teams' meetings in the Premiership.

HODGE
IS AT
BUTLIN'S
WATCHING
THE BILL

0-0

Middlesbrough o
Liverpool o

▶ Ugo Ehiogu is a picture of concentration

Event Line	
28 O ▪ Alonso	
33 O ▪ Parlour	
42 O ▪ Garcia	
Half time 0-0	
51 O ▪ Sissoko	
57 O ⇄ Cisse > Garcia	
65 O ⇄ Nemeth > Mendieta	
67 O ⇄ Baros > Morientes	
67 O ⇄ Viduka > Hasselbaink	
74 O ▪ Ehiogu	
Foul	
75 O ⇄ Bates > Yakubu	
84 O Queudrue	
Full time 0-0	

The opening day of the season saw the European Champions make the trip to the Riverside, where the spoils were shared after Liverpool dominated following Ugo Ehiogu's late dismissal.

Bolo Zenden, who had quit Boro for Anfield during the summer, made his return to the Riverside to a less than welcoming reception.

Steven Gerrard wasted a chance halfway through the first half, blasting his shot over the bar. Just before the break, good build up play between Queudrue and Mendieta led to a 25-yard drive from George Boateng. His powerful shot, however, was off target and so both teams went into the interval on even terms.

The game took a potentially decisive turn in the 73rd minute when a long ball found Ehiogu flat-footed and beaten for pace by Gerrard. As the Liverpool captain advanced to the edge of the box, Ehiogu's last-ditch tackle earned the Boro defender a red card.

Liverpool came close to snatching a late winner but England star Gerrard could only direct a back post header across the face of the goal and wide.

Fans Player of the Match

George Boateng

Quote

❝ Steve McClaren

It was a great point for us. It's always important to get something from the first game of the season.

Premiership Milestone

▶ Debut

Yakubu made his first Premiership appearance in the colours of Middlesbrough.

Venue: Riverside Stadium
Attendance: 31,908
Capacity: 35,100
Occupancy: 91%

Referee: M.R.Halsey - 05/06
Matches: 1
Yellow Cards: 0
Red Cards: 0

Middlesbrough
Liverpool

Form Coming into Fixture

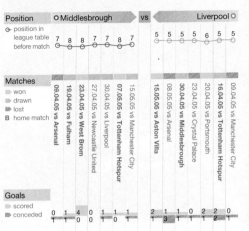

Position

o- position in league table before match

Middlesbrough	vs	Liverpool
7 8 8 7 7 8 7		5 5 5 5 6 5 5

Matches

- won
- drawn
- lost
- B home match

Middlesbrough:
09.04.05 vs Arsenal
19.04.05 vs Fulham
23.04.05 vs West Brom
27.04.05 vs Newcastle United
30.04.05 vs Liverpool
07.05.05 vs Tottenham Hotspur
15.05.05 vs Manchester City

Liverpool:
15.05.05 vs Aston Villa
08.05.05 vs Arsenal
30.04.05 vs Middlesbrough
23.04.05 vs Crystal Palace
20.04.05 vs Portsmouth
16.04.05 vs Tottenham Hotspur
09.04.05 vs Manchester City

Goals

scored	0	1	4	0	1	1	1	2	1	1	0	2	2	0
conceded	1	1	0	0	0	1	0	1	3	1	1	1	2	1

Goal Statistics

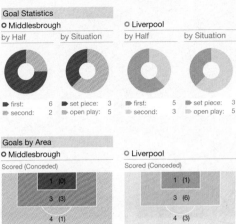

Middlesbrough
by Half / by Situation

- first: 6
- second: 2
- set piece: 3
- open play: 5

Liverpool
by Half / by Situation

- first: 5
- second: 3
- set piece: 3
- open play: 5

Goals by Area

Middlesbrough — Scored (Conceded)

1 (0)
3 (3)
4 (1)

Liverpool — Scored (Conceded)

1 (1)
3 (6)
4 (3)

Team Statistics

Starting Line-Ups

Middlesbrough

Schwarzer
Queudrue, Downing
Southgate, Boateng
Yakubu / Bates
Ehiogu, Parlour / Hasselbaink / Viduka
Reiziger, Mendieta / Nemeth
Morientes / Baros

Liverpool

Garcia / Cisse, Finnan
Sissoko
Carragher
Gerrard
Reina
Hyypia
Alonso
Zenden, Warnock

Middlesbrough: 4/4/2
Unused Sub: Jones, Doriva

Liverpool: 4/5/1
Unused Sub: Carson, Whitbread, Riise

Premiership Totals

	Boro	Liverpool
Premiership Appearances	2,383	1,069
Team Appearances	1,003	889
Goals Scored	317	97
Assists	236	97
Clean Sheets (goalkeepers)	69	0
Yellow Cards	278	109
Red Cards	19	8
Full Internationals	12	11

Age/Height

Middlesbrough Age: **29 yrs, 1 mo**
Liverpool Age: **26 yrs**

Middlesbrough Height: **6'**
Liverpool Height: **6'**

Match Statistics

League Table after Fixture

	Played	Won	Drawn	Lost	For	Against	Pts
9 Liverpool	1	0	1	0	0	0	1
10 Man City	1	0	1	0	0	0	1
11 Middlesbrough	1	0	1	0	0	0	1
12 West Brom	1	0	1	0	0	0	1
13 Arsenal	0	0	0	0	0	0	0
14 Chelsea	0	0	0	0	0	0	0
15 Newcastle	0	0	0	0	0	0	0
16 Wigan	0	0	0	0	0	0	0
17 Blackburn	1	0	0	1	1	3	0

Statistics

	Boro	Liverpool
Goals	0	0
Shots on Target	2	7
Shots off Target	2	9
Hit Woodwork	0	0
Possession %	42	58
Corners	5	0
Offsides	3	1
Fouls	17	11
Disciplinary Points	20	12

2-0

Tottenham Hotspur ○
Middlesbrough ○

▶ Gareth Southgate demonstrates his aerial prowess

Event Line

Half time 0-0

46 ○ ⇄	Morrison > Mendieta	
46 ○ ⇄	Viduka > Yakubu	
49 ○ ⊕	Defoe / RF / OP / OA	
	Assist: Tainio	
50 ○ ▢	Defoe	
52 ○ ▢	Tainio	
67 ○ ▢	Davids	
68 ○ ▢	Hasselbaink	
73 ○ ⇄	Doriva > Bates	
75 ○ ⊕	Mido / LF / OP / OA	
	Assist: Defoe	
76 ○ ⇄	Keane > Defoe	

Full time 2-0

Despite an encouraging display, Boro were still looking for their first goal of the season as they lost 2-0 to Spurs in the Premier League campaign's first away game.

The home team set a ferocious pace to the match but Boro soaked up the pressure well early on and managed to start attacks of their own. Stewart Downing outpaced Teemu Tainio to create problems down the left. New boy Yakubu also threatened, powering his way past two defenders before hitting a shot from the edge of the box, which was deflected for a corner.

Spurs took the lead three minutes in to the second half. Jermain Defoe was given time and space to run at the Boro defence before hitting a 22-yard shot that seemed to swerve in flight, beating Schwarzer at his left hand post.

As Boro chased the game and went to three at the back, Spurs attacked on the break to double their lead, Mido's low, weak shot rolling under Schwarzer.

Boro were left even more frustrated as Paul Robinson pulled off another stunning one-handed save four minutes from time, turning away a 22-yard Hasselbaink free kick.

Fans' Player of the Match

Mark Viduka

Quote

❝ **Steve McClaren**

It is hard to take a defeat like that. We missed some glorious chances and on another day we would have come away with a victory.

Venue:	White Hart Lane	Referee:	M.Atkinson - 05/06		Tottenham Hotspur
Attendance:	35,844	Matches:	1		Middlesbrough
Capacity:	36,247	Yellow Cards:	3		
Occupancy:	99%	Red Cards:	0		

Form Coming into Fixture

Goal Statistics

Tottenham Hotspur

by Half / by Situation

- first: 5
- second: 5
- set piece: 4
- open play: 5
- own goals: 1

Middlesbrough

by Half / by Situation

- first: 6
- second: 2
- set piece: 3
- open play: 5

Goals by Area

Tottenham Hotspur — Scored (Conceded)

- 2 (0)
- 6 (3)
- 2 (3)

Middlesbrough — Scored (Conceded)

- 1 (0)
- 3 (2)
- 4 (1)

Team Statistics

Starting Line-Ups

Tottenham Hotspur: 4/4/2
Middlesbrough: 4/4/2

Unused Sub: Cerny, Naybet, Mendes, Lennon

Unused Sub: Jones, Wheater

Premiership Totals	Tottenham	Boro
Premiership Appearances	710	2,013
Team Appearances	363	862
Goals Scored	113	275
Assists	68	221
Clean Sheets (goalkeepers)	31	70
Yellow Cards	53	246
Red Cards	1	15
Full Internationals	11	11

Age/Height

	Tottenham Hotspur	Middlesbrough
Age	25 yrs, 3 mo	28 yrs, 6 mo
Height	5'11"	5'11"

Match Statistics

League Table after Fixture

		Played	Won	Drawn	Lost	For	Against	Pts
↑ 1	Tottenham	2	2	0	0	4	0	6
...		...	...	...	...	...	...	...
↓ 14	Fulham	2	0	1	1	1	2	1
↓ 15	Middlesbrough	2	0	1	1	0	2	1
↑ 16	Newcastle	2	0	1	1	0	2	1
↑ 17	Everton	1	0	0	1	0	2	0
↓ 18	Wigan	2	0	0	2	0	2	0
↑ 19	Portsmouth	2	0	0	2	1	4	0
↓ 20	Sunderland	2	0	0	2	1	4	0

Statistics	Tottenham	Boro
Goals	2	0
Shots on Target	8	3
Shots off Target	10	9
Hit Woodwork	0	0
Possession %	60	40
Corners	5	6
Offsides	5	2
Fouls	16	10
Disciplinary Points	12	4

0-3

Birmingham City ○
Middlesbrough ○

▶ Franck Queudrue celebrates making sure of the points

Event Line

14 ○ ⊕	Viduka / LF / OP / IA
	Assist: Morrison
28 ○ ▯	Boateng
45 ○ ⊕	Viduka / RF / OP / IA
Half time 0-2	
46 ○ ⇄	Izzet > Clemence
46 ○ ⇄	Forssell > Tebily
68 ○ ⇄	Gray > Pandiani
71 ○ ⊕	Queudrue / LF / IFK / 6Y
	Assist: Downing
74 ○ ⇄	Maccarone > Hasselbaink
78 ○ ⇄	Job > Viduka
89 ○ ⇄	Bates > Morrison
Full time 0-3	

Mark Viduka scored one of the goals of the season and managed an equally unlikely miss as Boro recorded a hugely impressive first league win of the new campaign.

He struck Boro's first goal of the season – and his first for nine months – with 14 minutes gone. Viduka blasted home James Morrison's right-wing cross to put his side ahead.

Viduka was denied a second five minutes later when he was tackled by Matthew Upson with the goal at his mercy.

But Viduka made it count with a stunning strike in the final few minutes of the half. Receiving the ball via Franck Queudrue's throw-in on the edge of Birmingham's box, he left opposition defenders for dead with a neat turn before hitting a swerving half-volley past Maik Taylor.

The second half saw City come out with more purpose but Boro always looked the more likely to score. Queudrue hit Boro's third of the night. A 71st minute free-kick from Stewart Downing was completely misjudged by the City defence, allowing the French defender to slide in at the back post.

Fans' Player of the Match

Mark Viduka

Quote

🔘 **Steve McClaren**

When Mark Viduka's fit there is nobody better in the Premiership at what he does and the two finishes were superb.

Venue:	St Andrew's	Referee:	P.Dowd - 05/06		Birmingham City
Attendance:	27,998	Matches:	3		Middlesbrough
Capacity:	30,016	Yellow Cards:	11		
Occupancy:	93%	Red Cards:	0		

Form Coming into Fixture

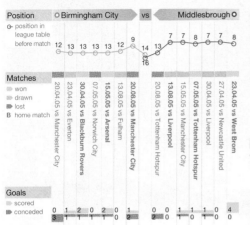

Position
- position in league table before match

Matches
- won
- drawn
- lost
- B home match

Birmingham City matches: 20.04.05 vs Manchester City, 23.04.05 vs Everton, 30.04.05 vs Blackburn Rovers, 07.05.05 vs Norwich City, 15.05.05 vs Arsenal, 13.08.05 vs Fulham, 20.08.05 vs Manchester City

Middlesbrough matches: 20.08.05 vs Tottenham Hotspur, 13.08.05 vs Liverpool, 15.05.05 vs Manchester City, 07.05.05 vs Tottenham Hotspur, 30.04.05 vs Liverpool, 27.04.05 vs Newcastle United, 23.04.05 vs West Brom

Goals
- scored
- conceded

Birmingham City: scored 0 1 2 0 2 0 1 / conceded 3 1 1 1 0 2
Middlesbrough: scored 0 0 1 1 1 0 4 / conceded 2 0 0 0 0

Goal Statistics

○ Birmingham City

by Half		by Situation	
first:	2	set piece:	1
second:	4	open play:	5

○ Middlesbrough

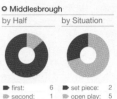

by Half		by Situation	
first:	6	set piece:	2
second:	1	open play:	5

Goals by Area

○ Birmingham City

Scored (Conceded)

0 (3)
4 (6)
2 (0)

○ Middlesbrough

Scored (Conceded)

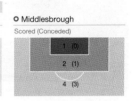

1 (0)
2 (1)
4 (3)

Team Statistics

Starting Line-Ups

Birmingham City: Taylor Maik; Lazaridis, Clemence (Izzet); Upson, Tebily (Forssell); Jarosik, Hasselbaink (Maccarone); Cunningham, Butt, Pandiani (Gray); Melchiot, Pennant

Middlesbrough: Morrison, Reiziger (Bates); Parlour, Ehiogu; Viduka (Job), Boateng, Southgate; Schwarzer; Downing, Queudrue

4/4/2   **4/4/2**

Unused Sub: Vaesen, Clapham   Unused Sub: Jones, Doriva

Premiership Totals

	○ Birmingham	Boro ○
Premiership Appearances	1,789	2,351
Team Appearances	621	1,038
Goals Scored	110	294
Assists	160	222
Clean Sheets (goalkeepers)	36	70
Yellow Cards	198	280
Red Cards	12	20
Full Internationals	11	11

Age/Height

Birmingham City Age	Middlesbrough Age
▶ 28 yrs, 11 mo	**▶ 28 yrs, 6 mo**
Birmingham City Height	Middlesbrough Height
▶ 6'	**▶ 6'**

Match Statistics

League Table after Fixture

		Played	Won	Drawn	Lost	For	Against	Pts
↑ 1	Man City	3	2	1	0	4	2	7
↓ 2	Tottenham	2	2	0	0	4	0	6
↓ 3	Charlton	2	2	0	0	4	1	6
↓ 4	Man Utd	2	2	0	0	3	0	6
↓ 5	Chelsea	2	2	0	0	2	0	6
↓ 6	West Ham	2	1	1	0	3	1	4
↑ 7	Middlesbrough	3	1	1	1	3	2	4
...	...	...	...	...	...	...	...	...
↓ 18	Birmingham	3	0	1	2	1	5	1

Statistics

	○ Birmingham	Boro ○
Goals	0	3
Shots on Target	8	3
Shots off Target	6	5
Hit Woodwork	1	0
Possession %	54	46
Corners	2	2
Offsides	3	5
Fouls	14	15
Disciplinary Points	0	4

0-3

Middlesbrough ○
Charlton Athletic ○

▶ Emanuel Pogatetz tries to organise things at the back

Event Line

38 ○ ⊕	Rommedahl / LF / OP / IA
	Assist: Murphy
Half time 0-1	
46 ○ ⇄	Mendieta > Morrison
46 ○ ⇄	Pogatetz > Queudrue
58 ○ ⇄	Maccarone > Mendieta
72 ○ ▪	Southgate
78 ○ ⇄	Bartlett > Thomas
79 ○ ▪	Reiziger
81 ○ ⊕	Perry / RF / IFK / IA
	Assist: Murphy
83 ○ ⇄	Hughes > Smertin
86 ○ ▪	Hreidarsson
90 ○ ⊕	Bent D / LF / OP / OA
	Assist: Hughes
Full time 0-3	

Boro followed up their midweek trouncing of Birmingham with a dismal display in front of their own fans, losing heavily to Charlton.

Boro simply had no answer for Charlton's quick passing, pacy football, and Steve McClaren clearly had some thinking to do as the players were booed off at the end of the game.

Charlton took the lead on 38 minutes. Boro lost possession from their own throw-in and the ball was played forward for the lightening-quick Dennis Rommedahl. He sprinted past the Boro defence with ease before hitting a first-time, left-footed effort from just inside the penalty area.

Boro had a couple of chances to score after the break, Viduka forcing a save from a volley, but both teams were guilty of poor distribution and wasted possession.

With 10 minutes left, Boro failed to clear a free kick from the edge of the box, allowing Chris Perry the opportunity to side-foot home from seven yards out. And Charlton hit a third with just seconds remaining. A long ball caught the Boro defence flat-footed, giving Darren Bent ample time to control and hit a low shot for his fourth goal in three games.

Quote

❝ Steve McClaren

It was very poor, not the Middlesbrough we have come to know. It was possibly the worst performance I have seen since I came here.

Premiership Milestone

▶ Debut

Emanuel Pogatetz made his Premiership debut.

Venue:	Riverside Stadium	Referee:	M.L.Dean - 05/06		Middlesbrough
Attendance:	26,206	Matches:	0		Charlton Athletic
Capacity:	35,100	Yellow Cards:	0		
Occupancy:	75%	Red Cards:	0		

Form Coming into Fixture

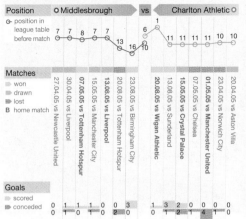

Goal Statistics

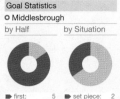

○ Middlesbrough

by Half   by Situation

▶ first: 5   ▶ set piece: 2
▶ second: 1   ▶ open play: 4

○ Charlton Athletic

by Half   by Situation

▶ first: 3   ▶ set piece: 2
▶ second: 3   ▶ open play: 4

Goals by Area

○ Middlesbrough

Scored (Conceded)

1 (0)
2 (1)
3 (3)

○ Charlton Athletic

Scored (Conceded)

2 (2)
3 (5)
1 (2)

Team Statistics

Starting Line-Ups

▶ 4/4/2

Unused Sub: Jones, Doriva

▶ 4/5/1

Unused Sub: Myhre, Fortune, Spector

Premiership Totals	○ Boro	Charlton ○
Premiership Appearances	2,133	1,574
Team Appearances	958	769
Goals Scored	196	89
Assists	166	94
Clean Sheets (goalkeepers)	71	1
Yellow Cards	249	179
Red Cards	18	4
Full Internationals	12	9

Age/Height

Middlesbrough Age

▶ 28 yrs, 3 mo

Charlton Athletic Age

▶ 28 yrs, 8 mo

Middlesbrough Height

▶ 6'

Charlton Athletic Height

▶ 5'11"

Match Statistics

League Table after Fixture

		Played	Won	Drawn	Lost	For	Against	Pts
↑ 3	Charlton	3	3	0	0	7	1	9
...		...	...	...	...	...	...	...
↓ 12	Middlesbrough	4	1	1	2	3	5	4
● 13	Birmingham	4	1	1	2	4	7	4
● 14	Fulham	4	1	1	2	3	6	4
● 15	West Brom	4	1	1	2	4	8	4
● 16	Wigan	3	1	0	2	1	2	3
● 17	Everton	3	1	0	2	1	3	3
● 18	Portsmouth	4	0	1	3	3	7	1

Statistics	○ Boro	Charlton ○
Goals	0	3
Shots on Target	6	8
Shots off Target	4	4
Hit Woodwork	0	0
Possession %	44	56
Corners	6	1
Offsides	2	1
Fouls	18	15
Disciplinary Points	8	4

2-1

Middlesbrough ○
Arsenal ○

▶ Ray Parlour in action against his old club

It was a gritty and determined team effort that gave Boro their first ever Premiership win over Arsenal. New signings Fabio Rochemback and Abel Xavier made their Boro debuts and 18-year old Adam Johnson made his first league start.

Arsenal, who were without their influential captain Thierry Henry, earned four corners in the first 10 minutes but Boro defended well before taking the lead six minutes before the break. Good build-up play led to a low ball in to Yakubu, who made up for a poor first touch with a sharp turn that left Kolo Toure stranded. His 16-yard strike was his first in a Boro shirt.

Boro started the second half brightly, urged on by an impressive Rochemback. A second goal came from a Schwarzer long goal-kick, Pascal Cygan failing to play Yakubu offside and the stumbling striker picking out Massimo Maccarone. With just Lehmann to beat, he hit a low shot away to the German's right from just inside the penalty area.

Three minutes into injury time, Jose Reyes scored a consolation goal, beating the offside trap to race through the middle and round Schwarzer before tucking the ball into the back of the net from a narrow angle.

Fans' Player of the Match	Quote	Premiership Milestone
Massimo Maccarone	❝ **Steve McClaren**	▶ **Debut**

The first ten minutes were hectic and we were hesitant, but we settled down superbly after that.

Fabio Rochemback, Adam Johnson and Abel Xavier all made their Boro Premiership debuts.

Venue:	Riverside Stadium	Referee:	M.A.Riley - 05/06
Attendance:	28,075	Matches:	3
Capacity:	35,100	Yellow Cards:	11
Occupancy:	80%	Red Cards:	1

Middlesbrough
Arsenal

Form Coming into Fixture

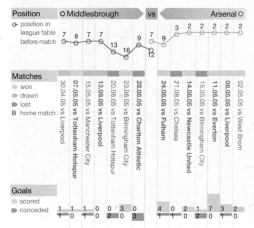

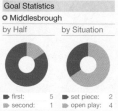

Goal Statistics

○ Middlesbrough

by Half	by Situation

- first: 5
- second: 1
- set piece: 2
- open play: 4

○ Arsenal

by Half	by Situation

- first: 6
- second: 13
- set piece: 5
- open play: 14

Goals by Area

○ Middlesbrough
Scored (Conceded)

1 (0)
2 (3)
3 (4)

○ Arsenal
Scored (Conceded)

2 (0)
16 (4)
1 (1)

Team Statistics

Starting Line-Ups

▶ 4/5/1

Unused Sub: Jones, Kennedy

▶ 4/4/2

Unused Sub: Almunia, Clichy, Senderos

Premiership Totals	○ Boro	Arsenal ○
Premiership Appearances	1,973	1,179
Team Appearances	871	1,179
Goals Scored	124	185
Assists	117	204
Clean Sheets (goalkeepers)	71	27
Yellow Cards	243	132
Red Cards	17	3
Full Internationals	11	10

Age/Height

Middlesbrough Age	Arsenal Age
▶ 27 yrs, 10 mo	**▶ 27 yrs**
Middlesbrough Height	Arsenal Height
▶ 6'	**▶ 6'**

Match Statistics

League Table after Fixture

		Played	Won	Drawn	Lost	For	Against	Pts
●	1 Chelsea	5	5	0	0	10	0	15
↑	2 Charlton	4	4	0	0	8	1	12
↓	3 Man City	5	3	2	0	7	4	11
●	4 Man Utd	4	3	1	0	6	1	10
↑	5 Tottenham	5	2	2	1	4	2	8
↓	6 Bolton	4	2	1	1	6	4	7
↑	7 Middlesbrough	5	2	1	2	5	6	7
↓	8 Arsenal	4	2	0	2	7	4	6
↑	9 Wigan	4	2	0	2	3	3	6

Statistics	○ Boro	Arsenal ○
Goals	2	1
Shots on Target	5	8
Shots off Target	1	5
Hit Woodwork	0	1
Possession %	49	51
Corners	6	7
Offsides	4	2
Fouls	17	16
Disciplinary Points	12	16

2-0

Middlesbrough ○
Skoda Xanthi ○

▶ Mark Viduka fires the ball goalwards

Event Line

28 ○ ⊕ Boateng / RF / OP / IA
   Assist: Maccarone

Half time 1-0

61 ○ ⇄ Queudrue > Johnson

63 ○ ▢ Bates

67 ○ ⇄ Quintana > Torosidis

74 ○ ⇄ Yakubu > Maccarone

74 ○ ⇄ Morrison > Parlour

76 ○ ⇄ Santos Conzalves > Maghradze

83 ○ ⊕ Viduka / LF / OP / IA

87 ○ ⇄ Kazakis > Paviot

Full time 2-0

Boro made a positive start to their second season in Europe against a side that had added ex-Riverside hero Emerson to its line-up since finishing fourth in the Greek top flight the previous season.

After being forced to sit out the opening six weeks through suspension, new signing Emanuel Pogatetz was cleared to make his first start and was favoured ahead of Franck Queudrue at left-back. With Fabio Rochemback cup-tied, Doriva started, while Mark Viduka returned to replace Yakubu.

Brazilian Emerson was given a warm reception on his first return to Teesside and promptly set about turning in a display that was energetically effective.

The breakthrough came after 28 minutes. Adam Johnson played a long diagonal ball in from the left and Massimo Maccarone controlled well, only to see his powerful shot pushed away. George Boateng was left with the simple task of drilling the ball into an empty net from 12 yards.

Boro started the second half brightly, good work down the right setting up Boateng, who had a close-range shot blocked. Xanthi twice went close. Levan Maghradze turned neatly inside the penalty area and sent a low shot at Mark Schwarzer. Stavros Labriakos was next to apply pressure, a curling shot from the edge of the penalty area only just clearing the bar.

Boro were suddenly under pressure and Maghradze, a Georgian midfielder, sent a low shot inches wide of Schwarzer's left-hand post after getting the better of Matthew Bates.

► George Boateng celebrates a rare goal

Match Statistics

Starting Line-Ups

▶ 4/4/2   ▶ 4/4/2

Unused Sub: Jones, Southgate, Kennedy, Graham

Unused Sub: Anastasopoulos, Zapropoulos, Carabas, Lafata

Statistics	○ Boro	Xanthi ○
Goals	2	0
Shots on Target	7	1
Shots off Target	5	10
Hit Woodwork	0	0
Possession %	52	48
Corners	3	3
Offsides	6	4
Fouls	12	13
Disciplinary Points	4	0

Xanthi coach Ioannis Matzourakis made a bold change midway through the second half as he replaced a defender with an attacker. Luciano then sent a free-kick just wide.

McClaren made a double change 16 minutes from time as Maccarone and Ray Parlour made way for Yakubu and James Morrison.

Boro went two-up with eight minutes remaining. Pizanowski fumbled a low left-wing cross, Viduka shot for goal and French central defender Jacques Paviot deflected the ball past his own goalkeeper.

Fans' Player of the Match

Massimo Maccarone

Quote

○ **Steve McClaren**

We made more mistakes than usual. Maybe we were afraid of our opponents or maybe we overestimated them.

23

1-1

Wigan Athletic ○
Middlesbrough ○

► Fabio Rochemback in midfield action

What appeared at the time to be a disappointing point against newly promoted Wigan seems far better in light of the Premiership new boys' excellent season.

Event Line

14 ○ ⊕ Yakubu / RF / IFK / IA
    Assist: Viduka

41 ○ ▮ Pogatetz

44 ○ ⇄ Doriva > Morrison

Half time 0-1

61 ○ ⇄ Maccarone > Viduka

64 ○ ⇄ Camara > Connolly

68 ○ ⊕ Camara / RF / OP / IA
    Assist: Baines

Full time 1-1

There was a lively start from both teams, although neither goalkeeper was overly troubled by the early exchanges. However, it did not take Boro long to open the scoring, Yakubu giving them the lead after just 13 minutes. Abel Xavier's free-kick was flicked on via Viduka to Yakubu, who took one touch to control before hitting a low drive from seven yards out beyond Mike Pollitt in the Wigan goal.

Wigan got their deserved equaliser midway through the second half. A long ball from Leighton Baines curled its way behind the Boro defence. As Ugo Ehiogu attempted to clear the ball, it hit substitute Henri Camara on the chest. Ehiogu's appeals for handball were dismissed by the referee and Camara, who had played on, tucked the ball into the net as Southgate tried in vain to close him down.

Boro struggled to get a foothold in the game during the second half and, in the end, a draw was a fair reflection of a match in which neither side was inventive enough to create an abundance of chances.

Fans' Player of the Match

Gareth Southgate

Quote

❶❶ Steve McClaren

We controlled the game and we had chances. If we had got that second goal then I think we'd have won it, but Wigan are a team who'll fight all season.

Venue:	JJB Stadium	Referee:	U.D.Rennie - 05/06		Wigan Athletic
Attendance:	16,641	Matches:	4		Middlesbrough
Capacity:	25,023	Yellow Cards:	4		
Occupancy:	67%	Red Cards:	0		

Form Coming into Fixture

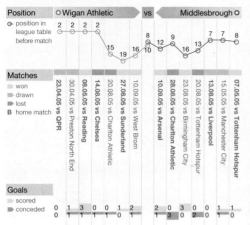

Goal Statistics

○ Wigan Athletic

by Half	by Situation

first:	5	set piece:	2
second:	2	open play:	5

○ Middlesbrough

by Half	by Situation

first:	5	set piece:	2
second:	2	open play:	5

Goals by Area

○ Wigan Athletic

Scored (Conceded)

○ Middlesbrough

Scored (Conceded)

Team Statistics

Starting Line-Ups

Wigan Athletic: Pollitt; Baines, McCulloch, Henchoz, Kavanagh, Chimbonda, Bullard, De Zeeuw, Francis, Connolly (Camara), Roberts

▶ 4/4/2

Unused Sub: Filan, Jackson, McMillan, Taylor

Middlesbrough: Schwarzer; Morrison, Xavier, Boateng, Ehiogu, Southgate, Queudrue, Pogatetz, Rochemback, Yakubu, Viduka (Maccarone), Doriva

▶ 4/4/2

Unused Sub: Jones, Bates, Graham

Premiership Totals

	○ Wigan	Middlesbrough ○
Premiership Appearances	482	1,771
Team Appearances	38	872
Goals Scored	30	170
Assists	19	112
Clean Sheets (goalkeepers)	1	71
Yellow Cards	66	203
Red Cards	1	16
Full Internationals	7	11

Age/Height

Wigan Athletic Age	Middlesbrough Age
▶ 28 yrs, 8 mo	▶ 28 yrs, 5 mo
Wigan Athletic Height	Middlesbrough Height
▶ 6'	▶ 6'

Match Statistics

League Table after Fixture

		Played	Won	Drawn	Lost	For	Against	Pts
●	1 Chelsea	6	6	0	0	12	0	18
●	2 Charlton	5	4	0	1	8	3	12
↑	3 Man Utd	5	3	2	0	6	1	11
↑	4 Bolton	6	3	2	1	7	4	11
↓	5 Man City	6	3	2	1	7	5	11
↓	6 West Ham	5	3	1	1	10	4	10
↓	7 Tottenham	6	2	3	1	5	3	9
●	8 Middlesbrough	6	2	2	2	6	7	8
↑	9 Wigan	5	2	1	2	4	4	7

Statistics

	○ Wigan	Middlesbrough ○
Goals	1	1
Shots on Target	4	3
Shots off Target	7	7
Hit Woodwork	0	1
Possession %	56	44
Corners	4	5
Offsides	1	2
Fouls	11	16
Disciplinary Points	0	4

0-2

Middlesbrough ○
Sunderland ○

▶ Abel Xavier beats Stephen Elliott to the ball

Event Line

2 ○ ⊕	Miller / RF / OP / IA	
29 ○ ▢	Queudrue	
37 ○ ⇄	Maccarone > Ehiogu	
Half time 0-1		
55 ○ ▢	Maccarone	
55 ○ ▢	Hoyte	
59 ○ ▢	Southgate	
60 ○ ⊕	Arca / LF / DFK / OA	
	Assist: Elliott	
64 ○ ⇄	Parlour > Morrison	
64 ○ ⇄	Hasselbaink > Yakubu	
66 ○ ▢	Whitehead	
84 ○ ⇄	Le Tallec > Elliott	
90 ○ ⇄	Lawrence > Whitehead	
Full time 0-2		

This was a dark day for Boro, as local rivals Sunderland lifted themselves off the bottom of the table with a 2-0 Riverside win – their first top-flight victory since December 2002.

The visitors took the lead after just 83 seconds. Emanuel Pogatetz misjudged the bounce on the halfway line, drawing Gareth Southgate out of position to cover. Although Boro had sufficient numbers back to defend, Tommy Miller pounced on a loose ball and drilled a low shot beyond Jones from 12 yards out.

Boro responded by piling the pressure on, but suffered from a lack of quality in the Sunderland penalty area. The Sunderland 'keeper was by far the busier but Boro were clearly missing an edge to their game.

With an hour played, the visitors won a free kick on the edge of the penalty area. Up stepped dead ball specialist Julio Arca to unleash one of his trademark efforts into the top left hand corner, well beyond Jones in the Boro goal.

It was a hugely embarrassing defeat for Boro, who were already earning something of a Jekyll and Hyde reputation, equally likely to perform poorly or turn on the style on different days.

Fans' Player of the Match
George Boateng

Quote
❻ Steve McClaren

We can beat Arsenal well one week and lose to Sunderland the next – it's very frustrating.

Venue:	Riverside Stadium	Referee:	H.M.Webb - 05/06		Middlesbrough
Attendance:	29,583	Matches:	6		Sunderland
Capacity:	35,100	Yellow Cards:	16		
Occupancy:	84%	Red Cards:	1		

Form Coming into Fixture

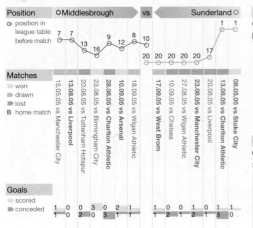

Position
Middlesbrough vs Sunderland

position in league table before match

Matches
- won
- drawn
- lost
- B home match

Middlesbrough matches:
- 15.05.05 vs Manchester City
- 13.08.05 vs Liverpool
- 20.08.05 vs Tottenham Hotspur
- 23.08.05 vs Birmingham City
- 28.08.05 vs Charlton Athletic
- 10.09.05 vs Arsenal
- 18.09.05 vs Wigan Athletic

Sunderland matches:
- 17.09.05 vs West Brom
- 19.09.05 vs Chelsea
- 24.08.05 vs Wigan Athletic
- 27.08.05 vs Wigan Athletic
- 23.08.05 vs Manchester City
- 20.08.05 vs Liverpool
- 13.08.05 vs Charlton Athletic
- 08.05.05 vs Stoke City

Goals
- scored: 1 0 0 3 0 2 1 | 1 0 0 1 0 1 1
- conceded: 1 0 2 0 3 1 1 | 1 2 1 2 1 3 0

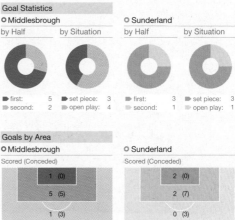

Goal Statistics

Middlesbrough

by Half | by Situation
- first: 5
- second: 2
- set piece: 3
- open play: 4

Sunderland

by Half | by Situation
- first: 3
- second: 1
- set piece: 3
- open play: 1

Goals by Area

Middlesbrough — Scored (Conceded)
- 1 (0)
- 5 (5)
- 1 (3)

Sunderland — Scored (Conceded)
- 2 (0)
- 2 (7)
- 0 (3)

Team Statistics

Starting Line-Ups

Middlesbrough:
- Jones
- Pogatetz, Queudrue
- Southgate, Rochemback
- Yakubu (Hasselbaink), Elliott (Le Tallec)
- Viduka, Gray
- Ehiogu (Maccarone), Boateng
- Xavier, Morrison (Parlour)

4/4/2

Unused Sub: Knight, Doriva

Sunderland:
- Whitehead (Lawrence), Nosworthy
- Bassila, Breen
- Davis
- Miller, Caldwell
- Arca, Hoyte

4/4/2

Unused Sub: Murphy J, Collins D, Welsh

Premiership Totals

Premiership Totals	Boro	Sunderland
Premiership Appearances	2,109	360
Team Appearances	672	123
Goals Scored	308	10
Assists	219	18
Clean Sheets (goalkeepers)	2	0
Yellow Cards	288	36
Red Cards	20	1
Full Internationals	11	4

Age/Height

Middlesbrough Age	Sunderland Age
28 yrs	25 yrs, 4 mo

Middlesbrough Height	Sunderland Height
6'	6'

Match Statistics

League Table after Fixture

		Played	Won	Drawn	Lost	For	Against	Pts
↓	11 Middlesbrough	7	2	2	3	6	9	8
•	12 Blackburn	7	2	2	3	5	9	8
•	13 Liverpool	5	1	4	0	3	2	7
•	14 Birmingham	7	1	3	3	7	11	6
•	15 Aston Villa	7	1	3	3	6	11	6
•	16 Fulham	6	1	2	3	5	9	5
•	17 Portsmouth	7	1	2	4	5	9	5
•	18 West Brom	7	1	2	4	7	13	5
↑	19 Sunderland	7	1	1	5	5	10	4

Statistics

Statistics	Boro	Sunderland
Goals	0	2
Shots on Target	11	2
Shots off Target	9	2
Hit Woodwork	0	0
Possession %	55	45
Corners	8	2
Offsides	6	2
Fouls	13	21
Disciplinary Points	12	8

0-0

Skoda Xanthi ○
Middlesbrough ○

➤ Jimmy Floyd Hasselbaink cannot find a way through

Event Line
Half time 0-0
46 ○ ⇄ Kazakis > Torosidis
47 ○ ▢ Queudrue
60 ○ ⇄ Santos Conzalves > Andrande
69 ○ ⇄ Garpozis > Maghradze
70 ○ ▢ Jones
71 ○ ⇄ Yakubu > Hasselbaink
71 ○ ⇄ Nemeth > Maccarone
73 ○ ▢ De Souza
79 ○ ⇄ Parnaby > Queudrue
Full time 0-0

Boro cruised through to the group stages of the UEFA Cup with a thoroughly professional display.

Luciano tested Brad Jones after just two minutes, the Australian parrying his effort from the edge of the box before Chris Riggott hooked the ball clear.

Emerson continued his impressive form from the first leg but was unable to engineer an opening from a quick free-kick near the edge of the box after a foul by Riggott and the ball was cleared. More good work by the Brazilian midfielder set up compatriot Luciano, whose rasping shot just sizzled by the post and past the outstretched fingertips of Jones.

Boro created a good chance on 28 minutes when Jimmy Floyd Hasselbaink showed superb control to bring down Doriva's pass before slotting the ball neatly to the advancing Massimo Maccarone. But under intense pressure from Antzas, the Italian drove his shot into the side-netting.

Steve McClaren's men came even closer on 31 minutes as Hasselbaink's piledriver was turned wide by Pizanowski at full stretch. Seconds later, Boro had the ball in the back of the net after the goalkeeper spilled James Morrison's shot and Maccarone tapped in the rebound, only to be denied by an offside flag.

Xanthi produced some neat approach play but rarely threatened to produce the goal they badly needed to stay in the tie. Boro, meanwhile, continued to battle for every ball, Southgate typifying the spirit as he dispossessed Emerson with a fine tackle inside the box.

➠ Massimo Maccarone makes forward progress

Match Statistics

Starting Line-Ups

4/4/1/1   **4/4/2**

Unused Sub: Anastasopoulos, Zaropoulos, Carabas, Lafata

Unused Sub: Knight, Bates, Mendieta, Johnson

Statistics	Xanthi	Boro
Goals	0	0
Shots on Target	2	3
Shots off Target	4	4
Hit Woodwork	0	0
Possession %	55	45
Corners	10	11
Offsides	1	8
Fouls	11	17
Disciplinary Points	4	8

Szilard Nemeth and Yakubu replaced Boro's two main strikers with 20 minutes remaining, Hasselbaink and Maccarone receiving generous applause from the home fans.

Queudrue, who had overcome a shin injury to play, limped off with 13 minutes remaining, being replaced by Stuart Parnaby.

Boro had a chance to seal the tie when Yakubu pounced on a misplaced pass and sprayed the ball wide to Nemeth, but the Slovakian shot tamely wide across the face of the goal. At the other end, Luciano's free-kick was headed over the bar by Xavier before a late flurry of chances for the visitors.

Fans' Player of the Match

Doriva

Quote

❝ Steve McClaren

A great team performance and I'm delighted. We were very professional and full of character.

29

2-3

Aston Villa ○
Middlesbrough ○

▶ Brad Jones climbs highest

Event Line

23 ○ ■ Barry
33 ○ ⊕ Yakubu / LF / OP / IA
Half time 0-1
46 ○ ⇄ Samuel > De la Cruz
50 ○ ⊕ Moore / RF / OP / IA
　　　Assist: Angel
61 ○ ■ Riggott
64 ○ ⊕ Boateng / LF / C / IA
　　　Assist: Pogatetz
65 ○ ⇄ Queudrue > Mendieta
69 ○ ⇄ Parnaby > Nemeth
75 ○ ■ Berger
76 ○ ⇄ Bakke > Bouma
80 ○ ■ Ridgewell
87 ○ ■ Samuel
88 ○ ⊕ Yakubu / RF / P / IA
　　　Assist: Boateng
90 ○ ⊕ Davis / RF / C / OA
Full time 2-3

Boro continued to treat Birmingham like a second home, winning for the second time in the city, despite their struggles at the Riverside.

Steve McClaren's side made the breakthough with just over half an hour played. A poor clearance allowed Yakubu to hit a powerful volley at goal. Although on target, it hit Liam Ridgewell before finding the back of the net.

The home side were level within five minutes of the restart, thanks to Luke Moore. He found himself with time and space to curl the ball around Brad Jones in the Boro goal. The parity did not last and, on the hour mark, Boro were back in the lead. Ex-Villa star George Boateng picked up on a loose ball from a corner to hit a swerving left-footed strike.

Boro sealed the win with a penalty with four minutes to play. Rochemback's perfectly timed through ball to Boateng saw the midfielder brought down by Samuel. Yakubu sent Sorenson the wrong way from the spot to secure the win.

There was still life in the Villa attack, however. Three minutes into injury time, Steven Davis pounced on a loose ball to hit a low shot through a crowded penalty box for Villa's second goal.

Fans' Player of the Match

Yakubu

Quote

❝ **Steve McClaren**

It wasn't just 11 players, it was the whole squad who got through this week and showed character.

Venue:	Villa Park	Referee:	M.L.Dean - 05/06		Aston Villa
Attendance:	29,719	Matches:	5		Middlesbrough
Capacity:	42,573	Yellow Cards:	10		
Occupancy:	70%	Red Cards:	0		

Form Coming into Fixture

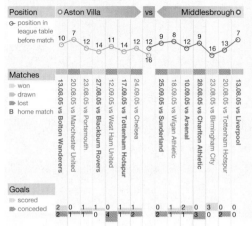

Goal Statistics

○ Aston Villa

by Half — by Situation

- first: 6
- second: 0
- set piece: 0
- open play: 5
- own goals: 1

○ Middlesbrough

by Half — by Situation

- first: 4
- second: 2
- set piece: 2
- open play: 4

Goals by Area

○ Aston Villa — Scored (Conceded)

| 2 (3) |
| 3 (6) |
| 1 (2) |

○ Middlesbrough — Scored (Conceded)

| 1 (0) |
| 5 (5) |
| 0 (4) |

Team Statistics

Starting Line-Ups

Bouma — Berger
Bakke
Ridgewell — Barry
Sorensen — Angel
Yakubu
Mellberg — Davis
Moore
De la Cruz — Milner
Samuel

Mendieta — Xavier
Queudrue
Doriva
Riggott
Rochemback — Jones
Southgate
Boateng
Nemeth — Pogatetz
Parnaby

▶ 4/4/2 ▶ 4/5/1

Unused Sub: Taylor, Cahill, Djemba-Djemba

Unused Sub: Knight, Hasselbaink, Maccarone

Premiership Totals	○ Aston Villa	Boro ○
Premiership Appearances	1,451	1,303
Team Appearances	921	694
Goals Scored	116	102
Assists	112	92
Clean Sheets (goalkeepers)	60	2
Yellow Cards	137	166
Red Cards	3	8
Full Internationals	9	9

Age/Height

Aston Villa Age

▶ 25 yrs, 10 mo

Middlesbrough Age

▶ 27 yrs, 8 mo

Aston Villa Height

▶ 5'11"

Middlesbrough Height

▶ 6'

Match Statistics

League Table after Fixture

		Played	Won	Drawn	Lost	For	Against	Pts.
↑ 8	Wigan	7	4	1	2	7	5	13
↓ 9	West Ham	7	3	3	1	11	5	12
↑ 10	Middlesbrough	8	3	2	3	9	11	11
↓ 11	Blackburn	8	3	2	3	7	9	11
↓ 12	Newcastle	8	2	3	3	5	7	9
● 13	Liverpool	6	1	4	1	4	6	7
↑ 14	Portsmouth	8	1	3	4	5	9	6
↓ 15	Birmingham	8	1	3	4	7	12	6
● 16	Aston Villa	8	1	3	4	8	14	6

Statistics	○ Aston Villa	Boro ○
Goals	2	3
Shots on Target	6	11
Shots off Target	7	3
Hit Woodwork	0	0
Possession %	50	50
Corners	6	5
Offsides	4	1
Fouls	17	10
Disciplinary Points	16	4

1-1

Middlesbrough ○
Portsmouth ○

▶ Yakubu celebrates scoring against his former employers

Event Line

Half time 0-0

46 ○	⇄	Mendieta > Queudrue
46 ○	⊕	O'Neil / RF / OP / IA
		Assist: Vukic
46 ○	⇄	Skopelitis > Griffin
46 ○	⇄	Todorov > Silva
54 ○	⊕	Yakubu / H / C / 6Y
		Assist: Rochemback
55 ○	⇄	Viduka > Maccarone
55 ○	⇄	Hasselbaink > Rochemback
58 ○	⇄	Vignal > Robert
66 ○	▢	Skopelitis
70 ○	▢	O'Neil
88 ○	▢	Pogatetz
90 ○	▢	Boateng
90 ○	▢	Vignal

Full time 1-1

Yakubu faced his old club for the first time and showed Portsmouth just what they were missing as he hit the equaliser to ensure Boro got a share of the points.

An uninspiring first half saw chances from both sides, but neither team took the initiative. Boro enjoyed the majority of possession but shots by both Rochemback and Maccarone were off target.

The game finally sprung into life in the first minute of the second half. Pogatetz was left stranded high up the pitch as Portsmouth attacked down the right. A miss-hit cross from Vukic dropped nicely for England youth international Gary O'Neil, who placed his shot beyond Schwarzer.

Fired into action, it took Boro just eight minutes to equalise. A deep corner reached Yakubu at the back post and his well-timed header proved unstoppable for Ashdown in the Portsmouth goal.

Boro could have taken all three points when Mendieta set up Boateng in injury time. The Dutch midfielder's low shot, however, was deflected away for a corner and the home side were forced to settle with a draw.

Fans' Player of the Match

Massimo Maccarone

Quote

ⓕ Steve McClaren

We are disappointing at home. It's the same old problem of consistency and we have to find answers for that.

Venue:	Riverside Stadium	Referee:	C.J.Foy - 05/06		Middlesbrough
Attendance:	26,551	Matches:	9		Portsmouth
Capacity:	35,100	Yellow Cards:	20		
Occupancy:	76%	Red Cards:	2		

Form Coming into Fixture

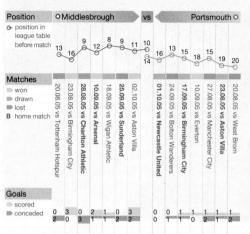

Goal Statistics

Middlesbrough

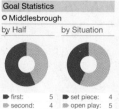

by Half		by Situation	
▶ first:	5	▶ set piece:	4
▶ second:	4	▶ open play:	5

Portsmouth

by Half		by Situation	
▶ first:	2	▶ set piece:	3
▶ second:	3	▶ open play:	1
		▶ own goals:	1

Goals by Area

Middlesbrough — Scored (Conceded)

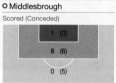

1 (0)
8 (6)
0 (5)

Portsmouth — Scored (Conceded)

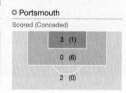

3 (1)
0 (6)
2 (0)

Team Statistics

Starting Line-Ups

▶ 4/4/1/1

▶ 5/4/1

Unused Sub: Knight, Bates

Unused Sub: Westerveld, Songo'o

Premiership Totals	○ Boro	Portsmouth ○
Premiership Appearances	1,833	748
Team Appearances	946	278
Goals Scored	279	46
Assists	192	66
Clean Sheets (goalkeepers)	71	4
Yellow Cards	222	92
Red Cards	12	8
Full Internationals	11	8

Age/Height

Middlesbrough Age	Portsmouth Age
▶ 28 yrs, 5 mo	▶ 27 yrs, 1 mo
Middlesbrough Height	Portsmouth Height
▶ 6'	▶ 5'11"

Match Statistics

League Table after Fixture

			Played	Won	Drawn	Lost	For	Against	Pts
↓	7	Bolton	9	4	2	3	10	11	14
↓	8	Arsenal	8	4	1	3	11	6	13
●	9	West Ham	7	3	3	1	11	5	12
●	10	Middlesbrough	9	3	3	3	10	12	12
●	11	Blackburn	9	3	2	4	7	10	11
↑	12	Liverpool	7	2	4	1	5	6	10
↓	13	Newcastle	9	2	3	4	5	8	9
↑	14	West Brom	9	2	2	5	9	16	8
↓	15	Portsmouth	9	1	4	4	6	10	7

Statistics	○ Boro	Portsmouth ○
Goals	1	1
Shots on Target	7	4
Shots off Target	7	5
Hit Woodwork	0	0
Possession %	48	52
Corners	6	3
Offsides	2	2
Fouls	12	12
Disciplinary Points	8	12

0-1

Grasshopper-Club ○
Middlesbrough ○

▶ Gaizka Mendieta shields the ball in midfield

Event Line

10 ○ ⊕	Hasselbaink / RF / OP / IA
	Assist: Doriva

Half time 0-1

65 ○ ▪	Pogatetz
67 ○ ▪	Nemeth
67 ○ ⇄	Morrison > Nemeth
79 ○ ⇄	Queudrue > Mendieta
82 ○ ⇄	Toure > Chihab
85 ○ ⇄	Yakubu > Viduka
87 ○ ⇄	Salatic > Renggli

Full time 0-1

It was backs-to-the-wall stuff at times, but a solitary goal was enough to secure victory for Boro in Switzerland.

Jimmy Floyd Hasselbaink, who limped off at the end of the game, scored after nine minutes to inflict the first home defeat of the season on Grasshoppers.

The 700-strong travelling army of fans soon had something to celebrate. Boro cut through the Swiss like a knife through butter, with Hasselbaink drilling a low shot beyond Fabio Coltorti from 14 yards.

Szilard Nemeth had a great chance to make it two a few minutes later when he was picked out with his back to goal seven yards out, but the Slovakian striker played a wayward pass, which was easily cleared.

Grasshoppers thought they had equalised after 21 minutes. A 22-yard drive from Rogerio was fumbled by Mark Schwarzer and his fellow Brazilian, Eduardo, tucked in the rebound.

But their joy was short-lived as they spotted a lineman's flag raised, Eduardo adjudged to have been offside when the initial shot was made. With 11 minutes of the half remaining, Eduardo curled a shot just wide of the angle.

Dos Santos was again guilty of a glaring miss four minutes from the break when, getting on the end of a Tarek Chihab chestdown, he shot well over with the goal at his mercy.

Ricardo Cabanas brought a diving save from Schwarzer with the first shot of the second half. Then Eduardo headed over when he ought to have done better.

Venue:	Hardturm Stadium	Referee:	E.Berntsen (NOR)
Attendance:	8,500		
Capacity:	17,766		
Occupancy:	48%		

**Grasshopper-Club
Middlesbrough**

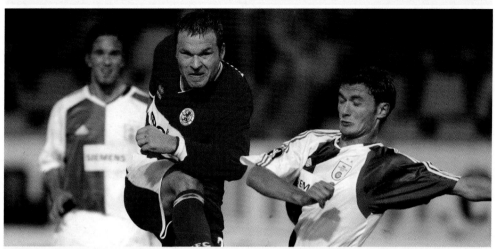

▶ Mark Viduka unleashes a venomous drive

Match Statistics

Starting Line-Ups

Grasshoppers
Jaggy — Antonio
Stepanovs I N — Cabanas
Eduardo — Viduka (Yakubu)
Collotti
Mitreski A — Renggli (Salatic)
Rogerio — Hasselbaink
Sutter — Chihab (Toure)

Mendieta (Queudrue) — Parnaby
Doriva — Riggott
Schwarzer
Boateng — Southgate
Nemeth (Morrison) — Pogatetz

▶ 4/4/2   ▶ 4/4/2

Unused Sub: Jehle, Hurlimann, Schwegler, Denicola, Luetolf

Unused Sub: Knight, Bates, Johnson, Maccarone

Statistics	Grasshoppers	Boro
Goals	0	1
Shots on Target	5	4
Shots off Target	13	2
Hit Woodwork	0	0
Possession %	55	45
Corners	5	2
Offsides	1	6
Fouls	10	12
Disciplinary Points	0	8

A glorious Boro chance was wasted when Doriva beat the offside trap only to shoot across the face of goal and just wide, with Viduka perfectly placed in the middle.

Grasshoppers continued to enjoy more possession and twice went close towards the end. Cabanas brought another save from Schwarzer just before Rogerio flashed a header across the face of goal.

In the closing minutes, Rogerio flashed another header across the face of goal, but the Boro fans were in full voice and cheered their team to victory in the first visit of the club to a Swiss ground.

Fans' Player of the Match

Chris Riggott

Quote

❝ Steve McClaren

It was hard work. When you come away and go a goal ahead you are going to have to soak up some pressure.

2-1

West Ham United ○
Middlesbrough ○

▶ Jimmy Floyd Hasselbaink keeps Danny Gabbidon at bay

Event Line

12 ○ ▮	Ferdinand
25 ○ ⇄	Queudrue > Southgate
29 ○ ▮	Doriva
Half time 0-0	
60 ○ ⇄	Hasselbaink > Maccarone
65 ○ ⇄	Sheringham > Zamora
66 ○ ⊕	Sheringham / LF / OP / IA
	Assist: Konchesky
74 ○ ⊕	Riggott / LF / OG / IA
	Assist: Konchesky
76 ○ ⇄	Newton > Etherington
77 ○ ▮	Boateng
78 ○ ⇄	Viduka > Doriva
87 ○ ⊕	Queudrue / H / C / 6Y
	Assist: Rochemback
90 ○ ⇄	Dailly > Benayoun
Full time 2-1	

Boro, who have a far from impressive record away at West Ham, lost out in the capital in controversial circumstances.

McClaren's men had the livelier start but, when West Ham did finally put together an attack, it caused significant problems for the visitors. The Hammers had a Nigel Reo-Coker goal disallowed for offside.

Within a minute of entering the game as a second half substitute, veteran striker Teddy Sheringham scored with his first touch. He connected with a cross from Paul Konchesky to hit a left-footed shot from eight yards out.

Controversy surrounded the home side's second goal 10 minutes later. Konchesky's well-hit cross was deflected goalwards by Chris Riggott. The deflection wrong-footed Mark Schwarzer but he managed to grab the ball on the line. The linesman, however, saw it differently. Despite Boro protests, he decided that Schwarzer had carried the ball over the line.

With four minutes remaining, Boro got a consolation goal, Franck Queudrue heading in a Rochemback cross from six yards out.

Fans' Player of the Match

Chris Riggott

Quote

❝ **Steve McClaren**

One decision has cost us the game and the Premiership is too big to trust decisions like that to human error.

Venue:	Upton Park	Referee:	S.G.Bennett - 05/06		**West Ham United**
Attendance:	34,612	Matches:	11		**Middlesbrough**
Capacity:	35,647	Yellow Cards:	41		
Occupancy:	97%	Red Cards:	3		

Form Coming into Fixture

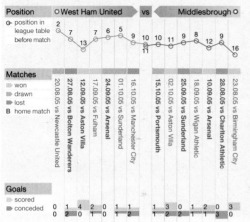

Goal Statistics

West Ham United

by Half   by Situation

- first: 2
- second: 7
- set piece: 4
- open play: 4
- own goals: 1

Middlesbrough

by Half   by Situation

- first: 5
- second: 5
- set piece: 5
- open play: 5

Goals by Area

West Ham United — Scored (Conceded)

2 (3)
7 (2)
0 (1)

Middlesbrough — Scored (Conceded)

2 (0)
8 (7)
0 (3)

Team Statistics

Starting Line-Ups

West Ham United: Hislop; Konchesky, Etherington, Newton, Gabbidon, Mullins, Zamora, Sheringham, Yakubu, Ferdinand, Reo-Coker, Harewood, Repka, Benayoun, Dailly

Middlesbrough: Schwarzer; Mendieta, Bates, Doriva, Viduka, Riggott, Maccarone, Hasselbaink, Boateng, Southgate, Queudrue, Rochemback, Pogatetz

▶ 4/4/2   **▶ 4/4/2**

Unused Sub: Bywater, Bellion   Unused Sub: Jones, Morrison

Premiership Totals

	West Ham	Boro
Premiership Appearances	1,188	1,797
Team Appearances	342	910
Goals Scored	161	280
Assists	127	190
Clean Sheets (goalkeepers)	54	71
Yellow Cards	115	222
Red Cards	9	12
Full Internationals	7	11

Age/Height

West Ham United Age	Middlesbrough Age
▶ 27 yrs, 10 mo	**▶ 28 yrs, 2 mo**
West Ham United Height	Middlesbrough Height
▶ 5'11"	**▶ 6'**

Match Statistics

League Table after Fixture

		Played	Won	Drawn	Lost	For	Against	Pts
↑	9 West Ham	9	4	3	2	14	8	15
↓	10 Blackburn	10	4	2	4	9	10	14
↑	11 Newcastle	10	3	3	4	8	10	12
↓	12 Middlesbrough	10	3	3	4	11	14	12
↓	13 Liverpool	8	2	4	2	5	8	10
•	14 Fulham	10	2	3	5	10	14	9
•	15 Aston Villa	10	2	3	5	9	16	9
•	16 West Brom	10	2	2	6	9	18	8
•	17 Portsmouth	10	1	4	5	7	12	7

Statistics

	West Ham	Boro
Goals	2	1
Shots on Target	8	9
Shots off Target	7	10
Hit Woodwork	0	0
Possession %	54	46
Corners	4	7
Offsides	4	5
Fouls	11	9
Disciplinary Points	4	8

0-1

Everton ○
Middlesbrough ○

▶ Franck Queudrue surges past James McFadden

A solitary goal from Jimmy Floyd Hasselbaink guided Boro to their first-ever cup success at Goodison Park.

Gareth Southgate, injured in the league defeat at West Ham, handed his place and captaincy to Ugo Ehiogu, who was started for the first time in almost a month. Matthew Bates, Gaizka Mendieta, Massimo Maccarone, Yakubu and George Boateng – missing his first game of the season – were replaced by Stuart Parnaby, Franck Queudrue, James Morrison, Mark Viduka and Jimmy Floyd Hasselbaink. Boro adopted a 3-5-2 formation with Parnaby and Emanuel Pogatetz deployed as wing-backs.

Emanuel Pogatetz produced the best early effort when his shot from a good angle brought a flying save from Nigel Martyn. The former England goalkeeper was in action again a couple of minutes later as Viduka shot across the face of goal after getting the better of Joseph Yobo.

The visitors scored their decisive goal after 38 minutes. A stray pass inside Everton's half was pounced on by Doriva, who supplied Viduka. The Aussie picked out Hasselbaink, whose low shot went through the legs of Martyn.

Steve McClaren was forced into a change during the break as Ehiogu was ruled out with injury to be replaced by Matthew Bates.

Fabio Rochemback sent Morrison clear with a long ball over the top. The bounce of the ball was awkward, but Martyn was slow to react and the winger had time to shoot narrowly wide.

Viduka was even closer a few minutes later when a low shot from the edge of the

▶ Fabio Rochemback looks to evade a sliding challenge

Match Statistics

Starting Line-Ups

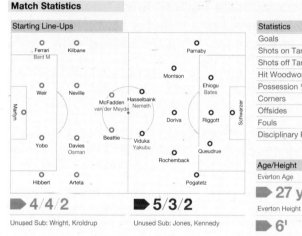

Everton: Ferrari, Kilbane, Parnaby, Bent M, Morrison, Weir, Neville, Ehiogu, Bates, Martyn, McFadden, van der Meyde, Hasselbaink, Nemeth, Doriva, Riggott, Schwarzer, Yobo, Davies, Osman, Beattie, Viduka, Yakubu, Queudrue, Hibbert, Arteta, Rochemback, Pogatetz

▶ 4/4/2   ▶ 5/3/2

Unused Sub: Wright, Kroldrup   Unused Sub: Jones, Kennedy

Statistics	○ Everton	Boro ○
Goals	0	1
Shots on Target	7	6
Shots off Target	4	5
Hit Woodwork	0	0
Possession %	61	39
Corners	10	1
Offsides	0	2
Fouls	13	15
Disciplinary Points	4	8

Age/Height

Everton Age	Middlesbrough Age
▶ 27 yrs, 7 mo	▶ 26 yrs, 9 mo
Everton Height	Middlesbrough Height
▶ 6'	▶ 6'

Everton box was turned round for a corner at full-stretch by Martyn. Boro continued to impress, with Viduka bringing a parry from Martyn and Hasselbaink thrashing the loose ball against the goalkeeper's left-hand post.

The second half was almost half an hour old before Mark Schwarzer was called upon to make another save, a flying effort to his left to turn away a left-footed shot from Arteta despatched from the edge of the Boro penalty area.

Boro hung on to their lead with some determined challenges. A magnificent tackle from Queudrue denied Bent seven minutes from time. Four minutes, the visitors were given a let-off after Rochemback handled 25 yards from goal. Arteta hit the bar from the resultant free-kick, with Schwarzer rooted to the spot.

Fans' Player of the Match

Gaizka Mendieta

Quote

💬 Steve McClaren

Our attitude was spot on. We broke well, made loads of chances and dominated in midfield.

4-1

Middlesbrough ○
Manchester United ○

▶ Yakubu is on target from the penalty spot

Event Line

2 ○ ⊕ Mendieta / RF / OP / OA	
	Assist: Pogatetz
18 ○ ▉ Pogatetz	
20 ○ ▉ van Nistelrooy	
25 ○ ⊕ Hasselbaink / RF / OP / IA	
	Assist: Mendieta
31 ○ ⇄ Richardson > Bardsley	
45 ○ ▉ Smith	
45 ○ ⊕ Yakubu / RF / P / IA	
	Assist: Parnaby
Half time 3-0	
60 ○ ⇄ Ronaldo > Park	
64 ○ ⇄ Doriva > Rochemback	
71 ○ ▉ Fletcher	
78 ○ ⊕ Mendieta / RF / OP / IA	
	Assist: Yakubu
79 ○ ⇄ Nemeth > Hasselbaink	
87 ○ ⇄ Brown > Ferdinand	
87 ○ ⇄ Morrison > Mendieta	
90 ○ ▉ O'Shea	
90 ○ ⊕ Ronaldo / H / C / IA	
	Assist: Scholes
Full time 4-1	

An exceptional team performance saw a Gaizka Mendieta-inspired Boro inflict a stunning defeat on a star-studded Manchester United side.

Mendieta turned back the clock to reproduce the form that once earned him a reputation as Europe's finest midfielder. The Spaniard gave Boro the best possible start with just one minute and 38 seconds played, firing in from 30 yards.

Mendieta then set up Jimmy Floyd Hasselbaink for Boro's second on 25 minutes. The Dutch striker shrugged off a challenge, gave himself room to shoot before unleashing a fierce shot that hit a powerless van der Sar on its route to goal.

Boro inflicted yet more damage before the break, taking an incredible three-goal lead. Deep into injury time, Stuart Parnaby was brought down in the box for a penalty. Yakubu sent the keeper the wrong way from the spot.

The second half was a high tempo affair in which United desperately searched for a way back into the game, but it only got worse for the visitors. With 13 minutes remaining, Yakubu powered forward, drawing in defenders before pulling the ball back for Mendieta to strike a low shot for his second goal of the game. Cristiano Ronaldo hit a 93rd minute consolation goal for United.

Fans' Player of the Match

Gaizka Mendieta

Quote

🎙 **Steve McClaren**

We deserved it as the players were fantastic. We played some good football and scored some very good goals.

Venue:	Riverside Stadium	Referee:	A.G.Wiley - 05/06	**Middlesbrough**
Attendance:	30,579	Matches:	12	**Manchester United**
Capacity:	35,100	Yellow Cards:	35	
Occupancy:	87%	Red Cards:	3	

Form Coming into Fixture

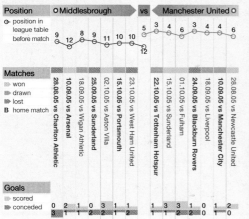

Position ○ Middlesbrough vs Manchester United ○

position in league table before match

Matches
- won
- drawn
- lost
- B home match

	28.08.05 vs Charlton Athletic	10.09.05 vs Arsenal	18.09.05 vs Wigan Athletic	25.09.05 vs Sunderland	02.10.05 vs Aston Villa	15.10.05 vs Portsmouth	23.10.05 vs West Ham United	22.10.05 vs Tottenham Hotspur	15.10.05 vs Sunderland	01.10.05 vs Fulham	24.09.05 vs Blackburn Rovers	18.09.05 vs Liverpool	10.09.05 vs Manchester City	28.08.05 vs Newcastle United

Goals
scored	0	2	1	0	3	1	1		1	3	3	1	0	1	2
conceded	3	1	1	2	2	1	1		1	1	2	2	0	1	0

Goal Statistics

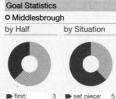

○ Middlesbrough

by Half — first: 3, second: 5

by Situation — set piece: 5, open play: 3

○ Manchester United

by Half — first: 6, second: 5

by Situation — set piece: 3, open play: 8

Goals by Area

○ Middlesbrough — Scored (Conceded)

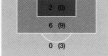

2 (0)

6 (9)

0 (3)

○ Manchester United — Scored (Conceded)

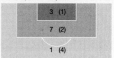

3 (1)

7 (2)

1 (4)

Team Statistics

Starting Line-Ups

Middlesbrough:
Schwarzer; Pogatetz, Rochemback, Doriva, Queudrue, Riggott, Boateng, Bates, Mendieta/Morrison, Parnaby; Yakubu, Rooney, Hasselbaink/Nemeth

Manchester United:
Fletcher, Bardsley/Richardson, Smith, Ferdinand/Brown, van der Sar, van Nistelrooy, Scholes, Silvestre, Park/Ronaldo, O'Shea

Unused Sub: Jones, Viduka

Unused Sub: Howard, Rossi

▶ 5/3/2

▶ 4/4/2

Premiership Totals	○ Boro	Man Utd ○
Premiership Appearances	1,370	1,762
Team Appearances	879	1,203
Goals Scored	205	272
Assists	151	188
Clean Sheets (goalkeepers)	71	46
Yellow Cards	175	198
Red Cards	9	13
Full Internationals	9	13

Age/Height

Middlesbrough Age	Manchester United Age
▶ **26 yrs, 8 mo**	▶ **25 yrs, 4 mo**
Middlesbrough Height	Manchester United Height
▶ **5'11"**	▶ **6'**

Match Statistics

League Table after Fixture

		Played	Won	Drawn	Lost	For	Against	Pts
↓ 6	Man Utd	10	5	3	2	15	11	18
↑ 7	Arsenal	10	5	2	3	13	7	17
↓ 8	Man City	10	5	2	3	11	8	17
↓ 9	West Ham	10	4	3	3	14	10	15
↑ 10	Middlesbrough	11	4	3	4	15	15	15
↓ 11	Blackburn	11	4	2	5	11	14	14
↑ 12	Liverpool	9	3	4	2	7	8	13
↓ 13	Newcastle	10	3	3	4	8	10	12
↑ 14	Portsmouth	11	2	4	5	11	13	10

Statistics	○ Boro	Man Utd ○
Goals	4	1
Shots on Target	5	8
Shots off Target	3	6
Hit Woodwork	0	0
Possession %	46	54
Corners	2	6
Offsides	0	1
Fouls	14	22
Disciplinary Points	4	16

3-0

Middlesbrough ○
Dnipro Dnipropetrovsk ○

► Stuart Parnaby prepares to control the ball

Event Line

36 ○ ⊕ Yakubu / RF / OP / IA
　　Assist: Mendieta
Half time 1-0
50 ○ ⊕ Viduka / RF / OP / OA
52 ○ ⇄ Melashchenko > Kostyshyn
56 ○ ⊕ Viduka / RF / OP / IA
　　Assist: Morrison
57 ○ ⇄ Maccarone > Yakubu
58 ○ ⇄ Lysytskiy > Rusol
60 ○ ⇄ Kennedy > Mendieta
64 ○ ⇄ Nemeth > Viduka
66 ○ ⇄ Motuz > Mykhaylenko
90 ○ ▨ Maccarone
Full time 3-0

Two goals from Mark Viduka and one from Yakubu sent Boro top of the group with a comfortable win over Ukrainian side, Dnipro.

Boro showed three changes from the side which comprehensively beat Manchester United a few days earlier.

After five minutes, Mark Viduka attempted to find Yakubu with a chip on the edge of the area. His effort was cleared but only to Gaizka Mendieta, who struck a low, first-time volley from 25 yards.

Less than a minute later, Yakubu set up Mendieta on the edge of the Dnipro penalty area, and another low snapshot from the Spaniard went a yard wide.

Dnipro, as expected, moved swiftly on the break but found it difficult to get past the defence and were restricted to shots from outside the penalty area.

After 35 minutes, Yakubu exchanged passes with Mendieta before tucking the return ball low to keeper Kusliy's right. Five minutes after the restart, Boro doubled their advantage.

Pogatetz played a short ball to Mendieta, whose pass to Viduka looked to have fallen short. But the Australian international turned his nearest marker on the edge of the area and fired a thunderous shot past Kusliy.

Five minutes later came the third as James Morrison fired in a shot that was too powerful for Kusliy. His parried save fell to Viduka, who was left with the relatively simple task of sliding a low shot in between two defenders from 12 yards.

► Mark Viduka celebrates a goal with Gaizka Mendieta

Match Statistics

Starting Line-Ups

Pogatetz · Semochko · Rykun
Queudrue · Mendieta Kennedy · Yezerskiy
Schwarzer · Viduka Nemeth · Mykhaylenko Motuz · Kusliy
Riggott · Doriva · Kostyshyn MelashcHenko · Husol Lysytskiy
Bates · Yakubu Maccarone · Nazarenko · Shershun
Morrison · Shelayev
Parnaby · Radchenko

► 5/3/2   ► 5/4/1

Unused Sub: Jones, Boateng, Johnson, Hasselbaink

Unused Sub: Kernozenko, Bidnenko, Kravchenko, Kornilenko

Statistics	○ Boro	Dnipro ○
Goals	3	0
Shots on Target	10	0
Shots off Target	6	8
Hit Woodwork	0	0
Possession %	51	49
Corners	8	1
Offsides	3	2
Fouls	24	19
Disciplinary Points	4	0

Mark Schwarzer wasn't exactly overworked, but was called upon to make a smart save from a Dmytro Mykhaylenko free-kick.

Viduka was just wide with an angled shot as he went for his hat-trick. There was no let up in Boro's determination and Morrison brought an acrobatic save from the overworked Kusliy with a delightful effort from just inside the penalty area.

Morrison was a constant threat in the second half, turning in a performance that deserved a goal. Emanuel Pogatetz was just off target with a drive from the edge of the penalty area.

Deep in injury time, Morrison had another attempt saved by Kusliy.

Fans' Player of the Match

Mark Viduka

Quote

❝ **Steve McClaren**

It was important to win. It sets us up nicely and we only need another point from the next two games to progress.

1-0

Everton ○
Middlesbrough ○

➤ George Boateng holds off Simon Davies

Event Line

16 ○ ⊕ Beattie / H / C / 6Y	
	Assist: van der Meyde
Half time 1-0	
48 ○ ▢ Rochemback	
54 ○ ⇄ Viduka > Yakubu	
56 ○ ⇄ Kilbane > Davies	
61 ○ ▢ Neville	
66 ○ ▢ van der Meyde	
69 ○ ⇄ McFadden > van der Meyde	
76 ○ ⇄ Bent M > Ferguson	
76 ○ ⇄ Morrison > Rochemback	
81 ○ ⇄ Doriva > Ehiogu	
Full time 1-0	

Boro's frustrating inconsistency continued, as a first half goal was enough for Everton to take all three points and their first home win of the season.

With 16 minutes gone, Everton took the lead against the run of play. A well-worked short corner caught Ugo Ehiogu flat-footed, allowing James Beattie in to score with a glancing header from the edge of the six-yard box.

With their confidence raised, the home side knocked the ball around comfortably. Boro could have levelled before half time when Yakubu had only the 'keeper to beat, but former England international Nigel Martyn recovered sufficiently to save the striker's miss-hit shot.

Everton's direct approach in the second half threatened to put Boro further behind but, thanks to good defensive work, the home side were denied the opportunity to double their lead. With 10 minutes to go, Beattie broke through on goal but his effort struck the crossbar. Franck Queudrue went close in the final minute, but Boro were denied a point when his header from a corner struck the crossbar.

Fans' Player of the Match

Gaizka Mendieta

Quote

❝ **Steve McClaren**

We're disappointed with the result. We weren't ruthless and lacked creativity.

Premiership Milestone

➤ **250**

George Boateng made both his 250th Premiership appearance and 100th in the top-flight for Middlesbrough.

Venue:	Goodison Park	Referee:	M.A.Riley - 05/06		Everton
Attendance:	34,349	Matches:	10		Middlesbrough
Capacity:	40,569	Yellow Cards:	47		
Occupancy:	85%	Red Cards:	2		

Form Coming into Fixture

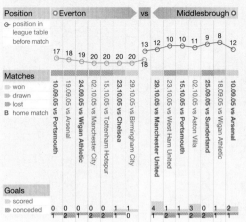

Position	Everton	vs	Middlesbrough
position in league table before match	17 18 19 20 20 20 20 18	13 12 10 10 11 9 8 12	

Matches
- won
- drawn
- lost
- B home match

	Everton	Middlesbrough
Matches	10.09.05 vs Portsmouth / 19.09.05 vs Arsenal / 24.09.05 vs Wigan Athletic / 02.10.05 vs Manchester City / 15.10.05 vs Tottenham Hotspur / 23.10.05 vs Chelsea / 29.10.05 vs Birmingham City	29.10.05 vs Manchester United / 23.10.05 vs West Ham United / 15.10.05 vs Portsmouth / 02.10.05 vs Aston Villa / 25.09.05 vs Sunderland / 18.09.05 vs Wigan Athletic / 10.09.05 vs Arsenal

Goals
- scored
- conceded

Goals scored	0	0	0	0	1	1		4	1	1	3	0	1	2
conceded	1	2	1	2	1	0		1	2	1	2	2	1	1

Goal Statistics

Everton

by Half		by Situation	
first:	2	set piece:	1
second:	0	open play:	1

Middlesbrough

by Half		by Situation	
first:	6	set piece:	6
second:	6	open play:	6

Goals by Area

Everton

Scored (Conceded)

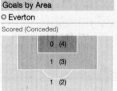

0 (4)
1 (3)
1 (2)

Middlesbrough

Scored (Conceded)

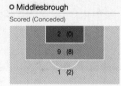

2 (0)
9 (8)
1 (2)

Team Statistics

Starting Line-Ups

Neville, van der Meyde, McFadden, Parnaby, Mendieta, Weir, Cahill, Ferguson, Bent M, Hasselbaink, Ehiogu, Doriva, Martyn, Boateng, Riggott, Schwarzer, Beattie, Yobo, Davies, Kilbane, Yakubu, Viduka, Queudrue, Rochemback, Morrison, Hibbert, Arteta, Pogatetz

4/4/2   5/3/2

Unused Sub: Wright, Kroldrup

Unused Sub: Jones, Bates

Premiership Totals	Everton	Boro
Premiership Appearances	2,072	1,759
Team Appearances	974	909
Goals Scored	221	271
Assists	150	175
Clean Sheets (goalkeepers)	132	71
Yellow Cards	209	231
Red Cards	17	16
Full Internationals	11	10

Age/Height

Everton Age	Middlesbrough Age
28 yrs, 3 mo	27 yrs, 10 mo
Everton Height	Middlesbrough Height
6'	6'

Match Statistics

League Table after Fixture

		Played	Won	Drawn	Lost	For	Against	Pts
↓	8 Charlton	11	6	1	4	16	14	19
↓	9 West Ham	11	5	3	3	15	10	18
●	10 Newcastle	12	5	3	4	12	10	18
●	11 Blackburn	12	5	2	5	15	15	17
●	12 Liverpool	10	4	4	2	9	8	16
●	13 Middlesbrough	12	4	3	5	15	16	15
●	14 Fulham	12	3	3	6	12	16	12
●	15 Portsmouth	12	2	4	6	11	15	10
↑	16 Everton	11	3	1	7	4	12	10

Statistics	Everton	Boro
Goals	1	0
Shots on Target	8	9
Shots off Target	4	8
Hit Woodwork	1	1
Possession %	45	55
Corners	9	3
Offsides	1	5
Fouls	21	16
Disciplinary Points	8	4

3-2

Middlesbrough ○
Fulham ○

Premiership
20.11.05

▶ James Morrison celebrates his 64th-minute equaliser

Event Line

9 ○ ⊕	John / LF / OP / IA
	Assist: Legwinski
31 ○ ▦	Jensen N
Half time 0-1	
46 ○ ⇄	Nemeth > Pogatetz
64 ○ ⊕	Morrison / RF / OP / 6Y
	Assist: Yakubu
70 ○ ⊕	Diop / H / C / IA
	Assist: John
76 ○ ⊕	Yakubu / RF / OP / 6Y
	Assist: Hasselbaink
78 ○ ⇄	Helguson > John
84 ○ ⊕	Hasselbaink / RF / OP / IA
	Assist: Nemeth
86 ○ ⇄	Doriva > Hasselbaink
Full time 3-2	

Boro showed great fighting spirit as they twice came from behind to win all three points, thanks to a late strike from last season's top scorer, Jimmy Floyd Hasselbaink.

The home side again conceded an early goal, Fulham taking the lead after just eight minutes. Collins John received the ball with his back to goal, controlled on his chest before turning to hit a left-footed volley beyond Brad Jones.

Boro finally equalised on the hour mark, Yakubu cutting in from the left and picking out James Morrison who hit his first ever Premiership goal.

Within five minutes, Fulham regained the lead when Papa Bouba Diop headed home from a corner. Boro equalised for a second time five minutes later when captain Gareth Southgate won a 50-50 challenge inside the Fulham half. His resulting pass found Rochemback, who crossed for a sliding Hasselbaink to convert off a prostrate Yakubu at the back post.

Having twice gone behind, Boro hit the winner in the 83rd minute. A right-wing cross picked out Hasselbaink. The striker controlled and cut inside before hitting his shot just inside the near post from 11 yards out.

Fans' Player of the Match	Quote	Premiership Milestone
Yakubu	🍏 **Steve McClaren**	▶ **First Goal**
	I said at half-time we might have to grind out this result. The players showed character and attitude as well as quality at the right time.	James Morrison netted his first Premiership goal.

Venue:	Riverside Stadium	Referee:	U.D.Rennie - 05/06
Attendance:	27,599	Matches:	13
Capacity:	35,100	Yellow Cards:	24
Occupancy:	79%	Red Cards:	2

Middlesbrough
Fulham

Form Coming into Fixture

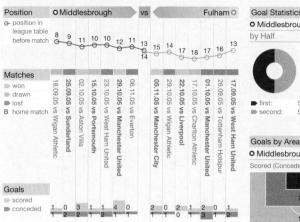

Position
⊙ position in league table before match

Middlesbrough vs Fulham

8 9 11 10 10 12 11 13 14 15 14 17 18 17 16 13

Matches
⏵ won
⏵ drawn
⏵ lost
B home match

18.09.05 vs Wigan Athletic
25.09.05 vs Sunderland
02.10.05 vs Aston Villa
15.10.05 vs Portsmouth
23.10.05 vs West Ham United
29.10.05 vs Manchester United
06.11.05 vs Everton
05.11.05 vs Manchester City
29.10.05 vs Wigan Athletic
22.10.05 vs Liverpool
17.10.05 vs Charlton Athletic
01.10.05 vs Manchester United
26.09.05 vs Tottenham Hotspur
17.09.05 vs West Ham United

Goals
⏵ scored
⏵ conceded

| 1 | 0 | 3 | 1 | 1 | 4 | 0 | | 2 | 0 | 2 | 1 | 2 | 0 | 1 |
| 1 | 2 | 2 | 1 | 2 | 1 | 1 | | 1 | 1 | 0 | 0 | 3 | 1 | 2 |

Goal Statistics

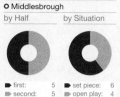

⊙ Middlesbrough

by Half / by Situation

⏵ first: 5   ⏵ set piece: 6
⏵ second: 5   ⏵ open play: 4

○ Fulham

by Half / by Situation

⏵ first: 6   ⏵ set piece: 2
⏵ second: 2   ⏵ open play: 6

Goals by Area

⊙ Middlesbrough

Scored (Conceded)

2 (0)
7 (7)
1 (2)

○ Fulham

Scored (Conceded)

0 (1)
6 (8)
2 (0)

Team Statistics

Starting Line-Ups

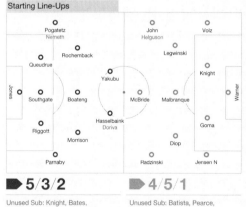

Pogatetz
Nemeth
Rochemback
Queudrue
Yakubu
Jones
Southgate   Boateng   McBride
Riggott   Hasselbaink   Doriva
Morrison
Parnaby

John
Helguson
Volz
Legwinski
Knight
Malbranque   Warner
Goma
Diop
Radzinski   Jensen N

⏵ **5/3/2**   ⏵ **4/5/1**

Unused Sub: Knight, Bates, Maccarone

Unused Sub: Batista, Pearce, Rehman, Rosenior

Premiership Totals	⊙ Boro	Fulham ○
Premiership Appearances	1,518	946
Team Appearances	761	765
Goals Scored	222	110
Assists	162	86
Clean Sheets (goalkeepers)	2	2
Yellow Cards	202	107
Red Cards	9	7
Full Internationals	8	8

Age/Height

Middlesbrough Age
⏵ **26 yrs, 11 mo**

Fulham Age
⏵ **28 yrs, 8 mo**

Middlesbrough Height
⏵ **6'**

Fulham Height
⏵ **5'11"**

Match Statistics

League Table after Fixture

		Played	Won	Drawn	Lost	For	Against	Pts
↑ 6	Tottenham	13	5	6	2	14	9	21
↓ 7	Man City	13	6	3	4	15	11	21
↑ 8	West Ham	12	5	4	3	16	11	19
↓ 9	Liverpool	11	5	4	2	12	8	19
↓ 10	Charlton	12	6	1	5	17	17	19
↑ 11	Middlesbrough	13	5	3	5	18	18	18
↓ 12	Blackburn	13	5	3	5	15	15	18
↓ 13	Newcastle	13	5	3	5	12	13	18
● 14	Fulham	13	3	3	7	14	19	12

Statistics	⊙ Boro	Fulham ○
Goals	3	2
Shots on Target	11	6
Shots off Target	9	3
Hit Woodwork	0	1
Possession %	57	43
Corners	9	4
Offsides	6	2
Fouls	9	16
Disciplinary Points	0	4

0-0

AZ Alkmaar ○
Middlesbrough ○

▶ Szilard Nemeth tries to find some space in which to operate

Event Line		
24 ○ ■	Schaars	
30 ○ ■	Hasselbaink	
Half time 0-0		
49 ○ ■	Pogatetz	
58 ○ ■	Boateng	
61 ○ ⇄	Meerdink > Sektioui	
64 ○ ⇄	Parnaby > Morrison	
64 ○ ⇄	Yakubu > Viduka	
71 ○ ■	Steinsson	
75 ○ ⇄	Queudrue > Nemeth	
77 ○ ⇄	Koevermans > Arveladze	
Full time 0-0		

Boro reached the last 32 of the UEFA Cup with a battling draw against the free-scoring Dutch side who were semi-finalists the previous season.

The match was played in heavy rain and blustery winds. Steve McClaren started with a 4-1-2-1-2 line-up, as Matthew Bates and Emanuel Pogatetz occupied the full-back berths and Ugo Ehiogu returned alongside Chris Riggott.

Morrison teamed up well with Mark Viduka and Jimmy Floyd Hasselbaink to set up an early chance, but Timmer raced off his line to smother the danger, while the goalkeeper saved well with his legs at his near post after a smart turn and shot from Viduka.

Alkmaar were unlucky to have a goal disallowed after 12 minutes. Brad Jones twice saved well as ex-Rangers striker Shota Arveladze and Dutch international midfielder Denny Landzaat caused problems, but Sektioui smashed home from close range only to have celebrations cut short by Italian referee Gianluca Paparesta after an infringement was flagged.

Boro had claims for a penalty after 30 minutes when Morrison, set up by a clever Viduka back heel, looked to have been upended when taking control. But the referee took no action.

Landzaat went close from distance before a Riggott header was deflected for a corner.

Ex-Holland star Van Galen shot from distance when Alkmaar next pressed, but Jones gathered comfortably.

▶ Doriva battles away in midfield

Match Statistics

Starting Line-Ups

AZ:
de Cler, van Galen, Mathijsen, Schaars, Arveladze, Koevermans, Timmer, Jaliens, Landzaat, Perez, Steinsson, Sektioui, Meerdink

Boro:
Bates, Morrison, Parnaby, Ehiogu, Jones, Hasselbaink, Nemeth, Queudrue, Doriva, Viduka, Yakubu, Boateng, Riggott, Pogatetz

▶ **4/4/1/1**   ▶ **4/4/2** (Diamond)

Unused Sub: Zwarthoed, Vlaar, Buskermolen, Ramzi, Huysegems.

Unused Sub: Knight, Southgate, Johnson, Maccarone

Statistics	AZ	Boro
Goals	0	0
Shots on Target	4	3
Shots off Target	7	2
Hit Woodwork	0	0
Possession %	67	33
Corners	2	3
Offsides	5	0
Fouls	12	12
Disciplinary Points	8	12

A neat move created a half-chance for Boro as the ball fell to George Boateng inside the area. His low shot brought a good save from Timmer.

Although Alkmaar enjoyed a lot of possession, there was little attacking threat from the Dutch hosts. Nevertheless it took a fine block from Ehiogu to thwart van Galen, whose low shot looked to have caught Jones out of position, the goalkeeper having weakly punched a sliced clearance from his defender.

Jones did better a few minutes later as Koevermans beat the offside trap and moved in on goal from a narrow angle. The keeper stood firm and got enough on the shot to send it spinning into the six-yard box, from where it was thumped clear.

Fans' Player of the Match

Brad Jones

Quote

❝ **Steve McClaren**

There were a few hectic moments, but they're a good side and we did well to keep a clean sheet.

2-2

Middlesbrough ○
West Bromwich Albion ○

▶ Doriva and Chris Riggott put Nathan Ellington under pressure

Event Line

12 ○ ⊕	Viduka / RF / OP / OA
18 ○ ⊕	Ellington / RF / OP / IA
	Assist: Kanu
Half time 1-1	
46 ○ ⇄	Nemeth > Queudrue
46 ○ ⇄	Albrechtsen > Watson
51 ○ ▪	Clement
57 ○ ⊕	Kanu / RF / OP / OA
	Assist: Robinson
62 ○ ⇄	Carter > Kamara
66 ○ ⊕	Yakubu / RF / P / IA
	Assist: Nemeth
70 ○ ▪	Parnaby
79 ○ ⇄	Doriva > Morrison
79 ○ ⇄	Hasselbaink > Viduka
Full time 2-2	

Goals from Yakubu and Mark Viduka were not enough to beat a battling West Brom as Bryan Robson and Jonathan Greening made happy Riverside returns.

Boro took the lead from their first meaningful attack. George Boateng attempted to play a one-two with Mark Viduka. When the return pass hit Junichi Inamoto, Viduka performed a drag-back before hitting a sensational shot with the outside of his right foot, beating Tomasz Kuszczak in goal.

Boro held the lead for just six minutes. An attempted clearance from Franck Queudrue hit Kanu just outside the Boro box. The Nigerian played in Nathan Ellington, who had time to drill his low shot across Schwarzer.

Kanu gave West Brom the lead in the second half with a low drive from the edge of the box. Boro were handed a lifeline midway through the second half when they were awarded a penalty for a push on Nemeth. Yakubu sent the goalkeeper the wrong way with another trademark casual penalty.

The visitors went close to a last-gasp victory, Ronnie Wallwork's 22-yard strike forcing a full-length save from Schwarzer.

Fans' Player of the Match	Quote	Premiership Milestone
Fabio Rochemback	🔘 **Steve McClaren**	▶ **50**
	We're scoring goals, but we're also conceding and we need to stop that to move up the Premiership.	Chris Riggott made his 50th Premiership appearance in the colours of Middlesbrough.

Venue:	Riverside Stadium	Referee:	P.Walton - 05/06	Middlesbrough
Attendance:	27,041	Matches:	16	West Bromwich Albion
Capacity:	35,100	Yellow Cards:	52	
Occupancy:	77%	Red Cards:	4	

Form Coming into Fixture

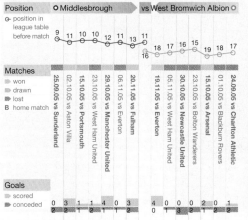

Position — position in league table before match

Matches: won, drawn, lost, B home match

Goals: scored, conceded

Goal Statistics

○ Middlesbrough

by Half — first: 4, second: 8
by Situation — set piece: 5, open play: 7

○ West Bromwich Albion

by Half — first: 2, second: 5
by Situation — set piece: 3, open play: 4

Goals by Area

○ Middlesbrough — Scored (Conceded)

4 (1)
7 (8)
1 (2)

○ West Bromwich Albion — Scored (Conceded)

2 (3)
2 (6)
3 (2)

Team Statistics

Starting Line-Ups

Middlesbrough: Pogatetz, Rochemback, Queudrue (Nemeth), Schwarzer, Yakubu, Ellington, Southgate, Boateng, Riggott, Viduka (Hasselbaink), Kanu, Morrison (Doriva), Parnaby

West Bromwich Albion: Greening, Watson (Albrechtsen), Wallwork, Davies C, Kuszczak, Inamoto, Clement, Kamara (Carter), Robinson

▶ 5/3/2

▶ 4/4/2

Unused Sub: Jones, Bates

Unused Sub: Hoult, Earnshaw, Horsfield

Premiership Totals

	○Boro	West Brom○
Premiership Appearances	1,922	1,053
Team Appearances	1,035	354
Goals Scored	291	86
Assists	191	84
Clean Sheets (goalkeepers)	71	2
Yellow Cards	221	102
Red Cards	12	3
Full Internationals	10	5

Age/Height

Middlesbrough Age ▶ **27 yrs, 10 mo**

West Bromwich Albion Age ▶ **26 yrs**

Middlesbrough Height ▶ **6'**

West Bromwich Albion Height ▶ **6'**

Match Statistics

League Table after Fixture

		Played	Won	Drawn	Lost	For	Against	Pts
●	9 West Ham	13	5	4	4	17	13	19
↑	10 Middlesbrough	14	5	4	5	20	20	19
↓	11 Charlton	13	6	1	6	17	18	19
●	12 Newcastle	14	5	3	6	12	14	18
●	13 Blackburn	14	5	3	6	15	18	18
↑	14 Fulham	14	4	3	7	16	20	15
↓	15 Aston Villa	14	4	3	7	14	22	15
↑	16 Everton	13	4	1	8	5	16	13
↓	17 West Brom	14	3	3	8	15	24	12

Statistics

	○Boro	West Brom○
Goals	2	2
Shots on Target	9	6
Shots off Target	5	3
Hit Woodwork	0	0
Possession %	46	54
Corners	6	5
Offsides	1	1
Fouls	15	13
Disciplinary Points	4	4

2-1

Middlesbrough ○
Crystal Palace ○

▶ Ugo Ehiogu is too strong for Jon Macken

Two second half goals saw Boro come from behind against their second division opponents to claim a place in the quarter-finals of the Carling Cup.

Chris Riggott was rested as Ugo Ehiogu returned, Szilard Nemeth replaced James Morrison, Doriva came in for Emanuel Pogatetz while Jimmy Floyd Hasselbaink started ahead of Yakubu. A crowd of less than 11,000 was at the Riverside to see Boro continue their challenge in a competition they won in 2004.

Boro enjoyed most of the early possession but there was not enough quality in their final ball to cause Palace keeper Julian Speroni undue concern. The home side went on to concede an own goal after 31 minutes. Mikele Leigertwood raced to the edge of the Boro penalty area from where he sent over a teasing cross that Franck Queudrue – under no pressure - turned past Mark Schwarzer from the edge of the six-yard box.

When Fabio Rochemback shot for goal from 22 yards a couple of minutes later, Speroni spilled the ball and Palace were forced to scramble clear. Four minutes from half-time, Boro created their best chance so far when Doriva won possession. George Boateng picked up the loose ball just up from the edge of the Palace penalty area and a neat backheel sent Mark Viduka away. But the Australia international went for power over placement and Speroni made a comfortable save.

Six minutes into the second-half Boro got the equaliser when Viduka unleashed an unstoppable shot from 30 yards that flew past Speroni. They went ahead four minutes later, Nemeth squeezing in his shot from a tight angle.

▶ Szilard Nemeth celebrates his winning goal

Match Statistics

Starting Line-Ups

Statistics	○ Boro	C. Palace ○
Goals	2	1
Shots on Target	6	3
Shots off Target	8	6
Hit Woodwork	1	0
Possession %	47	53
Corners	2	4
Offsides	4	4
Fouls	17	15
Disciplinary Points	8	4

▶ 4/4/2   ▶ 4/4/2

Unused Sub: Jones, Yakubu   Unused Sub: Kiraly, Ward

Within seconds, Hasselbaink unleashed a powerful shot that thudded against the bar. Steve McClaren made two changes, withdrawing Nemeth in favour of Emanuel Pogatetz and taking off Hasselbaink for Massimo Maccarone.

Far from crumbling, Palace fought their way back into the game, enjoying the better of the 50-50 challenges, and had three unlikely claims for penalties turned away.

Matthew Bates replaced Fabio Rochemback, releasing Stuart Parnaby to move further upfield. The switch almost paid dividends, as twice Parnaby went close with decent shots. Despite an energetic finish from the visitors, Boro determinedly held on.

Fans' Player of the Match

Mark Viduka

Quote

66 Steve McClaren

Despite trailing, I thought we played some of our best football at home this season in the first half.

53

1-0

Chelsea ○
Middlesbrough ○

▶ Matthew Bates puts Damien Duff under pressure

Event Line

Half time 0-0	
62 ○ ⊕ Terry / H / C / IA	
Assist: Duff	
64 ○ ⇄ Geremi > Gudjohnsen	
72 ○ ⇄ Viduka > Hasselbaink	
74 ○ ⇄ Wright-Phillips > Robben	
78 ○ ⇄ Cole C > Drogba	
81 ○ ⇄ Queudrue > Morrison	
Full time 1-0	

Despite their best efforts, Boro were unable to upset the champions Chelsea, who continued their unbeaten home run.

Boro came close to taking a shock lead with 14 minutes played. A deflected Yakubu shot fell to ex-Chelsea star Jimmy Floyd Hasselbaink, whose low shot from 16 yards out hit the post. It was the home team, however, that upped the pressure and looked the more likely to score.

After getting through the first half unscathed, it was Boro who gained in confidence. Hasselbaink won a free-kick eight yards from the Chelsea penalty area but then hit the ball well over the bar.

Chelsea grabbed what proved to be the game's only goal on the hour. John Terry headed home from a Damien Duff corner despite Rochemback's best efforts at keeping the ball out.

Once in the lead, the champions were bursting with confidence and Frank Lampard and Drogba were both guilty of missing good chances. Boro, however, refused to lie down and gave a good account of themselves without threatening an equaliser.

Fans' Player of the Match

Fabio Rochemback

Quote

❝ **Steve McClaren**

We showed fantastic attitude and character. We played to win and very nearly did it.

Venue:	Stamford Bridge	Referee:	M.A.Riley - 05/06		Chelsea
Attendance:	41,666	Matches:	14		Middlesbrough
Capacity:	42,449	Yellow Cards:	55		
Occupancy:	98%	Red Cards:	2		

Form Coming into Fixture

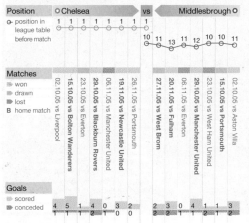

Position

○ Chelsea vs Middlesbrough ○

◑ position in league table before match

Chelsea: 1 1 1 1 1 1 1 1
Middlesbrough: 10 11 13 11 12 10 10 11

Matches
- won
- drawn
- lost
- B home match

Chelsea matches:
- 02.10.05 vs Liverpool
- 15.10.05 vs Bolton Wanderers
- 23.10.05 vs Everton
- 29.10.05 vs Blackburn Rovers
- 06.11.05 vs Manchester United
- 19.11.05 vs Newcastle United
- 26.11.05 vs Portsmouth

Middlesbrough matches:
- 27.11.05 vs West Brom
- 20.11.05 vs Fulham
- 06.11.05 vs Everton
- 29.10.05 vs Manchester United
- 23.10.05 vs West Ham United
- 15.10.05 vs Portsmouth
- 02.10.05 vs Aston Villa

Goals
- scored
- conceded

Chelsea: 4/1 5/1 1/1 4/2 0/0 3/1 2/0
Middlesbrough: 2/2 3/2 0/1 4/1 1/1 1/2 3/2

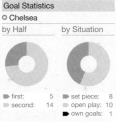

Goal Statistics

○ Chelsea

by Half / by Situation
- first: 5
- second: 14
- set piece: 8
- open play: 10
- own goals: 1

○ Middlesbrough

by Half / by Situation
- first: 5
- second: 9
- set piece: 6
- open play: 8

Goals by Area

○ Chelsea — Scored (Conceded)
- 3 (1)
- 12 (5)
- 4 (0)

○ Middlesbrough — Scored (Conceded)
- 4 (1)
- 8 (8)
- 2 (2)

Team Statistics

Starting Line-Ups

Chelsea: Cech; Del Horno, Terry, Carvalho, Gallas; Lampard, Essien, Gudjohnsen (Geremi), Duff; Robben Wright-Phillips, Drogba (Cole C)

4/3/3

Unused Sub: Cudicini, Ferreira

Middlesbrough: Schwarzer; Bates, Riggott, Southgate, Pogatetz; Boateng, Doriva, Morrison (Queudrue); Rochemback; Hasselbaink (Viduka), Yakubu

4/4/2 (Diamond)

Unused Sub: Jones, Ehiogu, Johnson

Premiership Totals

	○ Chelsea	Boro ○
Premiership Appearances	1,398	1,767
Team Appearances	942	880
Goals Scored	238	270
Assists	212	174
Clean Sheets (goalkeepers)	31	71
Yellow Cards	109	216
Red Cards	6	12
Full Internationals	13	9

Age/Height

Chelsea Age	Middlesbrough Age
25 yrs, 6 mo	27 yrs, 6 mo
Chelsea Height	Middlesbrough Height
6'	6'

Match Statistics

League Table after Fixture

		Played	Won	Drawn	Lost	For	Against	Pts
● 1	Chelsea	15	13	1	1	34	7	40
...		...	...	...	...	...	...	...
● 10	Middlesbrough	15	5	4	6	20	21	19
● 11	Charlton	13	6	1	6	17	18	19
● 12	Newcastle	15	5	4	6	13	15	19
● 13	Blackburn	15	5	3	7	15	20	18
● 14	Fulham	15	4	4	7	16	20	16
● 15	Aston Villa	15	4	4	7	15	23	16
● 16	Everton	14	5	1	8	7	16	16

Statistics

	○ Chelsea	Boro ○
Goals	1	0
Shots on Target	9	5
Shots off Target	8	5
Hit Woodwork	0	1
Possession %	56	44
Corners	6	4
Offsides	1	0
Fouls	15	14
Disciplinary Points	0	0

2-0

Liverpool ○
Middlesbrough ○

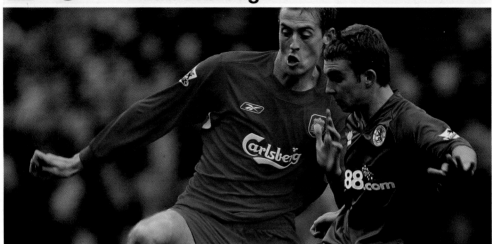

► James Morrison tries to find a way past the giant figure of Peter Crouch

Event Line

Half time 0-0

66 ○ ▨	Sissoko	
66 ○ ▨	Bates	
67 ○ ⇄	Garcia > Crouch	
72 ○ ⊕	Morientes / RF / OP / IA	
	Assist: Garcia	
75 ○ ⇄	Hasselbaink > Morrison	
77 ○ ⊕	Morientes / RF / OP / OA	
82 ○ ⇄	Cisse > Kewell	
84 ○ ◢	Riggott	
	2nd Bookable Offence	
86 ○ ⇄	Ehiogu > Yakubu	
87 ○ ⇄	Josemi > Morientes	

Full time 2-0

Boro were unable to stop Liverpool equalling a club record of successive clean sheets as they went down 2-0 at Anfield.

John-Arne Riise caused problems with a left-wing cross that dropped favourably for Morientes, whose header was tipped acrobatically over the bar by Mark Schwarzer.

Boro came out flying after the break and, in the first couple of minutes, came close to scoring. Mark Viduka looked set to put Boro ahead but was unfortunate to have his low shot saved by Jose Reina's legs.

It was an open game that saw chances for both sides, but it was the home team that took the lead with 19 minutes remaining. Morientes hit a low shot from 10 yards out that gave Schwarzer no chance.

Liverpool killed the game off just six minutes later. Franck Queudrue attempted to head back a Liverpool long ball to Schwarzer but, instead, the ball fell to Morientes, who lobbed the stranded Boro keeper from 20 yards. A miserable trip was concluded with Chris Riggott receiving a second yellow card, a harsh decision that saw the defender miss the last seven minutes of the game.

Fans' Player of the Match	Quote	Premiership Milestone
Chris Riggott	❝ **Steve McClaren**	➤ **150**

We are frustrated as we felt the second goal was a clear two yards offside and that the sending off was harsh.

Gareth Southgate made his 150th Premiership appearance in the colours of Middlesbrough.

Venue:	Anfield	Referee:	S.G.Bennett - 05/06		Liverpool
Attendance:	43,510	Matches:	17		Middlesbrough
Capacity:	45,362	Yellow Cards:	64		
Occupancy:	96%	Red Cards:	4		

Form Coming into Fixture

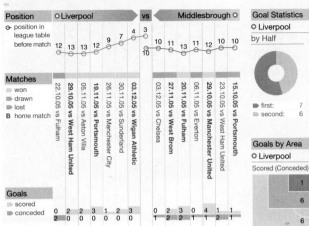

Position

O Liverpool vs Middlesbrough O

ᴏ position in league table before match

Liverpool: 12 13 13 12 9 7 4 3
Middlesbrough: 10 10 11 13 11 12 10 10

Matches
- won
- drawn
- lost
- B home match

Liverpool matches:
- 22.10.05 vs Fulham
- 29.10.05 vs West Ham United
- 05.11.05 vs Aston Villa
- 19.11.05 vs Portsmouth
- 26.11.05 vs Manchester City
- 30.11.05 vs Sunderland
- 03.12.05 vs Wigan Athletic

Middlesbrough matches:
- 03.12.05 vs Chelsea
- 27.11.05 vs West Brom
- 20.11.05 vs Fulham
- 06.11.05 vs Everton
- 29.10.05 vs Manchester United
- 23.10.05 vs West Ham United
- 15.10.05 vs Portsmouth

Goals
	scored	conceded
Liverpool	0 2 2 3 1 2 3	2 0 0 0 0 0 0
Middlesbrough	0 2 3 0 4 1 1	1 2 2 1 1 2 1

Goal Statistics

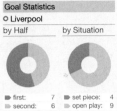

O Liverpool — by Half / by Situation

| first: | 7 | set piece: | 4 |
| second: | 6 | open play: | 9 |

O Middlesbrough — by Half / by Situation

| first: | 4 | set piece: | 4 |
| second: | 7 | open play: | 7 |

Goals by Area

O Liverpool — Scored (Conceded)

1 (0)
6 (2)
6 (0)

O Middlesbrough — Scored (Conceded)

4 (1)
5 (8)
2 (1)

Team Statistics

Starting Line-Ups

Liverpool:
Reina; Finnan, Carragher, Hyypia, Riise; Gerrard, Sissoko, Alonso, Kewell (Cisse); Morientes (Josemi), Crouch (Garcia)

Middlesbrough:
Schwarzer; Bates, Riggott, Southgate, Queudrue; Morrison (Hasselbaink), Doriva, Boateng, Viduka; Rochemback, Yakubu (Ehiogu)

▶ 4/4/2

▶ 4/4/2 (Diamond)

Unused Sub: Dudek, Warnock

Unused Sub: Jones, Pogatetz, Johnson

Premiership Totals

Premiership Totals	O Liverpool	Boro O
Premiership Appearances	1,487	2,112
Team Appearances	1,172	996
Goals Scored	171	289
Assists	163	178
Clean Sheets (goalkeepers)	11	71
Yellow Cards	144	255
Red Cards	10	17
Full Internationals	13	9

Age/Height

Liverpool Age	Middlesbrough Age
▶ 26 yrs, 4 mo	▶ 28 yrs, 3 mo
Liverpool Height	Middlesbrough Height
▶ 6'1"	▶ 6'

Match Statistics

League Table after Fixture

		Played	Won	Drawn	Lost	For	Against	Pts
↑ 2	Liverpool	15	9	4	2	20	8	31
...		...	...	...	...	...	...	...
↓ 13	Middlesbrough	16	5	4	7	20	23	19
↑ 14	Aston Villa	16	4	5	7	16	24	17
↓ 15	Fulham	16	4	4	8	16	21	16
↑ 16	West Brom	16	4	4	8	17	24	16
↓ 17	Everton	14	5	1	8	7	16	16
↑ 18	Birmingham	15	3	3	9	10	19	12
↓ 19	Portsmouth	15	2	4	9	11	23	10

Statistics

Statistics	O Liverpool	Boro O
Goals	2	0
Shots on Target	13	3
Shots off Target	10	3
Hit Woodwork	0	0
Possession %	54	46
Corners	11	2
Offsides	2	3
Fouls	10	18
Disciplinary Points	4	14

2-0

Middlesbrough ○
PFC Litex Lovech ○

➡ Jason Kennedy competes for the ball in midfield

Event Line

40 ○ ▪ Venkov	
Half time 0-0	
59 ○ ▪ Berberovic	
74 ○ ⇄ Lyubenov > Zlatinov	
77 ○ ⇄ Kirilov > Palankov	
80 ○ ⊕ Maccarone / H / OP / 6Y	
Assist: Johnson	
83 ○ ⊕ Cattermole > Hasselbaink	
86 ○ ⊕ Maccarone / LF / OP / OA	
Assist: Doriva	
87 ○ ⇄ Hazurov > Sandrinho	
89 ○ ▪ Cattermole	
Full time 2-0	

Two goals from Massimo Maccarone plus another clean sheet in Europe helped Boro end top of UEFA Cup Group D.

Steve McClaren included four teenagers, with Jason Kennedy starting for the first time. Boro began at a scorching pace, with Adam Johnson twice bringing near-post saves from Vutov with flashing drives from a yard either side of the penalty area.

The Bulgarians weathered the storm and created a fine opportunity to take the lead when left-back Mihail Venkov powered his way down Boro's right. After beating Matthew Bates relatively comfortably, he pulled a low ball back into the path of Milivoje Novakovic, whose shot whistled past Brad Jones.

Petar Zlatinov almost caught out Jones with a speculative effort from the left wing. An inswinging shot was dipping under the bar until the Australian keeper back-pedalled to tip over.

Boro started the second half brightly and nearly won a penalty after 53 minutes. Todor Palankov brought down Hasselbaink on the edge of the penalty area, but the visitors wasted the free-kick.

It didn't take Lovech long to get into stride, however, and Jones came racing two yards out of his area to deny Novakovic who was clean through after beating the offside trap.

The same player almost put Lovech into the lead a couple of minutes later, a low instinctive effort from 12 yards bringing a smart save from the keeper.

With 10 minutes left, Boro made the breakthrough.

▶ Massimo Maccarone competes for possession

Match Statistics

Starting Line-Ups

Jones

Queudrue Johnson

Riggott Doriva
       Maccarone Sandrinho
                  Hazurov
       Hasselbaink Novakovic
       Cattermole
Ehiogu Kennedy

Bates Morrison

Genchev Berberovic

Palankov Caillet
Kirilov

Jelenkovic Cichero

Vutov

Zlatinov Venkov
Lyubenov

▶ 4/4/2   ▶ 4/4/1/1

Unused Sub: Schwarzer, Southgate, Wheater, Boateng, Yakubu, Viduka

Unused Sub: Todorov, Zhelev, Zanev, Manolev

Statistics	o Boro	Litex o
Goals	2	0
Shots on Target	4	1
Shots off Target	6	10
Hit Woodwork	0	0
Possession %	51	49
Corners	6	4
Offsides	2	4
Fouls	16	9
Disciplinary Points	4	8

Johnson's perfect cross was met by Massimo Maccarone, who dived full-length on the edge of the six-yard box to head home.

A few minutes later, another product of Boro's Academy made his debut with 17-year-old Lee Cattermole replacing Jimmy Floyd Hasselbaink.

Boro wrapped it all up in spectacular fashion after 86 minutes as Maccarone despatched a strong shot from 25 yards that flew into Vutov's top right-hand corner.

Fans' Player of the Match

Massimo Maccarone

Quote

❝ **Steve McClaren**

We had a job to do and we did it well. It was not a very good game, but it gave our young players a bit of experience.

3-3

Middlesbrough ○
Tottenham Hotspur ○

▶ Franck Queudrue celebrates giving Boro a 3-2 lead

Event Line

6 ○ ▨	Dawson	
15 ○	Doriva	
19 ○	Davids	
25 ○ ⊕	Keane	/ RF / OP / IA
30 ○ ⊕	Yakubu	/ RF / C / IA
	Assist: Southgate	
41 ○	Bates	
43 ○ ⊕	Yakubu	/ LF / OP / IA
	Assist: Morrison	

Half time 2-1

56 ○ ⇄	Defoe > Reid	
63 ○ ⊕	Jenas	/ RF / DFK / OA
	Assist: Davids	
69 ○ ⊕	Queudrue	/ H / C / IA
	Assist: Rochemback	
70 ○	Robinson	
81 ○ ⇄	Rasiak > Jenas	
83 ○ ⊕	Mido	/ H / C / IA
	Assist: Carrick	
89 ○ ⇄	Maccarone > Morrison	
90 ○ ⇄	Brown > Defoe	

Full time 3-3

Boro's second clash of the season with Champions League-chasing Spurs was an entertaining goal-fest – with a dash of controversy added to the mix for good measure.

Tottenham hit the first goal with 25 minutes played. Young-Pyo Lee crossed the ball in from the left and, under pressure from Mido, Schwarzer dropped the ball, leaving Robbie Keane the simple task of slotting the ball in from 12 yards.

Boro were level within four minutes, Southgate flicking the ball on in the penalty area for Yakubu to volley in his ninth Premiership goal of the season.

Boro took the lead with just two minutes left of the first half. James Morrison beat a defender before hitting a powerful shot that deflected in off Yakubu.

Spurs came out fighting in the second half and Jermaine Jenas equalised thanks to a superbly taken free-kick from the top of the D Franck Queudrue countered for Boro with a header from Fabio Rochemback's corner.

Boro were denied all three points eight minutes from time when Mido was allowed a free header from a right-wing corner.

Fans' Player of the Match	Quote
James Morrison	🔊 **Steve McClaren**

We keep shooting ourselves in the foot. However, there was some terrific play today and we are not far from being a very good side.

Venue:	Riverside Stadium	Referee:	H.M.Webb - 05/06		Middlesbrough
Attendance:	27,614	Matches:	16		Tottenham Hotspur
Capacity:	35,100	Yellow Cards:	48		
Occupancy:	79%	Red Cards:	1		

Form Coming into Fixture

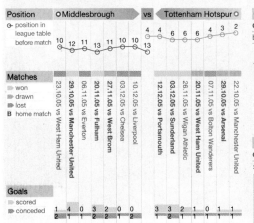

Position	Middlesbrough	vs	Tottenham Hotspur
position in league table before match	10 12 11 13 11 10 10 13		4 4 6 6 6 4 3 2

Matches
- won
- drawn
- lost
- B home match

Middlesbrough matches:
23.10.05 vs West Ham United / 29.10.05 vs Manchester United / 06.11.05 vs Everton / 20.11.05 vs Fulham / 27.11.05 vs West Brom / 03.12.05 vs Chelsea / 10.12.05 vs Liverpool

Tottenham matches:
12.12.05 vs Portsmouth / 03.12.05 vs Sunderland / 26.11.05 vs Wigan Athletic / 20.11.05 vs West Ham United / 07.11.05 vs Bolton Wanderers / 29.10.05 vs Arsenal / 22.10.05 vs Manchester United

Goals
	scored	1 4 0 3 2 0 0	3 3 2 1 0 1 1
	conceded	2 1 1 2 2 1 2	1 2 1 1 1 1 1

Goal Statistics

Middlesbrough

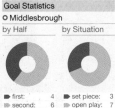

by Half / by Situation
- first: 4
- second: 6
- set piece: 3
- open play: 7

Tottenham Hotspur

by Half / by Situation
- first: 4
- second: 7
- set piece: 5
- open play: 6

Goals by Area

Middlesbrough

Scored (Conceded)

3 (1)
5 (8)
2 (2)

Tottenham Hotspur

Scored (Conceded)

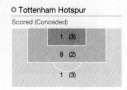

1 (3)
9 (2)
1 (3)

Team Statistics

Starting Line-Ups

Queudrue, Rochemback, Jenas, Stalteri, Raslak
Southgate, Doriva, Viduka, Keane, Carrick, Dawson
Schwarzer, Robinson
Ehiogu, Boateng, Yakubu, Mido, Davids, King
Bates, Morrison, Reid, Lee
Maccarone, Defoe

4/4/2   **4/4/2**

Unused Sub: Jones, Pogatetz, Wheater, Johnson

Unused Sub: Cerny, Pamarot

Premiership Totals

	Boro	Tottenham
Premiership Appearances	1,815	1,068
Team Appearances	973	590
Goals Scored	180	146
Assists	115	102
Clean Sheets (goalkeepers)	71	36
Yellow Cards	206	83
Red Cards	15	4
Full Internationals	9	12

Age/Height

Middlesbrough Age	Tottenham Hotspur Age
27 yrs, 11 mo	**25 yrs, 9 mo**
Middlesbrough Height	Tottenham Hotspur Height
6'	**5'11"**

Match Statistics

League Table after Fixture

		Played	Won	Drawn	Lost	For	Against	Pts
• 4	Tottenham	17	8	7	2	25	16	31
...		...	...	...	...	...	...	...
• 13	Middlesbrough	17	5	5	7	23	26	20
• 14	Fulham	17	5	4	8	18	22	19
• 15	Aston Villa	17	4	5	8	16	26	17
• 16	Everton	17	5	2	10	9	23	17
• 17	West Brom	17	4	4	9	17	25	16
• 18	Portsmouth	17	3	4	10	13	26	13
• 19	Birmingham	16	3	3	10	11	23	12

Statistics

	Boro	Tottenham
Goals	3	3
Shots on Target	8	5
Shots off Target	3	3
Hit Woodwork	0	0
Possession %	53	47
Corners	14	4
Offsides	0	5
Fouls	17	13
Disciplinary Points	8	12

0-1

Middlesbrough ○
Blackburn Rovers ○

▶ Massimo Maccarone hits the post in the last minute

Event Line

41 ○ ■ Savage	
Half time 0-0	
46 ○ ⇄ Parnaby > Bates	
64 ○ ■ Pedersen	
68 ○ ⇄ Emerton > Pedersen	
70 ○ ⇄ Maccarone > Johnson	
83 ○ ⇄ Queudrue > Boateng	
84 ○ ■ Tugay	
90 ○ ⊕ Dickov / RF / OP / 6Y	
Assist: Kuqi	
90 ○ ⇄ Reid > Bentley	
Full time 0-1	

Paul Dickov's last-gasp goal ended Boro's Carling Cup hopes on a miserable night at the Riverside, with George Boateng leaving the field with ankle ligament damage.

Dickov, in tandem with striking partner Shefki Kuqi, had troubled Boro throughout, the Rovers duo forcing a series of saves from Mark Schwarzer. But Schwarzer was finally beaten in the 90th minute when Dickov turned in Kuqi's deflected shot.

Substitute Massimo Maccarone almost forced the game into extra time, but his angled shot came back off the post.

Chris Riggott returned from suspension to replace Ugo Ehiogu and Emanuel Pogatetz recovered from injury to replace Franck Queudrue. James Morrison was out with a facial injury and was replaced by Adam Johnson. Jimmy Floyd Hasselbaink replaced Mark Viduka, who was suffering with a heavy cold.

Kuqi and Dickov both enjoyed good chances in the first half, with Boro's strikeforce unable to test Brad Friedel in Blackburn's goal. Despite Blackburn's dominance, Boro should have gone in ahead at half-time when the ball fell to Gareth Southgate eight yards out, but he stabbed his effort wide.

Within a minute of the restart, Boro missed another good opportunity after Hasselbaink played the ball out to Rochemback on the right. The Brazilian's pull-back found Yakubu, who opted to dummy the ball, allowing Blackburn to clear.

Venue:	Riverside Stadium	Referee:	A.G.Wiley - 05/06
Attendance:	14,710	Matches:	20
Capacity:	35,100	Yellow Cards:	58
Occupancy:	42%	Red Cards:	3

Middlesbrough
Blackburn Rovers

▶ George Boateng only has eyes for the ball

Match Statistics

Starting Line-Ups

Statistics	○ Boro	Blackburn ○
Goals	0	1
Shots on Target	3	8
Shots off Target	3	8
Hit Woodwork	0	0
Possession %	53	47
Corners	1	7
Offsides	1	6
Fouls	18	13
Disciplinary Points	0	12

▶ 4/4/2   ▶ 4/4/2

Unused Sub: Jones, Ehiogu

Unused Sub: Enckelman, Khizanishvili, Thompson

Age/Height

Middlesbrough Age	Blackburn Rovers Age
▶ 26 yrs, 11 mo	▶ 29 yrs, 2 mo
Middlesbrough Height	Blackburn Rovers Height
▶ 6'	▶ 5'11"

With extra time looming, Stuart Parnaby could only head Lucas Neill's 90th minute long ball out to Kuqi, whose deflected shot fell perfectly for Dickov to win it at the far post and find the net.

The defeat angered manager Steve McClaren and it was one of the lowest points of the season for Boro, who suffered the indignity of losing twice to Blackburn in five days. Rovers returned to the Riverside in Premier League action on Boxing Day, this time winning 2-0.

Fans' Player of the Match

Adam Johnson

Quote

❝ Steve McClaren

The performance was poor. We meet Blackburn again in five days time and we must play better.

0-2

Middlesbrough ○
Blackburn Rovers ○

▶ Mark Viduka is brought crashing to the ground

Event Line

9 ○	◼	Khizanishvili
21 ○		Mendieta
38 ○	⊕	Kuqi / H / OP / IA
		Assist: Emerton
45 ○		Riggott
Half time 0-1		
52 ○	◼	Queudrue
56 ○	⇄	Mokoena > Todd
61 ○	⇄	Johnson > Rochemback
67 ○	⇄	Bellamy > Bentley
74 ○	⇄	Reid > Thompson
75 ○	◼	Emerton
78 ○	⇄	Kennedy > Doriva
78 ○	⇄	Hasselbaink > Mendieta
79 ○	⊕	Kuqi / RF / OP / 6Y
		Assist: Bellamy
81 ○	◼	Hasselbaink
Full time 0-2		

Five days after beating Boro in the Carling Cup quarter-final, Rovers returned to take three points from their league clash at the Riverside.

Boro had the first chance of the match with just over a minute played, Yakubu heading over from pointblank range.

But it was Blackburn's direct approach that created the first goal. With 37 minutes played, Emerton hit a cross from the left that Shefki Kuqi headed beyond Mark Schwarzer.

Boro had the lion's share of possession in the second half but, with much of the play in front of them, the Rovers defence was rarely troubled.

Mark Hughes' side finished the game off with their second goal with 78 minutes played. Substitute Craig Bellamy's cross was deflected into the path of Kuqi, who was left with a close-range tap-in for his second of the match.

Kuqi was close to becoming the first visiting player to score a hat-trick at the Riverside, but his injury time effort was cleared thanks to a timely intervention by Gareth Southgate.

Fans' Player of the Match	Quote	Premiership Milestone
Chris Riggott	💬 **Steve McClaren**	▶ **250**
	We are in a spell where we cannot score and we cannot keep a clean sheet. Our midfield has been decimated by injuries and that is a key area.	Mark Schwarzer made his 250th Premiership appearance.

Venue:	Riverside Stadium	Referee:	U.D.Rennie - 05/06		Middlesbrough
Attendance:	29,881	Matches:	19		Blackburn Rovers
Capacity:	35,100	Yellow Cards:	32		
Occupancy:	85%	Red Cards:	3		

Form Coming into Fixture

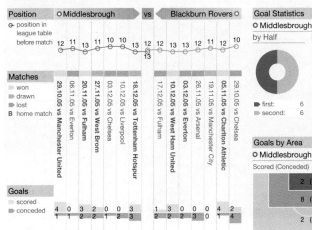

Goal Statistics

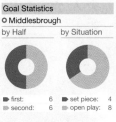

○ Middlesbrough

by Half

- first: 6
- second: 6

by Situation

- set piece: 4
- open play: 8

○ Blackburn Rovers

by Half

- first: 4
- second: 6

by Situation

- set piece: 3
- open play: 6
- own goals: 1

Goals by Area

○ Middlesbrough

Scored (Conceded)

| 2 (1) |
| 8 (8) |
| 2 (3) |

○ Blackburn Rovers

Scored (Conceded)

| 1 (3) |
| 9 (7) |
| 0 (4) |

Team Statistics

Starting Line-Ups

Middlesbrough:
Schwarzer; Pogatetz, Rochemback Johnson, Queudrue, Yakubu; Southgate, Doriva Kennedy, Viduka; Riggott, Mendieta Hasselbaink; Parnaby

Blackburn Rovers:
Thompson Reid, Khizanishvili; Tugay, Todd Mokoena; Bentley Bellamy, Kuqi; Savage, Nelson; Friedel; Emerton, Gray

▶ 5/3/2

▶ 4/4/1/1

Unused Sub: Jones, Bates

Unused Sub: Enckelman, Peter

Premiership Totals

	○ Boro	Blackburn ○
Premiership Appearances	1,617	1,490
Team Appearances	880	742
Goals Scored	263	100
Assists	175	134
Clean Sheets (goalkeepers)	71	56
Yellow Cards	162	221
Red Cards	12	12
Full Internationals	9	11

Age/Height

Middlesbrough Age
▶ 27 yrs, 3 mo

Blackburn Rovers Age
▶ 28 yrs, 5 mo

Middlesbrough Height
▶ 6'

Blackburn Rovers Height
▶ 5'11"

Match Statistics

League Table after Fixture

		Played	Won	Drawn	Lost	For	Against	Pts
↑	11 Blackburn	18	7	3	8	21	24	24
↓	12 Charlton	17	7	1	9	21	27	22
●	13 Middlesbrough	18	5	5	8	23	28	20
↑	14 Aston Villa	18	5	5	8	20	26	20
↓	15 Fulham	18	5	4	9	20	25	19
●	16 Everton	18	5	2	11	9	27	17
●	17 West Brom	18	4	4	10	17	28	16
●	18 Portsmouth	18	3	5	10	14	27	14
●	19 Birmingham	17	3	3	11	11	25	12

Statistics

	○ Boro	Blackburn ○
Goals	0	2
Shots on Target	5	4
Shots off Target	3	3
Hit Woodwork	0	0
Possession %	56	44
Corners	2	3
Offsides	7	8
Fouls	14	16
Disciplinary Points	16	8

0-0 Middlesbrough ○
Manchester City ○

➡ Yakubu protects the ball from danger

Event Line

45 ○ ▢	Onuoha
Half time 0-0	
46 ○ ⇄	Ireland > Sibierski
79 ○ ⇄	Bates > Parnaby
79 ○ ⇄	Hasselbaink > Yakubu
80 ○ ⇄	Wright-Phillips > Vassell
85 ○ ⇄	Maccarone > Pogatetz
Full time 0-0	

Boro's first clean sheet since August earned them a share of the points but Steve McClaren's side slipped to a sixth game without a win.

The game's opening stages were played at a frenetic pace with the action swinging from end to end but neither keeper was troubled.

Just after the hour mark, Boro had claims for a penalty dismissed. Mark Viduka appeared to be caught by City captain Sylvain Distin as he lined up to shoot. As the ref waved play on, Yakubu reacted quickest and hit a shot on the turn, which forced a save from David James.

City looked the more dangerous during the second half as they kept Mark Schwarzer busy. Boro's distribution became erratic and they dropped deeper into their own half. It took an outstanding save from Schwarzer to deny Joey Barton a goal from a diving header. The same City player had the chance to win the game when the Boro keeper's punch from a corner dropped at his feet. His shot, however, was embarrassingly wide and Boro fans and players breathed a sigh of relief.

Fans' Player of the Match

Gaizka Mendieta

Quote

 Steve McClaren

We have players coming back from injury and we are looking up the table not down. We are riding through our sticky patch.

Premiership Milestone

➡ **50**

Jimmy Floyd Hasselbaink made his 50th Premiership appearance in the colours of Middlesbrough.

Venue:	Riverside Stadium	Referee:	M.Atkinson - 05/06	Middlesbrough
Attendance:	28,022	Matches:	19	Manchester City
Capacity:	35,100	Yellow Cards:	44	
Occupancy:	80%	Red Cards:	1	

Form Coming into Fixture

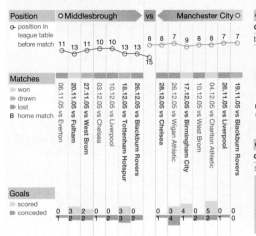

Position
- position in league table before match

Middlesbrough: 11 13 11 10 10 13 13
15
vs
Manchester City: 8 8 7 9 8 8 7 7

Matches
- won
- drawn
- lost
- B home match

Middlesbrough:
- 06.11.05 vs Everton
- 20.11.05 vs Fulham
- 27.11.05 vs West Brom
- 03.12.05 vs Chelsea
- 10.12.05 vs Liverpool
- 18.12.05 vs Tottenham Hotspur
- 26.12.05 vs Blackburn Rovers

Manchester City:
- 28.12.05 vs Chelsea
- 26.12.05 vs Wigan Athletic
- 17.12.05 vs Birmingham City
- 10.12.05 vs West Brom
- 04.12.05 vs Charlton Athletic
- 26.11.05 vs Liverpool
- 19.11.05 vs Blackburn Rovers

Goals
- scored
- conceded

Middlesbrough: 0 3 2 0 0 3 0 / 1 2 2 1 2 3 2
Manchester City: 0 3 4 0 5 0 0 / 1 4 1 2 2 1 0

Goal Statistics

Middlesbrough

by Half
by Situation

- first: 3
- second: 5
- set piece: 3
- open play: 5

Manchester City

by Half
by Situation

- first: 6
- second: 6
- set piece: 4
- open play: 8

Goals by Area

Middlesbrough
Scored (Conceded)

- 2 (2)
- 5 (8)
- 1 (3)

Manchester City
Scored (Conceded)

- 2 (1)
- 10 (7)
- 0 (3)

Team Statistics

Starting Line-Ups

Middlesbrough:
Schwarzer
Pogatetz, Maccarone
Mendieta
Queudrue
Yakubu Hasselbaink, Cole
Southgate, Doriva
Viduka, Vassell Wright-Phillips
Riggott
Morrison
Parnaby, Bates

5/3/2

Manchester City:
Sinclair, Onuoha
Barton, Dunne
James
Jihai, Distin
Sibierski, Ireland, Jordan

4/4/2

Unused Sub: Jones, Cattermole

Unused Sub: De Vlieger, Sommeil, Croft

Premiership Totals	Boro	Man City
Premiership Appearances	1,715	1,990
Team Appearances	978	749
Goals Scored	280	303
Assists	188	208
Clean Sheets (goalkeepers)	71	128
Yellow Cards	174	193
Red Cards	12	14
Full Internationals	9	6

Age/Height

Middlesbrough Age
27 yrs, 6 mo

Manchester City Age
26 yrs, 10 mo

Middlesbrough Height
6'

Manchester City Height
6'

Match Statistics

League Table after Fixture

		Played	Won	Drawn	Lost	For	Against	Pts
●	8 Man City	20	8	4	8	27	24	28
↑	9 Blackburn	19	8	3	8	24	24	27
↓	10 West Ham	20	7	5	8	26	27	26
↓	11 Newcastle	19	7	4	8	18	21	25
●	12 Charlton	18	8	1	9	23	27	25
●	13 Aston Villa	20	5	7	8	23	29	22
↑	14 Middlesbrough	19	5	6	8	23	28	21
↓	15 Fulham	20	5	5	10	23	29	20
↑	16 Everton	20	6	2	12	11	30	20

Statistics	Boro	Man City
Goals	0	0
Shots on Target	4	3
Shots off Target	8	5
Hit Woodwork	0	0
Possession %	46	54
Corners	4	7
Offsides	1	5
Fouls	6	12
Disciplinary Points	0	4

2-2

Newcastle United ○
Middlesbrough ○

▶ Gareth Southgate brings the ball out of defence

27 ○ ⊕	Solano / RF / DFK / OA	
	Assist: Ameobi	
Half time 1-0		
46 ○ ⇄	N'Zogbia > Ameobi	
46 ○ ⇄	Babayaro > Elliott	
54 ○ ⊕	Yakubu / RF / OP / IA	
	Assist: Morrison	
69 ○ ⇄	Bates > Mendieta	
74 ○ ⇄	Hasselbaink > Yakubu	
83 ○	Hasselbaink	
87 ○ ⊕	Hasselbaink / LF / OP / IA	
	Assist: Viduka	
90 ○	Bates	
90 ○ ⊕	Clark / LF / C / IA	
Full time 2-2		

Yet another late goal meant Boro missed a wonderful opportunity to record a first-ever Premiership win at St James' Park.

Lee Cattermole made his senior team debut for injury-hit Boro but the 17-year-old midfielder was hugely impressive in the heart of the midfield.

United took the lead with 25 minutes played when a free-kick from the edge of the box was curled in by Nolberto Solano. Boro players were then furious when the referee failed to award a penalty after defender Robbie Elliott handled the ball on the edge of the six-yard box.

Boro equalised with 53 minutes played. Yakubu got on the end of Morrison's low cross to score his 11th goal of the season from the edge of the six-yard box.

Boro looked to have clinched a crucial win when sub Jimmy Floyd Hasselbaink beat Boumsong for pace before powering his shot past Shay Given.

Boro were just seconds from victory when, almost three minutes into injury time, a clearance from a corner fell to Lee Clark. The midfielder's low shot zipped through a packed penalty area for his first Newcastle goal for almost nine years.

Fans' Player of the Match	Quote	Premiership Milestone
Lee Cattermole	⑥ **Steve McClaren**	▶ **Debut**
	I thought our team showed fantastic character and played some fantastic football. To have those points snatched away at the very end was extremely cruel.	Lee Cattermole made his Premiership debut.

Venue:	St James' Park	Referee:	S.G.Bennett - 05/06		Newcastle United
Attendance:	52,302	Matches:	22		Middlesbrough
Capacity:	52,327	Yellow Cards:	82		
Occupancy:	100%	Red Cards:	7		

Form Coming into Fixture

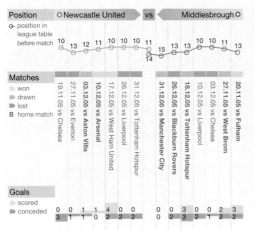

Position ○ Newcastle United vs Middlesbrough ○

position in league table before match

10 13 12 11 10 10 10 11 15 13 13 10 10 10 11 13
14

Matches
- won
- drawn
- lost
- B home match

	19.11.05 vs Chelsea	27.11.05 vs Everton	03.12.05 vs Aston Villa	10.12.05 vs Arsenal	17.12.05 vs West Ham United	26.12.05 vs Liverpool	31.12.05 vs Tottenham Hotspur	31.12.05 vs Manchester City	26.12.05 vs Blackburn Rovers	18.12.05 vs Tottenham Hotspur	10.12.05 vs Liverpool	03.12.05 vs Chelsea	27.11.05 vs West Brom	20.11.05 vs Fulham
Goals scored	0	0	1	1	4	0	0	0	0	3	0	0	2	3
conceded	3	1	1	0	2	2	2	2	3	2	1	2	2	2

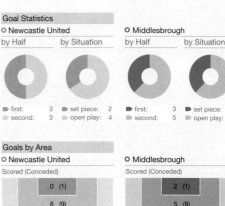

Goal Statistics

○ Newcastle United

by Half | by Situation
- first: 3
- second: 3
- set piece: 2
- open play: 4

○ Middlesbrough

by Half | by Situation
- first: 3
- second: 5
- set piece: 3
- open play: 5

Goals by Area
○ Newcastle United
Scored (Conceded)

0 (1)
6 (9)
0 (1)

○ Middlesbrough
Scored (Conceded)

2 (1)
5 (8)
1 (3)

Team Statistics

Starting Line-Ups

Elliott Ameobi Morrison Parnaby
Babayaro N'Zogbia

Boumsong Clark Cattermole Riggott
Luque Viduka
Given Schwarzer

Bramble Faye Shearer — Yakubu Doriva Southgate
Hasselbaink

Ramage Solano Mendieta Pogatetz
Bates

▶ 4/4/2   ▶ 4/4/2

Unused Sub: Harper, Brittain, Chopra

Unused Sub: Jones, Johnson, Maccarone

Premiership Totals

	○ Newcastle	Boro ○
Premiership Appearances	1,781	1,523
Team Appearances	1,303	786
Goals Scored	342	253
Assists	211	161
Clean Sheets (goalkeepers)	75	72
Yellow Cards	180	140
Red Cards	9	7
Full Internationals	7	8

Age/Height

Newcastle United Age
▶ 27 yrs, 10 mo

Middlesbrough Age
▶ 26 yrs, 10 mo

Newcastle United Height
▶ 5'11"

Middlesbrough Height
▶ 6'

Match Statistics

League Table after Fixture

		Played	Won	Drawn	Lost	For	Against	Pts
●	11 Newcastle	20	7	5	8	20	23	26
↑	12 Aston Villa	21	6	7	8	25	30	25
↓	13 Charlton	19	8	1	10	24	30	25
↑	14 Fulham	21	6	5	10	25	30	23
↑	15 Everton	21	7	2	12	14	31	23
↓	16 Middlesbrough	20	5	7	8	25	30	22
●	17 West Brom	21	5	4	12	20	31	19
●	18 Portsmouth	21	4	5	12	16	33	17
●	19 Birmingham	20	4	4	12	15	29	16

Statistics

	○ Newcastle	Boro ○
Goals	2	2
Shots on Target	5	3
Shots off Target	5	5
Hit Woodwork	1	0
Possession %	50	50
Corners	5	2
Offsides	11	6
Fouls	14	13
Disciplinary Points	0	8

1-1

Nuneaton Borough ○
Middlesbrough ○

▶ Lee Cattermole competes for the ball in midfield

Event Line

15 ○ ⊕	Mendieta / RF / DFK / OA	
	Assist: Yakubu	
23 ○ ⇄	Whittaker > Staff	
Half time 0-1		
77 ○ ⇄	Frew > Quailey	
82 ○ ⇄	Reeves > Fitzpatrick	
90 ○	Pogatetz	
90 ○ ⊕	Murphy / RF / P / IA	
Full time 1-1		

Gez Murphy's late equaliser earned battling Nuneaton a Riverside replay after a tense FA Cup tie at Manor Park.

Murphy, a 29-year-old sports development officer, struck two minutes from the end as the Midlanders kept alive their hopes of a giant-killing. Nuneaton were more than 100 places below Boro in the football pyramid. But it was not a mismatch – Roger Ashby's side fully deserved a replay after a hugely-committed performance.

Reserve keeper Brad Jones was called into the fray after Steve McClaren elected to leave out Mark Schwarzer, who had just made a surprise transfer request. Combative 17-year-old Lee Cattermole, who made his league debut at Newcastle five days earlier, was retained in midfield. Injuries had hit the squad hard, particularly in midfield, and the bench looked distinctly youthful, with three teenagers in Andrew Taylor, David Wheater and Adam Johnson.

Former Nuns striker Malcolm Christie received a hero's welcome when he was introduced to the crowd before the match. The Boro player, recovering from two years of injuries, spent his formative years with Nuneaton before turning full-time with Derby County. Also making a return to Manor Park was assistant manager Steve Round, who spent three months with Nuneaton at the end of his playing career 10 years ago.

Seeking to take advantage of Boro's worrying league form, Conference North side Nuneaton made it as difficult as possible for their visitors on a heavy, sloping pitch. Boro, however, got off to the best possible start when Gaizka Mendieta put them in front after just 14 minutes.

Venue:	Manor Park	Referee:	M.L.Dean - 05/06		Nuneaton Borough
Attendance:	6,000	Matches:	20		Middlesbrough
Capacity:	6,500	Yellow Cards:	56		
Occupancy:	92%	Red Cards:	4		

➤ Gaizka Mendieta wheels away after opening the scoring

Match Statistics

Starting Line-Ups

Statistics	○ Nuneaton	Boro ○
Goals	1	1
Shots on Target	6	5
Shots off Target	4	6
Hit Woodwork	0	0
Possession %	45	55
Corners	7	5
Offsides	3	3
Fouls	10	12
Disciplinary Points	0	4

4/4/2

4/4/2

Unused Sub: Poole, Wilkin

Unused Sub: Schwarzer, Taylor, Wheater, Johnson, Maccarone

Age/Height

Nuneaton Borough Age	Middlesbrough Age
➤ **28 yrs, 6 mo**	➤ **25 yrs, 6 mo**
Nuneaton Borough Height	Middlesbrough Height
➤ **5'11"**	➤ **5'11"**

The midfielder judged his long-range free-kick to perfection, and it curled past keeper Darren Acton into the corner. But his team-mates were unable to build on the advantage and Jones had to make some smart saves to keep the part-timers at bay.

Nuneaton had penalty claims turned down after Mark Noon fell under a challenge from Gareth Southgate. Midway through the second-half, full-back Rob Oddy made a well-timed challenge to stop Yakubu on the edge of the area.

Nuneaton kept fighting to the end and were rewarded when skipper Southgate was penalised for handling as he attempted to clear his lines. Murphy made no mistake from the spot.

Fans' Player of the Match

Gaizka Mendieta

Quote

🔊 Steve McClaren

It was very disappointing, but it could have been even worse. We live to fight another day.

7-0

Arsenal ○
Middlesbrough ○

▶ David Wheater tries to stop Aleksandr Hleb

Event Line

20 ○ ⊕	Henry / RF / OP / IA
	Assist: Ljungberg
22 ○ ⊕	Senderos / H / C / 6Y
	Assist: Reyes
30 ○ ⊕	Henry / RF / OP / OA
	Assist: Reyes
34 ○ ⇄	Cole > Cygan
45 ○ ⊕	Pires / RF / OP / IA
	Assist: Henry
Half time 4-0	
59 ○ ⊕	Gilberto Silva / H / IFK / IA
	Assist: Henry
61 ○ ⇄	Wheater > Taylor
68 ○ ⊕	Henry / RF / OP / IA
	Assist: Reyes
69 ○ ⇄	Hleb > Gilberto Silva
69 ○ ⇄	Flamini > Pires
70 ○ ⇄	Johnson > Rochemback
70 ○ ⇄	Cattermole > Viduka
73 ○ ◢	Doriva
	2nd Bookable Offence
79 ○	Lauren
84 ○ ⊕	Hleb / RF / OP / IA
	Assist: Reyes
90 ○	Cattermole
Full time 7-0	

Arsenal inflicted Boro's heaviest ever Premiership defeat in an embarrassingly one-sided game.

Thierry Henry opened the scoring after 20 minutes, volleying a cross from Ljungberg into the bottom corner of Brad Jones' goal. Minutes later their lead was doubled when Phillippe Senderos rose unchallenged to head the ball in from eight yards out.

Boro tried to play football but were again ripped apart by Arsenal. A pinpoint pass picked out Henry, who controlled effortlessly before drilling home goal number three. Robert Pires made it four in first half stoppage time, breezing through the midfield unchallenged and, from just inside the penalty area, curling a shot beyond the reach of Jones.

With an hour played, an Henry free-kick picked out Gilberto who headed home from eight yards. Minutes later, Henry equalled Cliff Bastin's all-time league scoring record for Arsenal as he hit his 150th goal for the club. The Frenchman latched onto a through-ball from Fabregas and hit a low shot past Jones. When Boro fans thought things could get no worse, Doriva was sent off for a second bookable offence and Alexander Hleb hit Arsenal's seventh with a simple tap in.

Quote

❝ Steve McClaren

We had to field a lot of teenagers today and it was hard for them. When Arsenal are in that mood, they can always rip you apart.

Premiership Milestone

▶ Debut

Both Andrew Taylor and David Wheater made their Premiership debuts.

Venue:	Highbury	Referee:	R.Styles - 05/06		Arsenal
Attendance:	38,186	Matches:	24		Middlesbrough
Capacity:	38,419	Yellow Cards:	84		
Occupancy:	99%	Red Cards:	2		

Form Coming into Fixture

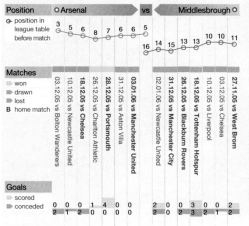

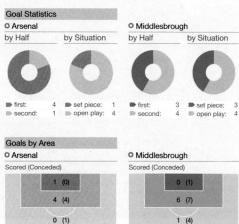

Goal Statistics

○ Arsenal

by Half / by Situation

- first: 4
- second: 1
- set piece: 1
- open play: 4

○ Middlesbrough

by Half / by Situation

- first: 3
- second: 4
- set piece: 3
- open play: 4

Goals by Area

○ Arsenal — Scored (Conceded)

- 1 (0)
- 4 (4)
- 0 (1)

○ Middlesbrough — Scored (Conceded)

- 0 (1)
- 6 (7)
- 1 (4)

Team Statistics

Starting Line-Ups

▶ 4/4/2   **▶ 4/4/2**

Unused Sub: Almunia, Lupoli

Unused Sub: Schwarzer, Hasselbaink

Premiership Totals	○ Arsenal	Boro ○
Premiership Appearances	1,313	618
Team Appearances	1,313	352
Goals Scored	290	119
Assists	232	70
Clean Sheets (goalkeepers)	36	2
Yellow Cards	149	67
Red Cards	3	3
Full Internationals	10	5

Age/Height

	Arsenal	Middlesbrough
Age	▶ 26 yrs, 4 mo	▶ 23 yrs, 6 mo
Height	▶ 6'	▶ 5'11"

Match Statistics

League Table after Fixture

		Played	Won	Drawn	Lost	For	Against	Pts
●	5 Arsenal	21	11	4	6	34	15	37
...		...	...	...	...	...	...	...
↑	14 Everton	22	8	2	12	15	31	26
↓	15 Aston Villa	22	6	7	9	26	32	25
●	16 Middlesbrough	21	5	7	9	25	37	22
●	17 West Brom	21	5	4	12	20	31	19
●	18 Portsmouth	22	4	5	13	16	34	17
●	19 Birmingham	21	4	4	13	15	31	16
●	20 Sunderland	20	1	3	16	15	38	6

Statistics	○ Arsenal	Boro ○
Goals	7	0
Shots on Target	17	2
Shots off Target	7	3
Hit Woodwork	1	0
Possession %	64	36
Corners	4	6
Offsides	1	7
Fouls	12	14
Disciplinary Points	4	14

5-2

Middlesbrough ○
Nuneaton Borough ○

► Andrew Taylor does well to prevent a free header

Event Line

29 ○	■	Parnaby
34 ○	⊕	Riggott / RF / OP / IA
		Assist: Bates
42 ○	⊕	Yakubu / RF / P / IA
		Assist: Mendieta
Half time 2-0		
50 ○	⊕	Parnaby / RF / OP / OA
58 ○	⊕	Yakubu / LF / OP / IA
		Assist: Viduka
59 ○	⇄	Frew > Quailey
63 ○	⊕	Viduka / RF / OP / IA
63 ○	⇄	Parlour > Parnaby
64 ○	⇄	Maccarone > Viduka
71 ○	⊕	Murphy / H / OP / OA
		Assist: Acton
75 ○	■	Love
77 ○	⇄	Wilkin > Whittaker
81 ○	⇄	Reeves > Collins
86 ○	⊕	Murphy / RF / P / IA
		Assist: Murphy
Full time 5-2		

Nuneaton brought 4,500 fans to the Riverside in search of an upset in the wake of Boro's 7-0 Premier League thumping at Arsenal. But despite a promising start, they could not match the power and pace of Boro on their home turf.

The prize of a fourth-round trip to near-neighbours Coventry City was a huge one for the part-timers, whose fans played such a big part in creating a terrific atmosphere at the Riverside. Boro were without the injured James Morrison, but Emanuel Pogatetz was available after serving a one-match ban at Highbury.

Chris Riggott, who missed the game at Manor Park, captained the side in the absence of ankle injury victim Gareth Southgate. Ray Parlour was back on the bench after making a successful comeback in a midweek reserve win over Sunderland.

Nuneaton started well, with danger man Gez Murphy forcing Brad Jones into an excellent one-handed save when given an early one-on-one chance. Boro looked distinctly nervy and lacking in confidence, but a goal 12 minutes from half-time gave them belief.

Riggott spotted Darren Acton off his line and beat him with a beautifully judged lob. The home side then had penalty claims denied when Yakubu appeared to have been pulled back by veteran centre-back Terry Angus.

Yakubu didn't have to wait long to get on the scoresheet, however. Four minutes from the break, Gaizka Mendieta was brought down inside the penalty area and the Nigerian sent Acton the wrong way from the spot.

▶ Brad Jones organises his defensive wall

Match Statistics

Starting Line-Ups

Taylor · Johnson · Pogatetz · Cattermole · Jones · Yakubu · Riggott · Parnaby (Parlour) · Viduka · Maccarone · Bates · Mendieta

Collins (Reeves) · Oddy · Noon · Moore · Quailey (Frew) · Murphy · Fitzpatrick · Angus · Acton · Whittaker (Wilkin) · Love

▶ 4/4/2   ▶ 4/4/2

Unused Sub: Schwarzer, Wheater, Rochemback

Unused Sub: Poole, Rea

Statistics	Boro	Nuneaton
Goals	5	2
Shots on Target	10	5
Shots off Target	6	4
Hit Woodwork	0	0
Possession %	57	43
Corners	4	2
Offsides	0	4
Fouls	15	13
Disciplinary Points	4	4

Three minutes after half-time, Boro went three up. Stuart Parnaby scored his first-ever goal with a 20-yard drive that went into the net with the aid of a deflection. Yakubu scored his second after 57 minutes with a delicate shot that rolled past Acton.

Five minutes later, it was five. Mark Viduka took advantage of a defensive mix-up to convert from close range. There seemed no way back for Nuneaton, but they battled to the end and were rewarded with two goals from Murphy.

For the first, after 71 minutes, Jones was beaten by a long ball up-field and Murphy had the simple task of hitting it over the line. His second, five minutes from the end, came from the penalty spot after Parlour brought down Martin Reeves.

Fans' Player of the Match

Lee Cattermole

Quote

🔒 Steve McClaren

This was a small step towards recovery, but there is still a long way to go and a lot of work to be done.

2-3

Middlesbrough ○
Wigan Athletic ○

► Lee Cattermole keeps a close eye on the ball

Event Line

2 ○ ⊕	Roberts / RF / OP / IA	
	Assist: Mellor	
27 ○ ⇄	Ehiogu > Riggott	
29 ○ ⊕	Thompson / H / OP / IA	
	Assist: Teale	
32 ○ ⇄	Johnson > Bates	
Half time 0-2		
46 ○ ⇄	Hasselbaink > Viduka	
56 ○ ⊕	Hasselbaink / H / C / 6Y	
	Assist: Downing	
65 ○	Scharner	
66 ○ ⊕	Yakubu / RF / C / 6Y	
	Assist: Southgate	
74 ○	Thompson	
90 ○ ⊕	Mellor / RF / C / 6Y	
	Assist: Roberts	
90 ○ ⇄	Johansson > Thompson	
Full time 2-3		

Yet more late goal misery stretched Boro's winless league run to two months and 11 games despite Stewart Downing's long-awaited return and a battling second half comeback.

Wigan took the lead after just two minutes, Jason Roberts hitting a powerful drive from the edge of the area.

Boro were left with a mountain to climb just before the half hour when Gary Teale picked out an unmarked David Thompson on the edge of the six-yard box. Thompson, on his Wigan debut, scored with a free header.

Boro came out rejuvenated from the break and a goal from sub Hasselbaink on 56 minutes gave renewed hope. Downing provided the inch-perfect cross for the Dutch striker to head home from six yards. Boro were level within 10 minutes, Gareth Southgate flicking on a corner for Yakubu to bundle over the line for his 15th goal of the season.

Boro were now the dominant team but it was Wigan who snatched a heartbreaking winner. A failed clearance from a corner was back-heeled by another Wigan debutant, Neil Mellor, who hit a shot from three yards to win the game.

Fans' Player of the Match	Quote
Stewart Downing	ⓖ **Steve McClaren**

These are testing times for everyone at the football club, but my job is to be positive, keep a clear head and not panic.

Venue:	Riverside Stadium	Referee:	A.Marriner - 05/06		Middlesbrough
Attendance:	27,208	Matches:	14		Wigan Athletic
Capacity:	35,100	Yellow Cards:	47		
Occupancy:	78%	Red Cards:	6		

Form Coming into Fixture

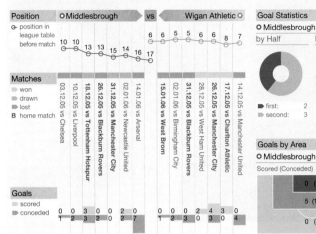

Position
o- position in league table before match

Middlesbrough: 10 10 13 13 15 14 16 17
Wigan Athletic: 6 6 5 5 6 6 8 7

Matches
- won
- drawn
- lost
- B home match

Middlesbrough:
03.12.05 vs Chelsea
10.12.05 vs Liverpool
18.12.05 vs Tottenham Hotspur
26.12.05 vs Blackburn Rovers
31.12.05 vs Manchester City
02.01.06 vs Newcastle United
14.01.06 vs Arsenal

Wigan Athletic:
15.01.06 vs West Brom
02.01.06 vs Birmingham City
31.12.05 vs Blackburn Rovers
28.12.05 vs West Ham United
26.12.05 vs Manchester City
17.12.05 vs Charlton Athletic
14.12.05 vs Manchester United

Goals
- scored
- conceded

Middlesbrough scored: 0 0 3 0 0 2 0
Middlesbrough conceded: 1 2 3 2 0 2 7

Wigan scored: 0 0 0 2 4 3 0
Wigan conceded: 1 2 3 0 3 0 4

Goal Statistics

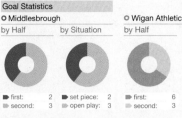

Middlesbrough

by Half
- first: 2
- second: 3

by Situation
- set piece: 2
- open play: 3

Wigan Athletic

by Half
- first: 6
- second: 3

by Situation
- set piece: 0
- open play: 9

Goals by Area

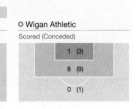

Middlesbrough — Scored (Conceded)

0 (2)
5 (11)
0 (4)

Wigan Athletic — Scored (Conceded)

1 (3)
8 (9)
0 (1)

Team Statistics

Starting Line-Ups

Middlesbrough

Pogatetz, Downing
Southgate, Cattermole, Yakubu, Mellor
Jones
Riggott / Ehiogu, Parlour, Viduka / Hasselbaink, Roberts
Bates / Johnson, Parnaby

4/4/2

Unused Sub: Schwarzer, Doriva

Wigan Athletic

Teale, Chimbonda
Bullard, Scharner
Pollitt
Kavanagh, Henchoz
Thompson / Johansson, Baines

4/4/2

Unused Sub: Filan, Jackson, Francis, Skoko

Premiership Totals

Premiership Totals	Boro	Wigan
Premiership Appearances	1,939	569
Team Appearances	640	156
Goals Scored	295	29
Assists	202	34
Clean Sheets (goalkeepers)	2	3
Yellow Cards	225	86
Red Cards	14	4
Full Internationals	8	5

Age/Height

Middlesbrough Age: 25 yrs, 10 mo
Wigan Athletic Age: 27 yrs, 9 mo
Middlesbrough Height: 6'
Wigan Athletic Height: 5'11"

Match Statistics

League Table after Fixture

	Played	Won	Drawn	Lost	For	Against	Pts
● 6 Wigan	23	12	1	10	28	29	37
...	...	...	...	...	...	...	...
↓ 14 Newcastle	22	7	5	10	20	25	26
● 15 Aston Villa	23	6	8	9	26	32	26
● 16 West Brom	23	6	4	13	21	32	22
● 17 Middlesbrough	22	5	7	10	27	40	22
↑ 18 Birmingham	22	5	4	13	20	31	19
↓ 19 Portsmouth	23	4	5	14	16	39	17
● 20 Sunderland	22	2	3	17	17	40	9

Statistics

Statistics	Boro	Wigan
Goals	2	3
Shots on Target	4	10
Shots off Target	3	6
Hit Woodwork	0	0
Possession %	41	59
Corners	8	8
Offsides	2	2
Fouls	9	11
Disciplinary Points	0	8

1-1

Coventry City ○
Middlesbrough ○

➡ Ugo Ehiogu prepares to receive the ball

Event Line

28 ○ ⇄	Bates > Ehiogu
Half time 0-0	
46 ○ ⊕	Hasselbaink / RF / OP / IA
	Assist: Yakubu
54 ○ ⊕	John / RF / OP / IA
	Assist: Hutchison
57 ○	Bates
60 ○	Cattermole
65 ○ ⇄	Viduka > Yakubu
72 ○ ⇄	Doriva > Rochemback
86 ○ ⇄	Jorgensen > Hutchison
90 ○ ⇄	Morrell > John
90 ○ ⇄	Impey > McSheffrey
Full time 1-1	

Boro made a return trip to Warwickshire and faced another tough hurdle in the shape of Championship side Coventry City, who gave their Premiership visitors a testing afternoon.

Steve McClaren made five changes from the side that lost at home to Wigan in the Premiership the previous week. Back-in-favour Mark Schwarzer replaced the injured Brad Jones, Ugo Ehiogu stood in for Chris Riggott, who had a back injury, while Gaizka Mendieta and Fabio Rochemback also returned.

The smart Ricoh Arena was seeing an FA Cup tie for the first time and the home side were determined to give their fans something to enjoy.

Less and less was seen of Boro as an attacking force as the first half wore on, a bright start beginning to dim. Thankfully, behind the front line the team appeared to be playing comfortably enough within themselves. Both sides had chances in an even first half.

Jimmy Floyd Hasselbaink blazed wildly over from the edge of the box, while Coventry striker Dele Adebola dragged a low shot wide. Midway through the opening period, Ehiogu was forced off with injury to be replaced by Matthew Bates.

The tie sprang to life with two goals at the start of the second half. First Hasselbaink converted past Martin Fulop and then slack marking allowed Stern John the chance to equalise from close range.

Venue:	Ricoh Arena	Referee:	C.J.Foy - 05/06		Coventry City
Attendance:	28,120	Matches:	23		Middlesbrough
Capacity:	32,000	Yellow Cards:	53		
Occupancy:	88%	Red Cards:	6		

➧ Mark Viduka competes with Don Hutchison

Match Statistics

Starting Line-Ups

➧ 4/4/2   ➧ 4/4/2

Unused Sub: Ince, Page   Unused Sub: Knight, Johnson

Statistics	○ Coventry	Boro ○
Goals	1	1
Shots on Target	7	5
Shots off Target	5	5
Hit Woodwork	0	0
Possession %	49	51
Corners	3	3
Offsides	1	2
Fouls	12	12
Disciplinary Points	0	8

Age/Height

Coventry City Age	Middlesbrough Age
➧ 29 yrs, 6 mo	➧ 27 yrs, 5 mo
Coventry City Height	Middlesbrough Height
➧ 6'	➧ 6'

The impressive Gary McSheffrey constantly caused Boro problems with his pace, while Trinidad and Tobago international John – who would face England in that summer's World Cup finals - showed good hold-up play as City went in search of the winner. There were some frantic moments as Schwarzer and his defence came under sustained pressure.

McClaren re-jigged his back line in an effort to stem the threat down the left and looked increasingly frustrated as Boro failed to make their extra quality count. Four minutes of injury time resulted in a nervy end to the contest, but the visitors held out for a replay at the Riverside.

Fans' Player of the Match

Gareth Southgate

Quote

❝ Steve McClaren

I was just disappointed we didnt ma ke better use of the ball in the final third.

0-3

Sunderland ○
Middlesbrough ○

▶ Emanuel Pogatetz celebrates scoring Boro's opening goal

Event Line

19 ○ ⊕	Pogatetz / H / IFK / IA
	Assist: Downing
31 ○ ⊕	Parnaby / RF / OP / IA
	Assist: Viduka
32 ○ ⇄	Kyle > Collins D
43 ○ ▪	Caldwell
Half time 0-2	
50 ○ ▪	Doriva
64 ○ ⇄	Davies > Viduka
71 ○ ⊕	Hasselbaink / RF / OP / OA
	Assist: Mendieta
77 ○ ⇄	Johnson > Downing
78 ○ ⇄	Murphy D > Stead
79 ○ ⇄	Yakubu > Hasselbaink
Full time 0-3	

Boro's clinical finishing gave them a morale-boosting victory over their north-east relegation rivals, ending an 11-game winless league run that had stretched back to mid-November.

The pressure was on Steve McClaren going into the match, with Boro fans fearful of bottom club Sunderland completing a derby double to record their first home success of the season.

But Boro took control of the game after 18 minutes. Stand-in centre-back Emanuel Pogatetz scored his first Boro goal from Downing's free-kick, a tremendous 12-yard header crashing in off the underside of the bar.

Sunderland created a couple of half chances but it was Boro who showed the killer instinct in front of goal. Stuart Parnaby raced down the right, played a one-two with Mark Viduka and hit a fantastic strike from 16 yards out.

The Black Cats came out fighting after the break but their own ineptitude in front of goal proved to be their downfall. Jimmy Floyd Hasselbaink delivered the killer blow for Sunderland. A simple through-ball split the Sunderland defence, allowing the striker to drill the ball beyond Kelvin Davis on 71 minutes.

Fans' Player of the Match

Emanuel Pogatetz

Quote

❝ Steve McClaren

The players deserved this victory. They have been under a lot of pressure, but showed tremendous spirit.

Premiership Milestone

▶ **First Goal**

Both Emanuel Pogatetz and Stuart Parnaby netted their first Premiership goals.

Venue:	Stadium of Light	Referee:	A.G.Wiley - 05/06	Sunderland
Attendance:	31,675	Matches:	29	Middlesbrough
Capacity:	48,300	Yellow Cards:	89	
Occupancy:	66%	Red Cards:	5	

Form Coming into Fixture

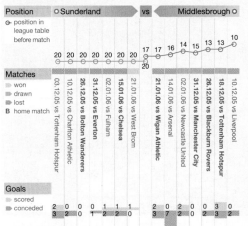

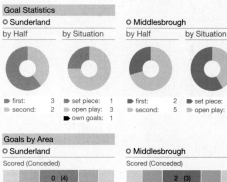

Goal Statistics

○ Sunderland

by Half / by Situation

- first: 3
- second: 2

- set piece: 1
- open play: 3
- own goals: 1

○ Middlesbrough

by Half / by Situation

- first: 2
- second: 5

- set piece: 4
- open play: 3

Goals by Area

○ Sunderland

Scored (Conceded)

- 0 (4)
- 3 (5)
- 2 (1)

○ Middlesbrough

Scored (Conceded)

- 2 (3)
- 5 (12)
- 0 (4)

Team Statistics

Starting Line-Ups

Unused Sub: Alnwick, Nosworthy, Bassila

Unused Sub: Jones, Maccarone

4/4/2

4/4/2

Premiership Totals

Premiership Totals	○ Sunderland	Boro ○
Premiership Appearances	526	1,468
Team Appearances	282	800
Goals Scored	27	254
Assists	27	176
Clean Sheets (goalkeepers)	3	72
Yellow Cards	63	119
Red Cards	2	7
Full Internationals	4	9

Age/Height

	Sunderland	Middlesbrough
Age	25 yrs	26 yrs, 2 mo
Height	6'	6'

Match Statistics

League Table after Fixture

	Played	Won	Drawn	Lost	For	Against	Pts
● 12 Everton	24	9	3	12	17	32	30
● 13 Fulham	24	8	5	11	28	32	29
● 14 Newcastle	22	7	5	10	20	25	26
● 15 Aston Villa	23	6	8	9	26	32	26
↑ 16 Middlesbrough	23	6	7	10	30	40	25
↓ 17 West Brom	24	6	5	13	21	32	23
● 18 Birmingham	22	5	4	13	20	31	19
● 19 Portsmouth	23	4	5	14	16	39	17
● 20 Sunderland	23	2	3	18	17	43	9

Statistics

Statistics	○ Sunderland	Boro ○
Goals	0	3
Shots on Target	7	4
Shots off Target	7	3
Hit Woodwork	0	0
Possession %	52	48
Corners	2	5
Offsides	2	1
Fouls	18	9
Disciplinary Points	4	4

0-4

Middlesbrough o
Aston Villa o

➡ Gaizka Mendieta battles for possession with Gareth Barry

Event Line

18 O ⊕ Moore / LF / OP / IA	
Assist: Phillips	
24 O ⊕ Phillips / H / OP / IA	
Assist: Milner	
Half time 0-2	
46 O ⇄ Maccarone > Hasselbaink	
46 O ⇄ Yakubu > Viduka	
52 O ▌ Doriva	
62 O ⊕ Moore / RF / OP / IA	
Assist: Barry	
64 O ⊕ Moore / RF / OP / IA	
Assist: Davis	
67 O ▌ Mendieta	
67 O ▌ Barry	
68 O ⇄ Davies > Mendieta	
73 O ▌ Maccarone	
78 O ⇄ Ridgewell > Mellberg	
81 O ⇄ Hendrie > Samuel	
83 O ⇄ Angel > Moore	
Full time 0-4	

Boro crashed back into crisis mode with a humiliating home defeat that left many Riverside regulars in mutinous mood.

The pressure was piling on manager Steve McClaren, whose side had now taken just seven points from 33, leaving them just five points above the bottom three.

Young Villa striker Luke Moore became the first visiting player to hit a Riverside hat-trick in a game perhaps best remembered for an incident midway through the second half when a Boro fan raced to the dug-out to throw his season ticket in McClaren's direction.

Boro fell behind on 18 minutes, a Kevin Phillips back-heel enabling Moore to volley home from six yards out. Six minutes later Villa were two up. A cross from the left was flicked backwards by Phillips, catching Mark Schwarzer by surprise as it flew across him and into the corner of the net.

Just after the hour mark, Gareth Barry rolled a low cross in from the left and Moore got the better of Pogatetz to side-foot his second goal. The defence was still reeling when Villa surged forward for a fourth goal with 25 minutes still to play. A low ball picked out Moore to complete his hat-trick from eight yards out.

Quote

❝ Steve McClaren

Our problems are there for everyone to see. We are conceding more goals than anyone and that is why we are in this position.

Venue:	Riverside Stadium	Referee:	L.Mason - 05/06		**Middlesbrough**
Attendance:	27,299	Matches:	20		**Aston Villa**
Capacity:	35,100	Yellow Cards:	52		
Occupancy:	78%	Red Cards:	2		

Form Coming into Fixture

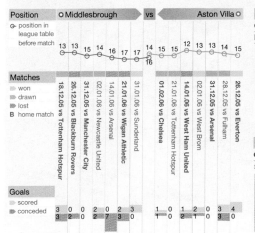

Goal Statistics

○ Middlesbrough

by Half
- first: 4
- second: 6

by Situation
- set piece: 5
- open play: 5

○ Aston Villa

by Half
- first: 3
- second: 8

by Situation
- set piece: 4
- open play: 7

Goals by Area

○ Middlesbrough
Scored (Conceded)

2 (3)
7 (11)
1 (3)

○ Aston Villa
Scored (Conceded)

7 (0)
4 (7)
0 (0)

Team Statistics

Starting Line-Ups

4/4/2

Unused Sub: Knight, Johnson

4/4/2

Unused Sub: Taylor, Gardner

Premiership Totals	○ Boro	Aston Villa ○
Premiership Appearances	1,543	2,178
Team Appearances	875	1,452
Goals Scored	273	212
Assists	192	169
Clean Sheets (goalkeepers)	73	65
Yellow Cards	127	249
Red Cards	7	9
Full Internationals	10	10

Age/Height

Middlesbrough Age
▶ 26 yrs, 9 mo

Aston Villa Age
▶ 26 yrs, 2 mo

Middlesbrough Height
▶ 6'

Aston Villa Height
▶ 5'11"

Match Statistics

League Table after Fixture

	Played	Won	Drawn	Lost	For	Against	Pts
↑ 12 Aston Villa	25	7	9	9	31	33	30
↓ 13 Charlton	22	9	3	10	27	31	30
↓ 14 Fulham	25	8	5	12	30	36	29
● 15 Newcastle	24	8	5	11	22	28	29
↑ 16 West Brom	25	7	5	13	23	32	26
↓ 17 Middlesbrough	24	6	7	11	30	44	25
● 18 Birmingham	24	5	5	14	21	34	20
● 19 Portsmouth	25	4	6	15	17	42	18
● 20 Sunderland	24	2	3	19	17	45	9

Statistics	○ Boro	Aston Villa ○
Goals	0	4
Shots on Target	4	5
Shots off Target	5	5
Hit Woodwork	0	0
Possession %	48	52
Corners	6	5
Offsides	1	6
Fouls	14	12
Disciplinary Points	12	4

1-0

Middlesbrough ○
Coventry City ○

FA Cup
08.02.06

▶ Chris Riggott gets to grips with Dele Adebola

Event Line

15 ○	▪	Scowcroft
20 ○	⊕	Hasselbaink / LF / OP / IA
		Assist: Yakubu

Half time 1-0

53 ○	▪	Taylor
59 ○	▪	Hutchison
68 ○		Yakubu
71 ○	⇄	Maccarone > Yakubu
81 ○	⇄	Bates > Mendieta
85 ○	⇄	Morrell > Whing
90 ○		Pogatetz

Full time 1-0

A solitary first-half strike from Jimmy Floyd Hasselbaink was enough to edge Boro into the fifth round of the FA Cup in a nervy replay at the Riverside.

The Boro side showed three changes to the one that had crashed to an embarrassing Premiership home defeat to Aston Villa four days earlier. Lee Cattermole was out through injury, Stewart Downing was suffering from a virus and Mark Viduka was rested. Their replacements were Chris Riggott, Fabio Rochemback and Yakubu.

The visitors looked determined to capitalise on Boro's brittle confidence and showed up well in the early stages, with James Scowcroft and Gary McSheffrey both influential.

Gaizka Mendieta blazed wildly over from 20 yards as Boro created space, but fine work saw them take the lead with 20 minutes played. Good hold-up play from Yakubu, followed by an inch-perfect pass, allowed Hasselbaink to beat the offside trap and round keeper Marton Fulop.

Four minutes later, Hasselbaink almost made it two after a good set-up from Mendieta. But Fulop was able to scramble the ball away.

As in the first match, McSheffrey was a constant danger and his low cross was flicked goalwards by Stern John, who brought a good save from Mark Schwarzer. City continued to look the brighter side and John wasted a good delivery from Marcus Hall. Then Doriva headed over his own bar as the defence came under more pressure.

➡ Jimmy Floyd Hasselbaink helps out at the back

Match Statistics

Starting Line-Ups

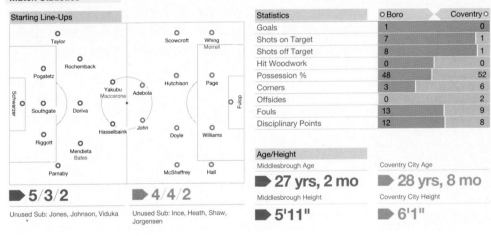

➡ 5/3/2

➡ 4/4/2

Unused Sub: Jones, Johnson, Viduka

Unused Sub: Ince, Heath, Shaw, Jorgensen

Statistics	Boro	Coventry
Goals	1	0
Shots on Target	7	1
Shots off Target	8	1
Hit Woodwork	0	0
Possession %	48	52
Corners	3	6
Offsides	0	2
Fouls	13	9
Disciplinary Points	12	8

Age/Height

Middlesbrough Age	Coventry City Age
➡ 27 yrs, 2 mo	➡ 28 yrs, 8 mo
Middlesbrough Height	Coventry City Height
➡ 5'11"	➡ 6'1"

There were chances for both sides in the closing stages. Nine minutes from time, Stuart Parnaby rifled in a drive from 25 yards that Fulop was glad to tip over the bar. The home defence was breached in the final minute of normal time as John wriggled free on the edge of the box and his low shot fizzed towards goal, Schwarzer producing a fine full-length save.

Deep into injury time, substitute Massimo Maccarone had a great chance to grab a second when beating the offside trap with an unchallenged run on goal. The run took him into the penalty area and around Fulop, but he slightly overran the ball and a low shot from a narrowing angle was cleared off the line by Robert Page.

Fans' Player of the Match

Gareth Southgate

Quote

❝ **Steve McClaren**

We asked the players for more commitment and we scored a good goal.

3-0

Middlesbrough ○
Chelsea ○

▶ Stewart Downing celebrates doubling the lead

Event Line

2 ○ ⊕ Rochemback / LF / OP / IA	
	Assist: Yakubu
17 ○ ⇄ Maniche > Gallas	
39 ○ ⇄ Boateng > Morrison	
42 ○ ▢ Terry	
45 ○ ▢ Gudjohnsen	
45 ○ ⊕ Downing / RF / OP / IA	
Half time 2-0	
46 ○ ⇄ Wright-Phillips > Cole J	
46 ○ ⇄ Cole C > Geremi	
68 ○ ⊕ Yakubu / RF / IFK / IA	
	Assist: Schwarzer
90 ○ ▢ Carvalho	
90 ○ ⇄ Davies > Mendieta	
90 ○ ⇄ Hasselbaink > Yakubu	
Full time 3-0	

In arguably the season's biggest shock result, Chelsea arrived at the Riverside with just one defeat in 54 games but left having suffered their heaviest league defeat for nearly four years.

Boro took the lead with only 77 seconds gone. Fabio Rochemback pressured ex-Boro player Geremi as he received a throw-in inside his own half. Yakubu took possession before returning the ball to Rochemback, whose shot squirmed under Petr Cech's body.

The champions – who would go on to retain their trophy - moved the ball around well but Boro's wholehearted performance made them unrecogniseable from the side that capitulated in such lack-lustre fashion seven days earlier.

Boro grabbed a second just before the break, Stewart Downing's low shot finding the bottom corner of the net with the help of a Mendieta dummy.

Chelsea poured forward in the second half but Boro kept the visitors at bay. The rout ws complete on 68 minutes when Yakubu latched on to a long goal-kick, raced to the edge of the penalty area, cut inside and drove the ball into the net for a fine solo effort.

Fans' Player of the Match	Quote	Premiership Milestone
Fabio Rochemback	❝ **Steve McClaren**	▶ **First Goal**

Today the team got their just rewards. I am especially delighted for the fans as they have not had much to shout about in the last few months.

Fabio Rochemback netted his first Premiership goal.

Venue:	Riverside Stadium	Referee:	S.G.Bennett - 05/06	
Attendance:	31,037	Matches:	28	
Capacity:	35,100	Yellow Cards:	95	
Occupancy:	88%	Red Cards:	9	

Middlesbrough
Chelsea

Form Coming into Fixture

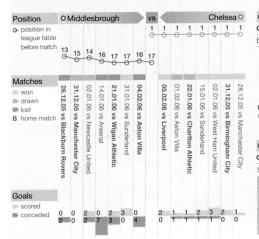

Position	Middlesbrough vs Chelsea
position in league table before match	13 15 14 16 17 17 16 17

Matches
- won
- drawn
- lost
- B home match

26.12.05 vs Blackburn Rovers
31.12.05 vs Manchester City
02.01.06 vs Newcastle United
14.01.06 vs Arsenal
21.01.06 vs Wigan Athletic
31.01.06 vs Sunderland
04.02.06 vs Aston Villa

05.02.06 vs Liverpool
01.02.06 vs Aston Villa
22.01.06 vs Charlton Athletic
15.01.06 vs Sunderland
02.01.06 vs West Ham United
31.12.05 vs Birmingham City
28.12.05 vs Manchester City

Goals
- scored
- conceded

0	0	2	0	2	3	0		1	1	2	3	2	1		
2	0	2	7	3	0	4		1	1	1	1	0	0		

Goal Statistics

Middlesbrough

by Half	by Situation
first: 2	set piece: 3
second: 5	open play: 4

Chelsea

by Half	by Situation
first: 7	set piece: 2
second: 5	open play: 10

Goals by Area

Middlesbrough
Scored (Conceded)

| 2 (3) |
| 4 (13) |
| 1 (2) |

Chelsea
Scored (Conceded)

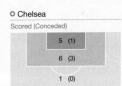

| 5 (1) |
| 6 (3) |
| 1 (0) |

Team Statistics

Starting Line-Ups

Middlesbrough:
Pogatetz, Downing, Rochemback, Southgate, Schwarzer, Doriva, Yakubu (Hasselbaink), Riggott, Mendieta (Davies), Parnaby, Morrison (Boateng)

Chelsea:
Cole J (Wright-Phillips), Geremi, Cole C, Gudjohnsen, Carvalho, Crespo, Essien, Cech, Terry, Lampard, Robben, Gallas (Maniche)

4/5/1

Unused Sub: Jones, Maccarone

4/3/3

Unused Sub: Cudicini, Huth

Premiership Totals	Boro	Chelsea
Premiership Appearances	1,742	1,514
Team Appearances	985	1,045
Goals Scored	211	240
Assists	173	194
Clean Sheets (goalkeepers)	73	36
Yellow Cards	190	144
Red Cards	7	8
Full Internationals	10	13

Age/Height

Middlesbrough Age	Chelsea Age
27 yrs, 3 mo	**25 yrs, 11 mo**

Middlesbrough Height	Chelsea Height
6'	**5'11"**

Match Statistics

League Table after Fixture

		Played	Won	Drawn	Lost	For	Against	Pts
●	1 Chelsea	26	21	3	2	52	16	66
...	...	...	...	...	...	...	...	...
↑	14 Newcastle	25	9	5	11	24	29	32
↓	15 Aston Villa	26	7	9	10	32	35	30
↑	16 Middlesbrough	25	7	7	11	33	44	28
↓	17 West Brom	26	7	5	14	24	38	26
●	18 Birmingham	24	5	5	14	21	34	20
●	19 Portsmouth	26	4	6	16	18	45	18
●	20 Sunderland	24	2	3	19	17	45	9

Statistics	Boro	Chelsea
Goals	3	0
Shots on Target	6	10
Shots off Target	1	7
Hit Woodwork	0	1
Possession %	39	61
Corners	5	9
Offsides	3	4
Fouls	17	7
Disciplinary Points	0	12

1-2

VfB Stuttgart ○
Middlesbrough ○

▶ Andrew Davies in action in Germany

Event Line

20 ○ ⊕	Hasselbaink / LF / OP / IA	
	Assist: Boateng	
22 ○ ■	Pogatetz	
33 ○ ■	Hitzlsperger	
Half time 0-1		
46 ○ ⊕	Parnaby / RF / OP / IA	
	Assist: Boateng	
46 ○ ⇄	Beck > Stranzl	
66 ○ ⇄	Gomez > Hitzlsperger	
68 ○	Davies	
73 ○ ⇄	Johnson > Downing	
80 ○ ⇄	Gentner > Meissner	
81 ○ ⇄	Kennedy > Boateng	
85 ○ ⇄	Yakubu > Hasselbaink	
86 ○ ⊕	Ljuboja / LF / DFK / OA	
	Assist: Ljuboja	
90 ○	Meira	
Full time 1-2		

Goals from Jimmy Floyd Hasselbaink and Stuart Parnaby guided Boro to a priceless away win in Germany in the UEFA Cup Round of 32.

After two minutes, Danijel Ljuboja raced into the box, bringing a fine save from Mark Schwarzer with a powerful cross shot. Former Newcastle United striker Jon Dahl Tomasson brought another save from Mark Schwarzer with a low shot from 20 yards as the home side continued to enjoy the best of the early possession.

The same player was just wide with a low shot from the edge of the six-yard box when meeting a low right-wing cross and it was another such delivery that almost brought the opening goal after 18 minutes.

An excellent delivery from the former Chelsea and Birmingham winger Jesper Gronkjaer fizzed low into the box and a vital touch from Gareth Southgate turned the ball off the feet of Ljuboja. A minute later Boro swept forward to take the lead.

Portuguese defender Fernando Meira's attempted clearance hit Boateng. Hasselbaink took possession and moved stealthily into the penalty area before shooting past German international goalkeeper Timo Hildebrand.

The goal knocked the edge off Stuttgart and all that could be heard in the £51m stadium were the celebrations of the 1,600-strong Teesside travelling army of supporters.

Boro got off to the best possible start in the second half. With just 55 seconds played, Boateng cleverly beat the full-back before crossing from the right to pick out Parnaby, who stroked home from seven yards.

Venue:	Gottlieb-Daimler Stadium	Referee:	A.Hamer (LUX)

Attendance: 21,000
Capacity: 54,088
Occupancy: 39%

**VfB Stuttgart
Middlesbrough**

Gareth Southgate, Emanuel Pogatetz and Chris Riggott salute the travelling fans

Match Statistics

Starting Line-Ups

Gerber Hitzlsperger
Gomez

Delpierre Meissner
Gentner Tomasson

Hasselbaink
Yakubu

Meira Soldo Ljuboja

Stranzl Gronkjaer
Beck

Hildebrand

Parnaby Davies

Boateng
Kennedy

Riggott

Doriva

Southgate

Rochemback

Downing Pogatetz
Johnson

Schwarzer

▶ 4/4/2   **▶ 4/5/1**

Unused Sub: Heinen, Babbel, Magnin, Tiffert

Unused Sub: Jones, McMahon, Bates, Taylor

Statistics	○ Stuttgart	Boro ○
Goals	1	2
Shots on Target	6	5
Shots off Target	11	1
Hit Woodwork	0	0
Possession %	64	36
Corners	4	1
Offsides	1	3
Fouls	12	19
Disciplinary Points	8	8

Confidence visibly drained from Stuttgart. Passes went astray and the crowd started to get on their backs. Boro flourished, controlling the game, and a low shot from Hasselbaink was saved by Hildebrand's outstretched left leg.

With nine minutes remaining, Schwarzer made a fine save when diving full-length to gather a header from Ljuboja. Stuttgart gave themselves a lifeline when scoring the first goal conceded by Boro in Europe this season.

Boro gave away a free-kick on the edge of the area and Ljuboja struck a superb delivery into Schwarzer's bottom right-hand corner.

Fans' Player of the Match

George Boateng

Quote

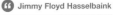 Jimmy Floyd Hasselbaink

We were a little bit unfortunate to concede a goal, but it was a very good performance.

89

0-2

Preston North End ○
Middlesbrough ○

FA Cup
19.02.06

➤ Stuart Parnaby demonstrates his ball skills

Boro travelled to Deepdale in good spirits after terrific wins against Chelsea and Stuttgart had turned around the club's fortunes.

Tony McMahon made his first appearance of the season following a lengthy shoulder problem, while Franck Queudrue returned following a two-month injury absence. Emanuel Pogatetz stood in for skipper Gareth Southgate, who was on the bench, Gaizka Mendieta returned in favour of Doriva and Yakubu was chosen ahead of Jimmy Floyd Hasselbaink up front. Preston, chasing promotion to the Premier League, sported a proud unbeaten run of 25 matches.

The early stages were dominated by the home side and a low 25-yard drive from David Nugent was deflected inches wide of a scrambling Schwarzer's left-hand post. Boro, again adopting a 4-5-1 approach, found it difficult to get going, with limited possession.

Preston had a great chance to open the scoring after 20 minutes when a free-kick was whipped into the area. Youl Mawene, unmarked, dived full-length to head wide from 12 yards. Boro suffered another injury blow in first-half injury time when Fabio Rochemback had to be stretchered off after hurting his ankle in a challenge. A second change came after the break as Hasselbaink replaced McMahon.

But Boro took just six minutes of the second period to take the lead. Yakubu pounced on slack marking to thrash an unstoppable left-footed shot beyond the reach of former Boro keeper Carlo Nash from the edge of the penalty area.

Preston striker David Nugent then caused a scare at the other end when he fired wide from long range. Schwarzer had to be alert to save a header from Mawene

Venue:	Deepdale	Referee:	P.Dowd - 05/06	Preston North End
Attendance:	19,877	Matches:	33	Middlesbrough
Capacity:	22,225	Yellow Cards:	129	
Occupancy:	89%	Red Cards:	5	

➡ Yakubu books a Quarter-Final place

Match Statistics

Starting Line-Ups

Preston: Nash; Mears, Sedgwick (Neal L), McKenna, Mawene, Davis, O'Neil (Dichio), Nugent, Hill, Davidson, Agyemang (Lucketti)

➡ 4/4/2

Unused Sub: Ward, Hibbert

Boro: Schwarzer; Queudrue, Pogatetz, Riggott, McMahon (Hasselbaink), Downing, Cattermole (Rochemback), Boateng, Parnaby, Mendieta, Yakubu (Southgate)

➡ 4/5/1

Unused Sub: Jones, Taylor

Statistics	○ Preston	Boro ○
Goals	0	2
Shots on Target	5	3
Shots off Target	7	2
Hit Woodwork	0	0
Possession %	52	48
Corners	6	0
Offsides	3	0
Fouls	14	16
Disciplinary Points	8	8

Age/Height

Preston North End Age	Middlesbrough Age
➡ 27 yrs, 8 mo	➡ 26 yrs, 7 mo
Preston North End Height	Middlesbrough Height
➡ 6'	➡ 6'

before the visitors doubled their advantage after 77 minutes. Stewart Downing delivered an excellent free-kick and Yakubu arrived at the back post to head past Nash.

Yakubu was then replaced by Gareth Southgate, who made his first appearance as a Boro substitute, as the visitors looked forward to the quarter-finals for the first time in four years. More than 3,000 Boro fans made the trip across the Pennines, one of the biggest away followings of the season.

With Steve McClaren's squad battling on three fronts, the match schedule was becoming increasingly hectic. But four successive wins had put everyone in good heart.

Fans' Player of the Match

Yakubu

Quote

🇬 Steve McClaren

I was disappointed with our first-half performance, so we decided to go for it in the second half and it paid off.

0-1

Middlesbrough ○
VfB Stuttgart ○

▶ George Boateng makes his presence felt in midfield

Event Line

13 ○ ⊕	Tiffert / RF / OP / IA	
	Assist: Ljuboja	
31 ○	Boateng	
Half time 0-1		
51 ○	Mendieta	
52 ○	Tiffert	
64 ○ ⇄	Gomez > Gronkjaer	
75 ○ ⇄	Cacau > Meissner	
80 ○ ⇄	Hitzlsperger > Magnin	
86 ○ ⇄	Yakubu > Hasselbaink	
86 ○ ⇄	Ehiogu > Mendieta	
90 ○	Cattermole	
90 ○ ⇄	Taylor > Downing	
Full time 0-1		

Despite this defeat, Boro reached the last 16 of the UEFA Cup for the second year running, the away-goals rule seeing them through.

Steve McClaren's side showed three changes from the first leg. Emanuel Pogatetz was suspended after picking up his third yellow card of the competition, Doriva was left out, while Fabio Rochemback was sidelined with an ankle injury. In came Franck Queudrue, Lee Cattermole and Gaizka Mendieta.

Boro got off to a nervous start as the German side went for an early goal. Much of the home side's problems were self-inflicted as they gave away a succession of free-kicks in dangerous positions.

Mark Schwarzer was kept alert as the visitors pressed from both flanks, and Danijel Ljuboja hit the side netting with a 20-yard free-kick. The goal that had been threatened came after 13 minutes.

Ljuboja won possession and released Christian Tiffert, who rode one challenge before hitting a sweet, low shot with the outside of his right foot beyond Schwarzer and into the keeper's bottom left-hand corner.

Five minutes from half-time Ljuboja fell in the area under a challenge from Gareth Southgate. But his penalty appeals were turned down.

Boro wasted a great chance to draw level early in the second half when Cattermole found Hasselbaink with a ball behind the Stuttgart defence. The Dutchman's low shot was smothered by the advancing goalkeeper, Timo Hildebrand.

Hasselbaink picked out Mendieta who, with Hildebrand out of position, took his

▶ Lee Cattermole is full of running

Match Statistics

Starting Line-Ups

▶ 4/4/1/1   ▶ 4/5/1

Unused Sub: Jones, McMahon, Viduka, Maccarone

Unused Sub: Heinen, Gerber, Beck, Carevic

Statistics	○ Boro	Stuttgart ○
Goals	0	1
Shots on Target	2	6
Shots off Target	5	6
Hit Woodwork	0	0
Possession %	41	59
Corners	1	4
Offsides	7	3
Fouls	21	14
Disciplinary Points	12	4

time and hit a low shot that was cleared off the line by former Germany and Liverpool defender Markus Babbel.

Schwarzer was forced to tip over a 30-yard free-kick from Ludovic Magnin and, when Stuttgart were awarded another free-kick, the same player forced the Australian into another save.

Five minutes from time, Steve McClaren made a double change, replacing Mendieta and Hasselbaink with Ugo Ehiogu and Yakubu. Boro played possession football in the closing stages in the knowledge that they had done enough to progress.

Fans' Player of the Match

Lee Cattermole

Quote

🔊 Steve McClaren

I changed tactics for the second half and we became more positive.

0-2

West Bromwich Albion ○
Middlesbrough ○

▶ Emanuel Pogatetz tries to find space in the box

Event Line

17 ○ ⊕	Hasselbaink / RF / OP / OA	
	Assist: Yakubu	
34 ○ ▪	Southgate	
44 ○ ⊕	Wallwork / LF / OG / IA	
	Assist: Hasselbaink	
Half time 0-2		
49 ○ ▪	Cattermole	
54 ○ ▪	Quashie	
	Violent Conduct	
58 ○ ⇄	Kozak > Campbell	
72 ○ ⇄	Maccarone > Hasselbaink	
80 ○ ⇄	Davies > Mendieta	
81 ○ ⇄	Inamoto > Albrechtsen	
81 ○ ⇄	Ellington > Kanu	
88 ○ ⇄	Viduka > Yakubu	
Full time 0-2		

Born-again Boro completed back-to-back Premiership wins for the first time in 50 games.

In fact, when combined with their UEFA and FA Cup progress, Steve McClaren's side were now in red hot form, so soon after being in an apparent downward spiral. Crucially, Boro moved five points clear of their hosts at the wrong end of the table.

After a good start Boro took the lead with 17 minutes played. Yakubu hit a perfectly weighted through ball for Jimmy Floyd Hasselbaink. The Dutch striker timed his run to perfection to beat the offside trap and score his 11th goal of the season from just inside the penalty area.

The home side saw plenty of the ball and it took good blocks from both Cattermole and Parnaby to prevent an equaliser. But a minute before half time Boro were awarded a free-kick on the edge of the Albion penalty area. Hasselbaink's well-struck effort took a deflection off Ronnie Wallwork, leaving his 'keeper stranded and giving Boro a commanding lead.

West Brom continued to press but their attacks were dealt with comfortably. Boro could have caused further misery for the home side had their final ball not let them down.

Fans' Player of the Match

Hasselbaink

Quote

❝ Steve McClaren

There is a great feeling in the dressing room at the moment after this run of results.

Venue:	The Hawthorns	Referee:	M.L.Dean - 05/06		West Bromwich Albion
Attendance:	24,061	Matches:	26		Middlesbrough
Capacity:	28,003	Yellow Cards:	72		
Occupancy:	86%	Red Cards:	6		

Form Coming into Fixture

Position

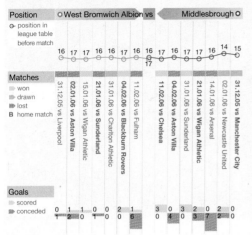

o→ position in league table before match

Matches
- won
- drawn
- lost
- B home match

Goals
- scored
- conceded

Goal Statistics

o West Bromwich Albion

by Half
by Situation

- first: 2
- second: 3
- set piece: 1
- open play: 4

o Middlesbrough

by Half
by Situation

- first: 4
- second: 6
- set piece: 4
- open play: 6

Goals by Area

o West Bromwich Albion

Scored (Conceded)

| 0 (3) |
| 4 (7) |
| 1 (0) |

o Middlesbrough

Scored (Conceded)

| 2 (2) |
| 7 (12) |
| 1 (2) |

Team Statistics

Starting Line-Ups

Robinson, Greening, Parnaby, Cattermole, Riggott, Clement, Quashie, Campbell (Kozak), Hasselbaink (Maccarone), Kuszczak, Mendieta (Davies), Southgate, Schwarzer, Davies C, Wallwork, Kanu (Ellington), Yakubu (Viduka), Queudrue, Albrechtsen (Inamoto), Kamara, Boateng, Pogatetz

4/4/2   **5/3/2**

Unused Sub: Kirkland, Martinez

Unused Sub: Jones, Ehiogu

Premiership Totals

	West Brom	Boro
Premiership Appearances	1,203	1,947
Team Appearances	494	1,060
Goals Scored	149	300
Assists	127	203
Clean Sheets (goalkeepers)	8	74
Yellow Cards	112	224
Red Cards	2	13
Full Internationals	6	9

Age/Height

West Bromwich Albion Age	Middlesbrough Age
26 yrs, 11 mo	**27 yrs, 6 mo**

West Bromwich Albion Height	Middlesbrough Height
6'	**6'**

Match Statistics

League Table after Fixture

		Played	Won	Drawn	Lost	For	Against	Pts
↓ 9	Wigan	27	12	4	11	32	34	40
• 10	Man City	27	11	4	12	36	31	37
• 11	Newcastle	27	10	6	11	26	29	36
• 12	Everton	27	11	3	13	19	34	36
• 13	Charlton	27	10	5	12	32	37	35
• 14	Fulham	27	9	5	13	37	39	32
• 15	Aston Villa	27	7	10	10	32	35	31
• 16	Middlesbrough	26	8	7	11	35	44	31
• 17	West Brom	27	7	5	15	24	40	26

Statistics

	West Brom	Boro
Goals	0	2
Shots on Target	9	4
Shots off Target	8	1
Hit Woodwork	0	0
Possession %	55	45
Corners	6	3
Offsides	2	3
Fouls	7	14
Disciplinary Points	12	8

1-0

Middlesbrough ○
Birmingham City ○

➡ Mark Viduka scores the crucial winner

Event Line

20 ○ ⇄ Davies > Parnaby
45 ○ ⊕ Viduka / LF / OP / 6Y
Assist: Cattermole

Half time 1-0

56 ○ ⇄ Campbell > Dunn
57 ○ ⇄ Jarosik > Kilkenny
68 ○ ⇄ Doriva > Mendieta
68 ○ ⇄ Maccarone > Viduka
78 ○ ⇄ Forssell > Johnson

Full time 1-0

Boro's stunning recovery continued as a battling performance earned a third successive Premiership clean sheet win – and a seventh win in nine in all competitions.

Crucially, the three points took Boro 11 points clear of third-bottom Birmingham to all but erase any lingering relegation concerns.

City could and perhaps should have taken an early lead when the ball fell to former England striker Emile Heskey. Chris Riggott failed to deal with a Melchiot cross, giving Heskey a free header that he contrived to put wide.

With seconds remaining in the first half, Boro took the lead. Lee Cattermole took on two players before releasing Mark Viduka with a well-timed pass. Viduka beat one defender and used his strength to hold off a second challenge before sliding the ball into the net from an acute angle.

Birmingham started the second half with more purpose and Schwarzer was called into action early on to make a save from a David Dunn header. With the exception of a couple of Boro half chances, it was one-way traffic for much of the second half but Boro held on for a vital win.

Fans' Player of the Match

Lee Cattermole

Quote

❝ **Steve McClaren**

It was a game where the result was vital. We got the result despite not playing well.

Venue:	Riverside Stadium	Referee:	G.Poll - 05/06		Middlesbrough
Attendance:	28,141	Matches:	31		Birmingham City
Capacity:	35,100	Yellow Cards:	107		
Occupancy:	80%	Red Cards:	6		

Form Coming into Fixture

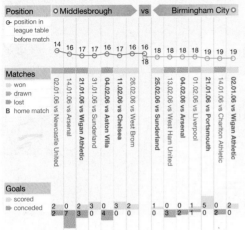

Position	O Middlesbrough	vs	Birmingham City O

position in league table before match

14 16 17 17 16 17 16 16 / 18 18 18 18 19 19 19
18

Matches
- won
- drawn
- lost
- B home match

02.01.06 vs Newcastle United
14.01.06 vs Arsenal
21.01.06 vs Wigan Athletic
31.01.06 vs Sunderland
04.02.06 vs Aston Villa
11.02.06 vs Chelsea
26.02.06 vs West Brom
25.02.06 vs Sunderland
13.02.06 vs West Ham United
04.02.06 vs Arsenal
01.02.06 vs Liverpool
21.01.06 vs Portsmouth
14.01.06 vs Charlton Athletic
02.01.06 vs Wigan Athletic

Goals
- scored
- conceded

| scored | 2 | 0 | 2 | 3 | 0 | 3 | 2 | | 1 | 0 | 0 | 1 | 5 | 0 | 2 |
| conceded | 2 | 7 | 3 | 0 | 4 | 0 | 0 | | 0 | 3 | 2 | 1 | 0 | 2 | 0 |

Goal Statistics

O Middlesbrough

by Half / by Situation

first:	6	set piece:	4
second:	6	open play:	7
		own goals:	1

O Birmingham City

by Half / by Situation

first:	5	set piece:	4
second:	4	open play:	4
		own goals:	1

Goals by Area

O Middlesbrough
Scored (Conceded)

| 2 (2) |
| 8 (12) |
| 2 (2) |

O Birmingham City
Scored (Conceded)

| 4 (3) |
| 5 (5) |
| 0 (0) |

Team Statistics

Starting Line-Ups

Pogatetz, Cattermole, Queudrue, Yakubu, Dunn/Campbell, Kilkenny/Jarosik, Pennant, Melchiot, Bruce, Schwarzer, Southgate, Boateng, Viduka/Maccarone, Heskey, Taylor Maik, Riggott, Mendieta/Doriva, Butt, Taylor Martin, Parnaby/Davies, Johnson/Forssell, Gray

▶ 5/3/2   ▶ 4/4/1/1

Unused Sub: Jones, Ehiogu   Unused Sub: Vaesen, Tebily

Premiership Totals	O Boro	Birmingham O
Premiership Appearances	1,772	1,575
Team Appearances	1,090	582
Goals Scored	179	181
Assists	131	163
Clean Sheets (goalkeepers)	75	39
Yellow Cards	201	162
Red Cards	12	14
Full Internationals	9	8

Age/Height

Middlesbrough Age
▶ **27 yrs, 6 mo**

Birmingham City Age
▶ **26 yrs, 7 mo**

Middlesbrough Height
▶ **6'**

Birmingham City Height
▶ **6'**

Match Statistics

League Table after Fixture

	Played	Won	Drawn	Lost	For	Against	Pts
↑ 10 Newcastle	28	11	6	11	29	30	39
↓ 11 Man City	27	11	4	12	36	31	37
● 12 Everton	28	11	4	13	21	36	37
● 13 Charlton	28	10	6	12	32	37	36
↑ 14 Aston Villa	28	8	10	10	33	35	34
↑ 15 Middlesbrough	27	9	7	11	36	44	34
↓ 16 Fulham	28	9	5	14	37	43	32
● 17 West Brom	28	7	5	16	25	42	26
● 18 Birmingham	27	6	5	16	22	38	23

Statistics	O Boro	Birmingham O
Goals	1	0
Shots on Target	6	5
Shots off Target	6	9
Hit Woodwork	0	0
Possession %	45	55
Corners	3	4
Offsides	1	4
Fouls	12	12
Disciplinary Points	0	0

1-0 Middlesbrough ○
AS Roma ○

▶ Andrew Davies is in control at the back

Event Line

2 ○ ⇄ Queudrue > Downing
12 ○ ⊕ Yakubu / RF / P / IA
    Assist: Hasselbaink
42 ○ ▪ Perrotta
Half time 1-0
61 ○ ⇄ Okaka Chuka > Taddei
72 ○ ▪ Riggott
73 ○ ⇄ Alvarez > Tommasi
81 ○ ⇄ Viduka > Yakubu
84 ○ ⇄ Aquilani > Dacourt
89 ○ ▪ Mexes
Full time 1-0

A solitary strike from Yakubu gave Boro a slender lead as "the small town in Europe" impressed against the cup favourites and one of Europe's form teams.

Boro tried to press home an early advantage, with Lee Cattermole and Gaizka Mendieta prominent. But it was the visitors who almost opened the scoring after six minutes as Mexes played a delightfully-weighted ball over the top from just inside the Boro half. Italian international star Perrotta controlled comfortably inside the penalty area and a low shot beat Mark Schwarzer before Gareth Southgate cleared off the line.

The all-important goal came after 12 minutes when Mendieta burst forward deep inside Roma territory and played a low ball in behind the visitors' defence. Hasselbaink took control inside the penalty area but was brought down by keeper Gianluca Curci. Yakubu put Boro in front with a cool finish from the spot.

With just five minutes of the first-half remaining, Brazilian Mancini was sent clear down the left but George Boateng powered his way back to recover lost ground and block an attempted cross.

Cattermole had a tremendous game and was a major influence in midfield. There was a scare when Boateng heavily limped off to take treatment on his left ankle, but he was able to return.

A flowing move saw Boro spring from defence into attack in devastating fashion. Hasselbaink suddenly shot low from edge of the Roma penalty area. Curci fumbled the fierce drive, but managed to beat it away.

Venue:	Riverside Staduim	Referee:	A.Sars (FRA)
Attendance:	25,354		
Capacity:	35,100		
Occupancy:	72%		

Middlesbrough
AS Roma

Yakubu tucks away the only goal of the game from the penalty spot

Match Statistics

Starting Line-Ups

4/4/1/1   4/5/1

Unused Sub: Jones, McMahon, Doriva, Parlour, Maccarone

Unused Sub: Pipolo, Chivu, Bovo, Rosi

Statistics	Boro	Roma
Goals	1	0
Shots on Target	3	2
Shots off Target	6	5
Hit Woodwork	0	0
Possession %	37	63
Corners	2	4
Offsides	2	3
Fouls	20	19
Disciplinary Points	4	8

Schwarzer then kept Boro ahead as he dived full-length across his goal to palm away a close-range cross from the right, with young sub Okaka waiting to capitalise.

Mendieta wasted a great chance to make it two nine minutes from time. Sent clear with the first touch of substitute Mark Viduka, the Spain international was left with just Curci to beat, but delayed his shot and blazed well over from 10 yards.

There was a heart-stopping moment in the final minute of injury time as Mancini was picked out midway inside the Boro half. The ball sat up nicely for him and a volley dipped and swerved. The lights and heavy rain could have made it difficult for Schwarzer. However, he stood his ground to make a vital save.

Fans' Player of the Match

Lee Cattermole

Quote

❝ **Steve McClaren**

It would have been nice to have scored more goals, but we would have taken a 1-0 win before the game.

2-1

Charlton Athletic ○
Middlesbrough ○

▶ Andrew Taylor looks to get forward

Event Line

8 ○	Hughes	
13 ○ ⇄	Davies > McMahon	
35 ○	Young	
Half time 0-0		
46 ○ ⇄	Euell > Bothroyd	
46 ○ ⇄	Thomas > Hughes	
60 ○	Parlour	
69 ○ ⇄	Cattermole > Parlour	
73 ○ ⊕	Bent D / H / OP / 6Y	
	Assist: Powell	
75 ○ ⇄	Bartlett > Ambrose	
76 ○ ⇄	Yakubu > Maccarone	
81 ○ ⊕	Viduka / RF / OP / OA	
86 ○ ⊕	Bent D / RF / OP / 6Y	
	Assist: Young	
Full time 2-1		

Two goals from in-form striker Darren Bent condemned Boro to their first Premiership loss since early February.

Boro created the first real chance when, with 22 minutes gone, Massimo Maccarone's low shot produced an outstanding one-handed save from Thomas Myhre in the Charlton goal. The away side continued to be the better team in the second half but it was Charlton who hit the target against the run of play. Bent beat Emanuel Pogatetz to a left wing cross and his powerful header from six yards out put Charlton ahead.

Boro got their well-deserved equaliser with a spectacular effort from Mark Viduka in the 79th minute. The Aussie striker received the ball on the right-hand edge of the penalty area, flicked the ball over two defenders and dispatched a volley over Myhre, who was barely off his line.

Having dominated for much of the game, Boro were just four minutes from a point when a lapse in concentration cost them the match. Young sent in a cross from the right that was completely untouched as it passed through the six-yard box. Bent ran in at the back post to score the easiest of goals for his 19th of the season.

Fans' Player of the Match

Adam Johnson

Quote

🍎 **Steve McClaren**

In the past I have been critical of our performances when we've won games, but today I was proud of the team.

Venue:	The Valley	Referee:	A.G.Wiley - 05/06		**Charlton Athletic**
Attendance:	24,830	Matches:	34		**Middlesbrough**
Capacity:	27,111	Yellow Cards:	103		
Occupancy:	92%	Red Cards:	7		

Form Coming into Fixture

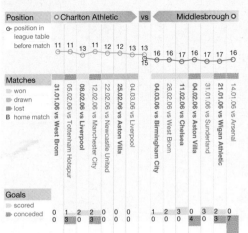

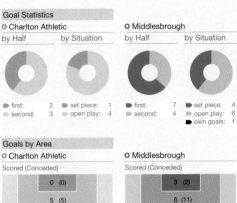

Goal Statistics

Charlton Athletic

by Half
- first: 2
- second: 3

by Situation
- set piece: 1
- open play: 4

Middlesbrough

by Half
- first: 7
- second: 4

by Situation
- set piece: 4
- open play: 6
- own goals: 1

Goals by Area

Charlton Athletic — Scored (Conceded)

0 (0)
5 (5)
0 (1)

Middlesbrough — Scored (Conceded)

3 (2)
6 (11)
2 (1)

Team Statistics

Starting Line-Ups

4/4/2

Unused Sub: Andersen, Spector

4/5/1

Unused Sub: Jones, Riggott

Premiership Totals	Charlton	Boro
Premiership Appearances	2,042	1,590
Team Appearances	1,139	831
Goals Scored	155	178
Assists	107	121
Clean Sheets (goalkeepers)	30	76
Yellow Cards	211	181
Red Cards	7	17
Full Internationals	9	8

Age/Height

	Charlton Athletic	Middlesbrough
Age	29 yrs, 1 mo	25 yrs, 10 mo
Height	6'	6'

Match Statistics

League Table after Fixture

		Played	Won	Drawn	Lost	For	Against	Pts
●	12 Newcastle	29	11	6	12	29	32	39
●	13 Charlton	29	11	6	12	34	38	39
●	14 Aston Villa	29	8	10	11	33	37	34
●	15 Middlesbrough	28	9	7	12	37	46	34
●	16 Fulham	29	9	5	15	38	46	32
●	17 West Brom	29	7	6	16	26	43	27
●	18 Birmingham	28	6	6	16	23	39	24
●	19 Portsmouth	29	5	6	18	20	49	21
●	20 Sunderland	29	2	4	23	19	52	10

Statistics	Charlton	Boro
Goals	2	1
Shots on Target	3	7
Shots off Target	2	2
Hit Woodwork	0	0
Possession %	52	48
Corners	0	4
Offsides	4	1
Fouls	17	20
Disciplinary Points	8	4

2-1 AS Roma ○
Middlesbrough ○

► Mark Schwarzer enjoyed a memorable night in Rome

Event Line

14 ○ ▢	Cattermole
30 ○ ▢	Boateng
31 ○ ▢	Mancini
32 ○ ⊕	Hasselbaink / H / OP / IA
	Assist: Downing
43 ○ ⊕	Mancini / RF / OP / IA
	Assist: Taddei
Half time 1-1	
46 ○ ⇄	Queudrue > Davies
58 ○ ⇄	Parlour > Yakubu
63 ○ ⇄	Okaka Chuka > Dacourt
66 ○ ⊕	Mancini / RF / P / IA
	Assist: Okaka Chuka
71 ○ ⇄	Aquilani > Alvarez
77 ○ ▢	Aquilani
85 ○ ▢	Pogatetz
86 ○ ▢	Bovo
86 ○ ⇄	Panucci > Chivu
90 ○ ◢	Mexes
	2nd Bookable Offence
Full time 2-1	

Boro progressed to the quarter-finals of the UEFA Cup for the first time by again taking the verdict on the away-goals rule.

There was a terrific atmosphere inside the Olympic Stadium as travelling Teessiders enthusiastically backed their team. The home side struck woodwork after 24 minutes when Stewart Downing mis-controlled. Bovo pounced and rattled the bar with a splendid effort from 22 yards.

Boro silenced the passionate Italian fans by taking a shock lead after 32 minutes. There looked little on as Downing moved down the left, but he swung over a good cross and Jimmy Floyd Hasselbaink stole in front of Mexes and glanced a sublime header across and beyond Gianluca Curci.

Roma grabbed an equaliser on 43 minutes, Taddei pulling the ball back for fellow Brazilian Mancini, who drilled a rising drive past Schwarzer from 11 yards.

A slip from substitute Franck Queudrue, playing in an unaccustomed right-back position, allowed the first break of the second half to go to Roma and Mancini cut in to hit a low shot against the chest of Schwarzer.

Roma lay siege to Boro's goal. Mancini saw a close-range shot deflected just wide before Schwarzer produced an outstanding stop to deny Italian international midfielder de Rossi one-handed from eight yards.

After 65 minutes, Roma were handed a way back into the tie when Ray Parlour was harshly adjudged to have caught Okaka on the edge of the box. Amidst furious protests, Norwegian referee Tom Henning Ovrebo awarded a penalty.

▶ The final whistle is greeted with delight by Lee Cattermole

Match Statistics

Starting Line-Ups

Statistics	Roma	Boro
Goals	2	1
Shots on Target	9	1
Shots off Target	10	0
Hit Woodwork	1	0
Possession %	63	37
Corners	13	2
Offsides	2	1
Fouls	19	16
Disciplinary Points	22	12

▶ 4/5/1

▶ 4/4/1/1

Unused Sub: Eleftheropoulos, Cufre, Kharja, Rosi

Unused Sub: Jones, Ehiogu, Doriva, Maccarone, Viduka

Mancini duly converted to Schwarzer's left. Deep into injury time Roma were reduced to 10 men when Mexes, booked for retaliation in the first half, pushed Downing and was shown a second yellow card.

After four and a half minutes of injury time, referee Ovrebo blew the whistle on one of the most memorable nights in Boro's history.

There were ecstatic celebrations from the travelling contingent of 3,500 Boro fans as the significance of the victory sank in. A note of regret, however, was that yellow cards shown to Lee Cattermole and George Boateng meant they were ruled out of the first leg of the quarter-final.

Fans' Player of the Match

Mark Schwarzer

Quote

🟢 Gareth Southgate

We knew we needed an away goal and Mark Schwarzer made some good saves to keep us in it.

103

3-2

Blackburn Rovers ○
Middlesbrough ○

▶ Ugo Ehiogu brings the ball under control

Event Line

11 ○ ⊕ Bellamy / LF / OP / IA	
16 ○ ⊕ Viduka / RF / OP / IA	
Assist: Morrison	
28 ○ ⊕ Pedersen / LF / DFK / OA	
Assist: Bellamy	

• Half time 2-1

46 ○ ⇄ Taylor > Johnson	
46 ○ ⇄ Yakubu > Parlour	
46 ○ ⇄ Pogatetz > Riggott	
54 ○ ◪ Savage	
2nd Bookable Offence	
58 ○ ▢ Pogatetz	
59 ○ ⇄ Mokoena > Emerton	
62 ○ ⊕ Rochemback / RF / OP / IA	
Assist: Morrison	
64 ○ ▢ Reid	
68 ○ ⊕ Bellamy / RF / OP / IA	
Assist: Pedersen	
72 ○ ⇄ Bentley > Sinama-Pongolle	
81 ○ ▢ Boateng	
84 ○ ▢ Neill	
86 ○ ▢ Queudrue	

Full time 3-2

A Craig Bellamy double was enough to give 10-man Rovers all three points as Steve McClaren chose to rest several members of the side that had done so well to beat Roma over two legs.

With 10 minutes played, Bellamy hit a low shot from the left-hand edge of the penalty area which curled beyond the reach of Mark Schwarzer. Rovers' lead lasted just six minutes. James Morrison intercepted a poor throw-in and played the ball in to Mark Viduka, who powered a fierce, low drive past Brad Friedel.

Rovers, however, took back their lead with a free-kick. Morten Gamst Pedersen made the most of the opportunity, re-positioning a free-kick in order to get a better angle, before beating Schwarzer with a left-footed drive.

When Rovers hard man Robbie Savage was sent off for a second bookable offence, Boro took advantage of their extra man to equalise with just over an hour played. Morrison set up Fabio Rochemback, who hit a low, hard shot into the net.

Boro should have gone on to win but, instead, they were left empty-handed when Pogatetz was caught out of position, allowing Bellamy to race into the area and strike a great match-winner.

Fans' Player of the Match

James Morrison

Quote

❝ Steve McClaren

Them going down to ten men gave us an opportunity, but again poor defending has cost us the game.

Venue:	Ewood Park	Referee:	C.J.Foy - 05/06	**Blackburn Rovers**
Attendance:	18,681	Matches:	32	**Middlesbrough**
Capacity:	31,367	Yellow Cards:	71	
Occupancy:	60%	Red Cards:	7	

Form Coming into Fixture

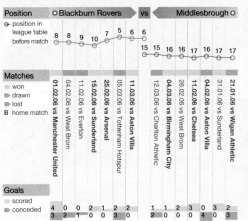

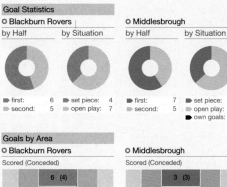

Goal Statistics

○ Blackburn Rovers

by Half — by Situation

- first: 6
- second: 5
- set piece: 4
- open play: 7

○ Middlesbrough

by Half — by Situation

- first: 7
- second: 5
- set piece: 4
- open play: 7
- own goals: 1

Goals by Area

○ Blackburn Rovers

Scored (Conceded)

| 6 (4) |
| 5 (4) |
| 0 (1) |

○ Middlesbrough

Scored (Conceded)

| 3 (3) |
| 6 (6) |
| 3 (0) |

Team Statistics

Starting Line-Ups

▶ 4/4/2

Unused Sub: Enckelman, Dickov, Kuqi

▶ 4/4/1/1

Unused Sub: Jones, Doriva

Premiership Totals	○ Blackburn	Boro ○
Premiership Appearances	1,409	1,872
Team Appearances	762	894
Goals Scored	104	185
Assists	126	127
Clean Sheets (goalkeepers)	63	76
Yellow Cards	193	241
Red Cards	7	18
Full Internationals	11	8

Age/Height

Blackburn Rovers Age
▶ 26 yrs, 11 mo

Middlesbrough Age
▶ 26 yrs

Blackburn Rovers Height
▶ 5'11"

Middlesbrough Height
▶ 6'

Match Statistics

League Table after Fixture

		Played	Won	Drawn	Lost	For	Against	Pts
● 6	Blackburn	30	15	4	11	41	36	49
...		...	...	...	...	...	...	...
● 14	Aston Villa	30	8	10	12	34	41	34
● 15	Middlesbrough	29	9	7	13	39	49	34
● 16	Fulham	30	9	5	16	39	51	32
● 17	West Brom	30	7	6	17	27	45	27
● 18	Birmingham	29	6	6	17	23	41	24
● 19	Portsmouth	30	6	6	18	24	51	24
● 20	Sunderland	30	2	4	24	19	54	10

Statistics	○ Blackburn	Boro ○
Goals	3	2
Shots on Target	3	5
Shots off Target	2	2
Hit Woodwork	0	0
Possession %	54	46
Corners	6	4
Offsides	3	2
Fouls	11	11
Disciplinary Points	18	12

0-0

Charlton Athletic ○
Middlesbrough ○

➤ Gareth Southgate gets a foot to the ball

Event Line
Half time 0-0
62 ○ ⇄ Rommedahl > Kishishev
64 ○ ⇄ Morrison > Mendieta
68 ○ ⇄ Viduka > Yakubu
76 ○ ⇄ Bothroyd > Bartlett
81 ○ ▢ Queudrue
Full time 0-0

A hard-working performance in a game short of clear-cut goal chances saw Boro clinch a Riverside replay.

This was the 11th time Boro had reached the FA Cup quarter-finals, but only twice had they progressed beyond the last eight. Charlton started as favourites as they had already beaten Boro twice in the league. The visitors showed seven changes from that which lost at Blackburn. Stuart Parnaby returned from a hamstring injury to replace cup-tied Andrew Davies. Chris Riggott was ruled out by a calf strain suffered in league action at Blackburn and his place was taken by returning skipper Gareth Southgate. Gaizka Mendieta was preferred ahead of James Morrison, Lee Cattermole came in for Ray Parlour, Stewart Downing for Adam Johnson, Jimmy Floyd Hasselbaink for Fabio Rochemback and Yakubu for Mark Viduka.

Boro had a great chance to open the scoring after three minutes. When Downing had a cross charged down, Franck Queudrue whipped over a fine cross but Yakubu, virtually unmarked, headed tamely over from seven yards. After 14 minutes, Matt Holland was narrowly off target with a powerful 20-yard drive.

Charlton enjoyed more possession in the opening period and created two good chances. After 34 minutes, a left-wing cross fell perfectly for Radostin Kishishev, but he blazed wide. Two minutes later, a right-wing cross was met by Hermann Hreidarsson, who stretched to volley from close range at the back post and Mark Schwarzer produced an outstanding one-handed save. Five minutes from half-time Charlton wasted another good chance when Bartlett, under pressure from Parnaby, volleyed well over in front of goal.

There was a worrying moment six minutes into the second half when Bartlett

Venue:	The Valley	Referee:	M.L.Dean - 05/06	**Charlton Athletic**
Attendance:	24,187	Matches:	30	**Middlesbrough**
Capacity:	27,111	Yellow Cards:	87	
Occupancy:	89%	Red Cards:	8	

▶ Mark Viduka brushes aside Luke Young

Match Statistics

Starting Line-Ups

▶ 4/4/2

Unused Sub: Andersen, Spector, Euell

▶ 4/4/1/1

Unused Sub: Jones, Pogatetz, Rochemback

Statistics	Charlton	Boro
Goals	0	0
Shots on Target	6	2
Shots off Target	3	6
Hit Woodwork	0	0
Possession %	53	47
Corners	3	5
Offsides	4	5
Fouls	12	10
Disciplinary Points	0	4

Age/Height

Charlton Athletic Age	Middlesbrough Age
▶ **29 yrs, 6 mo**	▶ **28 yrs**
Charlton Athletic Height	Middlesbrough Height
▶ **6'**	▶ **6'**

caught Ehiogu on the side of his head with his right elbow when both contested aerial possession. Ehiogu needed lengthy treatment and came back on the field sporting a huge white bandage around his head.

Charlton thought they had found a way through with 15 minutes remaining, as Dennis Rommedahl cut along the edge of the penalty area before firing a left-footed shot just over. In a final flurry of action, Morrison forced Thomas Myhre into a smart save at his near post.

The lively Charlton winger Jerome Thomas was presented with another chance for Charlton in the last five minutes, but a block from the impressive Ehiogu stopped the shot from the edge of the box.

Fans' Player of the Match

Ugo Ehiogu

Quote

🔵 **Steve McClaren**

They showed their experience. We had chances in the second half, but a draw was probably a fair result.

107

4-3

Middlesbrough ○
Bolton Wanderers ○

▶ Mark Viduka goes close with a header

Event Line

3 ○ ⊕	Giannakopoulos / RF / OP / IA	
8 ○ ⊕	Hasselbaink / RF / P / IA	
30 ○ ⊕	Viduka / RF / OP / IA	
	Assist: Hasselbaink	
41 ○ ■	Giannakopoulos	

Half time 2-1

47 ○ ⊕	Hasselbaink / RF / IFK / IA	
	Assist: Queudrue	
53 ○ ⇄	Borgetti > Pedersen	
56 ○ ■	Hasselbaink	
58 ○ ⊕	Okocha / RF / P / 6Y	
	Assist: Borgetti	
59 ○ ■	Jaaskelainen	
62 ○ ⇄	Cattermole > Morrison	
72 ○ ⇄	Nakata > Nolan	
73 ○ ⇄	Yakubu > Hasselbaink	
81 ○ ⊕	Jaidi / H / C / 6Y	
	Assist: Gardner	
83 ○ ⇄	Downing > Rochemback	
85 ○ ⇄	Diagne-Faye > Speed	
88 ○ ■	Pogatetz	
90 ○ ⊕	Parnaby / RF / OP / 6Y	
	Assist: Yakubu	

Full time 4-3

Boro warmed up for the first leg of their UEFA Cup quarter-final with Basel with an action-packed seven-goal thriller.

UEFA Cup-chasing Bolton opened the scoring after just three minutes. Stelios Giannakopoulos latched on to a header back from Ehiogu and pushed his way past Andrew Davies and Franck Queudrue to slam the ball home.

Boro levelled five minutes later following a deliberate handball in the area. Jimmy Floyd Hasselbaink stepped up and hit a low penalty off the goalkeeper and in. The home side then took the lead with half an hour played when Hasselbaink chested the ball into Viduka's path and the in-form Aussie raced through to score.

Boro extended their lead less than two minutes after half-time, Hasselbaink lobbing the keeper from the edge of the Bolton box. But Bolton were handed a lifeline 10 minutes later when awarded a penalty. Schwarzer saved Jay Jay Okocha's spot kick, only for the Nigerian to net the rebound.

Bolton equalised through a Radhi Jaidi header with nine minutes remaining, before that man Stuart Parnaby popped up, connecting with a Yakubu cross for a close-range winner two minutes into injury time.

Fans' Player of the Match	Quote	Premiership Milestone
Mark Viduka	❝ **Steve McClaren**	▶ **500**

Quote: Both teams conceded too many goals, but we are delighted with a great win. We kept going when it looked as though we did not have the energy.

Premiership Milestone: Jimmy Floyd Hasselbaink s second goal was the 500th scored by Middlesbrough in the Premiership.

Venue:	Riverside Stadium	Referee:	H.M.Webb - 05/06	Middlesbrough
Attendance:	25,971	Matches:	35	Bolton Wanderers
Capacity:	35,100	Yellow Cards:	93	
Occupancy:	74%	Red Cards:	4	

Form Coming into Fixture

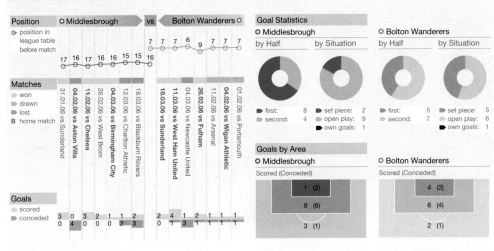

Position
○ Middlesbrough vs Bolton Wanderers
○- position in league table before match

Middlesbrough: 17 16 17 16 16 15 15 16
Bolton: 7 7 7 6 9 7 7 7

Matches
- won
- drawn
- lost
- B home match

Middlesbrough: 31.01.06 vs Sunderland · 04.02.06 vs Aston Villa · 11.02.06 vs Chelsea · 26.02.06 vs West Brom · 04.03.06 vs Birmingham City · 12.03.06 vs Charlton Athletic · 18.03.06 vs Blackburn Rovers

Bolton: 18.03.06 vs Sunderland · 11.03.06 vs West Ham United · 04.03.06 vs Newcastle United · 26.02.06 vs Fulham · 11.02.06 vs Arsenal · 04.02.06 vs Wigan Athletic · 01.02.06 vs Portsmouth

Goals
- scored
- conceded

Middlesbrough scored: 3 0 3 2 1 1 2
Middlesbrough conceded: 0 4 0 0 0 2 3

Bolton scored: 2 4 1 2 1 1
Bolton conceded: 0 1 3 1 1 1

Goal Statistics

○ Middlesbrough

by Half | by Situation

- first: 8
- second: 4
- set piece: 2
- open play: 9
- own goals: 1

○ Bolton Wanderers

by Half | by Situation

- first: 5
- second: 7
- set piece: 5
- open play: 6
- own goals: 1

Goals by Area

○ Middlesbrough — Scored (Conceded)

1 (2)
8 (6)
3 (1)

○ Bolton Wanderers — Scored (Conceded)

4 (3)
6 (4)
2 (1)

Team Statistics

Starting Line-Ups

Middlesbrough: Schwarzer, Pogatetz, Queudrue, Ehiogu, Davies, Rochemback (Downing), Boateng, Morrison (Cattermole), Parnaby, Viduka, Hasselbaink (Yakubu)

Bolton Wanderers: Jaaskelainen, Stelios, O'Brien, Nolan (Nakata), Ben Haim, Davies, Okocha, Jaidi, Speed (Faye), Pedersen (Borgetti), Gardner

5/3/2
Unused Sub: Jones, Mendieta

4/5/1
Unused Sub: Walker, Diouf

Premiership Totals	○ Boro	Bolton ○
Premiership Appearances	1,775	1,659
Team Appearances	994	1,117
Goals Scored	288	211
Assists	193	159
Clean Sheets (goalkeepers)	76	48
Yellow Cards	207	208
Red Cards	16	9
Full Internationals	9	12

Age/Height

Middlesbrough Age	Bolton Wanderers Age
26 yrs, 1 mo	**29 yrs, 1 mo**
Middlesbrough Height	Bolton Wanderers Height
6'	**5'11"**

Match Statistics

League Table after Fixture

		Played	Won	Drawn	Lost	For	Against	Pts
●	7 Bolton	29	13	9	7	42	32	48
●	8 Wigan	31	14	4	13	36	38	46
●	9 West Ham	30	13	6	11	46	45	45
●	10 Everton	31	13	4	14	29	41	43
↑	11 Charlton	31	12	6	13	37	42	42
↓	12 Man City	31	12	4	15	39	37	40
↓	13 Newcastle	31	11	6	14	31	38	39
↑	14 Middlesbrough	30	10	7	13	43	52	37
↓	15 Fulham	32	10	6	16	40	51	36

Statistics	○ Boro	Bolton ○
Goals	4	3
Shots on Target	12	6
Shots off Target	5	5
Hit Woodwork	0	0
Possession %	56	44
Corners	1	6
Offsides	2	6
Fouls	11	12

2-0

FC Basel ○
Middlesbrough ○

▶ Doriva makes a vital challenge

Event Line

29 ○	☐ Degen	
41 ○	☐ Majstorovic	
43 ○	⊕ Delgado / RF / OP / OA	
45 ○	⊕ Degen / RF / OP / IA	
	Assist: Eduardo	
Half time 2-0		
52 ○	☐ Downing	
64 ○	⇄ Chipperfield > Sterjovski	
68 ○	⇄ Ehiogu > Pogatetz	
74 ○	⇄ Yakubu > Hasselbaink	
74 ○	⇄ Rochemback > Mendieta	
77 ○	☐ Riggott	
85 ○	⇄ Ergic > Petric	
Full time 2-0		

Boro were left with a Swiss-sized mountain to climb after conceding two sloppy goals late in the first half of a game billed as one of the biggest in the club's history.

It could have been worse, had Chris Riggott not cleared a second half effort off the line, but the night was far from a success, as Emanuel Pogatetz also suffered a horrendous facial injury that ruled him out for the remainder of the season.

Boro started comfortably in front of a passionate Swiss crowd, creating the first real opportunity when Jimmy Floyd Hasselbaink struck a free-kick narrowly off target. Gaizka Mendieta then forced Swiss number one Pascal Zuberbuhler to tip over from long-range, before Hasselbaink headed wide from Stewart Downing's fine cross.

But all the good work was thrown away during a mad three-minute spell that left Boro two goals down. First, Matias Delgado skipped past Ray Parlour before unleashing a shot that Riggott inexplicably ducked under. The shot seemed to deceive Schwarzer, who was beaten on his near post.

A minute before half-time, the Swiss champions took a commanding position in the tie when Brazilian Eduardo's fine turn and pass sent David Degen racing into the box. The impressive Swiss international fired home from 12 yards.

Boro desperately searched to find an away goal to reduce the size of the task for the second leg, Hasselbaink forcing the keeper into full stretch with a header from Franck Queudrue's volley.

➡ Chris Riggott looks to make an interception

Match Statistics

Starting Line-Ups

➡ 4/3/3   ➡ 4/4/2

Unused Sub: Crayton, Quennoz, Kuzmanovic, Kulaksizoglu, Rakitic

Unused Sub: Jones, Davies, Taylor, Morrison

Statistics	Basel	Boro
Goals	2	0
Shots on Target	7	3
Shots off Target	4	9
Hit Woodwork	1	1
Possession %	45	55
Corners	5	8
Offsides	5	2
Fouls	19	21
Disciplinary Points	8	8

Riggott then came agonisingly close to a vital strike, hitting the bar from a corner. But Basel were also denied by the woodwork when Degen's free-kick struck the crossbar minutes later.

Pogatetz suffered a broken nose and fractured cheekbone in a horrendous clash of heads with Mladen Petric, the Austrian defender stretchered from the pitch to play no further part in Boro's season.

The tie could have been all but over minutes later had sub Scott Chipperfield scored from seven yards, but Riggott was the saviour with a desperate goal-line clearance. The final chance then fell to Ugo Ehiogu, whose header was blocked on the line by Zuberbuhler.

Fans' Player of the Match

Chris Riggott

Quote

❝ **Steve McClaren**

It was a tough night. We played reasonably well but gave away two poor goals.

111

0-1

Manchester City ○
Middlesbrough ○

▶ Lee Cattermole celebrates scoring the winner

Event Line

9 ○ ⇄	Taylor > Queudrue	
42 ○ ⊕	Cattermole / H / OP / IA	

Assist: Downing

Half time 0-1

60 ○ ⇄	Musampa > Ireland	
66 ○ ⇄	Croft > Sinclair	
72 ○ ⇄	Flood > Sibierski	
89 ○ ⇄	Davies > Morrison	

Full time 0-1

Lee Cattermole underlined his growing reputation by heading his first senior goal.

Steve McClaren chose to rest many of the players expected to feature in the crucial UEFA Cup second leg with Basel the following Thursday, making seven changes to the side that had lost the away leg in Switzerland.

It was 20 minutes before City troubled the Boro defence. Darius Vassell got in behind Boro's backline but wasted the first clear chance of the game by delaying his shot just long enough for George Boateng to bundle him off the ball.

Boro made the breakthrough shortly before half-time. A poor City clearance dropped to Rochemback, who played a first-time pass to Stewart Downing. His left wing cross was met perfectly by Cattermole, who headed Boro in front.

The teenage midfielder was nearly on target again in the second half, forcing a double save from James as a Boro side featuring five Academy players ripped City to shreds. Morrison missed chances too, but the nearest City came to an equaliser was an off-target Samaras header.

Fans' Player of the Match

Lee Cattermole

Quote

❝ **Steve McClaren**

We had enough chances to have won by a wider margin, but David James pulled off some very good saves.

Premiership Milestone

▶ **First Goal**

Lee Cattermole netted his first Premiership goal.

Venue:	City of Manchester Stadium	Referee:	M.A.Riley - 05/06		Manchester City
Attendance:	40,256	Matches:	35		Middlesbrough
Capacity:	48,000	Yellow Cards:	116		
Occupancy:	84%	Red Cards:	9		

Form Coming into Fixture

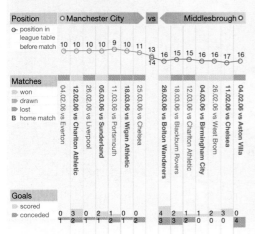

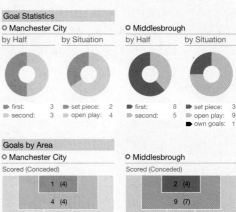

Goal Statistics

Manchester City

by Half / by Situation
- first: 3
- second: 3
- set piece: 2
- open play: 4

Middlesbrough

by Half / by Situation
- first: 8
- second: 5
- set piece: 3
- open play: 9
- own goals: 1

Goals by Area

Manchester City — Scored (Conceded)

1 (4)
4 (4)
1 (2)

Middlesbrough — Scored (Conceded)

2 (4)
9 (7)
2 (1)

Team Statistics

Starting Line-Ups

Manchester City: 4/4/2

Unused Sub: Sommeil, Wright-Phillips

Middlesbrough: 4/5/1

Unused Sub: Knight, Mendieta, Viduka

Premiership Totals

	Man City	Boro
Premiership Appearances	1,756	1,218
Team Appearances	594	703
Goals Scored	123	103
Assists	128	89
Clean Sheets (goalkeepers)	130	2
Yellow Cards	197	166
Red Cards	13	12
Full Internationals	8	5

Age/Height

Manchester City Age	Middlesbrough Age
26 yrs, 2 mo	24 yrs, 1 mo
Manchester City Height	Middlesbrough Height
6'	6'

Match Statistics

League Table after Fixture

	Played	Won	Drawn	Lost	For	Against	Pts
12 Newcastle	32	12	6	14	34	39	42
13 Man City	32	12	4	16	39	38	40
14 Middlesbrough	31	11	7	13	44	52	40
15 Fulham	33	10	6	17	41	54	36
16 Aston Villa	32	8	11	13	34	46	35
17 West Brom	32	7	6	19	28	49	27
18 Portsmouth	31	7	6	18	27	52	27
19 Birmingham	31	6	7	18	23	44	25
20 Sunderland	32	2	5	25	21	57	11

Statistics

	Man City	Boro
Goals	0	1
Shots on Target	2	9
Shots off Target	7	7
Hit Woodwork	0	0
Possession %	49	51
Corners	2	9
Offsides	5	3
Fouls	15	17
Disciplinary Points	0	0

4-1

Middlesbrough ○
FC Basel ○

▶ James Morrison is at full stretch

Event Line

23 ○ ⊕	Eduardo / RF / IFK / 6Y	
	Assist: Smiljanic	
24 ○ ▪	Riggott	
33 ○ ⊕	Viduka / RF / OP / IA	
	Assist: Yakubu	
Half time 1-1		
46 ○ ⇄	Hasselbaink > Morrison	
57 ○ ⊕	Viduka / LF / OP / IA	
	Assist: Yakubu	
58 ○ ▪	Degen	
61 ○ ⇄	Chipperfield > Degen	
67 ○ ⇄	Maccarone > Queudrue	
70 ○ ⇄	Ergic > Delgado	
73 ○ ◢	Majstorovic	
	2nd Bookable Offence	
79 ○ ⊕	Hasselbaink / RF / OP / OA	
	Assist: Boateng	
85 ○ ⇄	Quennoz > Sterjovski	
90 ○ ▪	Maccarone	
90 ○ ⊕	Maccarone / RF / OP / IA	
	Assist: Rochemback	
90 ○ ⇄	Taylor > Rochemback	
90 ○ ▪	Zuberbuhler	
Full time 4-1		

This was the game that had everything. Five goals, superb football, heart-stopping moments, a crucial red card and a dramatic last-minute winner by Massimo Maccarone to complete one of the greatest comebacks of all-time.

It was a night that will live forever in the memories of the fans privileged to have been there. But, like the magnificent players, the supporters played a huge part, screaming their team on to ever greater heights as Basel simply buckled under unrelenting pressure.

With George Boateng back from suspension in the heart of the midfield and captain Gareth Southgate fit again in central defence, there was belief that Boro could overturn the first leg deficit. But it was far from straight forward.

Yakubu almost put Boro back in it as early as the first minute, firing just wide after out-muscling Basel keeper Zuberbuhler.

Viduka then had what appeared a certain penalty waved away by the referee as the home side searched in vain for an early goal that would turn the tide their way.

Instead, disaster struck. Brazilian striker Eduardo gave Basel the lead on the night – making it 3-0 on aggregate – with the Swiss side's first attack midway through the opening period. It left Boro needing to score four without conceding another. But Viduka, playing arguably his best game in Boro colours, gave the home side an important psychological boost on 33 minutes with a skilful equaliser, his powerful drive from just inside the area levelling the scores on the night.

Venue:	Riverside Staduim	Referee:	I.Baskakov (RUS)		**Middlesbrough**
Attendance:	24,521				**FC Basel**
Capacity:	35,100				
Occupancy:	70%				

▶ Massimo Maccarone is ecstatic after completing Boro's amazing comeback

Match Statistics

Starting Line-Ups

▶ 4/4/2   ▶ 4/5/1

Unused Sub: Jones, Ehiogu, Davies, Doriva

Unused Sub: Crayton, Kulaksizoglu, Rakitic

Statistics	O Boro	Basel O
Goals	4	1
Shots on Target	12	3
Shots off Target	8	4
Hit Woodwork	0	0
Possession %	59	41
Corners	7	4
Offsides	2	3
Fouls	18	11
Disciplinary Points	8	18

Steve McClaren went for broke in the second half by throwing Hasselbaink into the fray and Boro's pressure paid off again when Viduka claimed his second just before the hour mark, rounding the keeper to convert.

"We only want two more!" chanted the Riverside faithful as buccaneering Boro ripped into Basel again. Next it was sub Hasselbaink's turn to send the volume levels soaring with a thunderbolt into the top corner of the net from the edge of the area.

A fourth striker, Massimo Maccarone, had been introduced as the clock ticked down and Boro's forgotten man clinched it at the death, firing in at the near post after Fabio Rochemback's shot had been palmed away by Zuberbuhler. Cue wild celebrations from fans and players alike.

Fans' Player of the Match

Mark Viduka

Quote

❝ **Steve McClaren**

I always knew we had goals in us and could do it. I didn't even mind conceding the first goal because I just felt we'd score.

1-2

Middlesbrough ○
Newcastle United ○

▶ Doriva puts Kieron Dyer under pressure

Event Line

26 ○ ▨	Emre
29 ○ ⊕	Boateng / H / OG / 6Y
	Assist: Ameobi
44 ○ ⊕	Ameobi / RF / OP / IA
	Assist: Carr
Half time 0-2	
46 ○ ⇄	Viduka > Johnson
46 ○ ⇄	Taylor > Queudrue
58 ○ ▨	Ameobi
62 ○ ⇄	Maccarone > Davies
66 ○ ▨	Rochemback
66 ○ ⇄	Dyer > Solano
68 ○ ▨	Moore
71 ○ ▨	Maccarone
79 ○ ⊕	Boateng / RF / IFK / OA
	Assist: Viduka
81 ○ ⇄	Faye > Emre
86 ○ ▨	N'Zogbia
Full time 1-2	

Three days after their sensational UEFA Cup comeback against Basel and three days before an FA Cup quarter-final replay with Charlton, Boro's players perhaps understandably played without the usual focus expected for a Tees-Tyne derby clash.

Newcastle's Shola Ameobi gave the visitors a deserved win as Boro put on a disappointing display in front of their home fans. United took the lead on 28 minutes. Nolberto Solano's corner was returned across the goalmouth by Ameobi, allowing Lee Bowyer to strike a header off the back of the unfortunate George Boateng.

Entering the final minute of the half, United extended their lead when a loose ball fell to Ameobi, who beat Schwarzer with a low shot into the bottom right hand corner.

Boro were offered a lifeline 11 minutes from time. A searing 20-yard shot from George Boateng took a wicked deflection off Titus Bramble to send Shay Given the wrong way and the ball into the net.

Fans' Player of the Match

Fabio Rochemback

Quote

❝ **Steve McClaren**

Conceding two goals in the first half was disappointing. Credit to the players though, they came back strongly after the break.

Venue:	Riverside Stadium	Referee:	A.G.Wiley - 05/06

Middlesbrough
Newcastle United

Attendance:	31,202
Capacity:	35,100
Occupancy:	89%

Matches:	39
Yellow Cards:	118
Red Cards:	7

Form Coming into Fixture

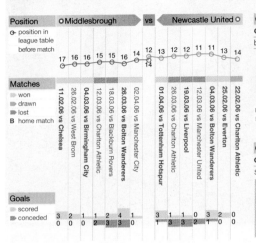

Position

o-position in league table before match

Middlesbrough 17 16 16 15 15 16 14 12 13 / 14
vs Newcastle United 12 12 11 11 13 14

Matches
- won
- drawn
- lost
- B home match

Middlesbrough matches:
11.02.06 vs Chelsea
26.02.06 vs West Brom
04.03.06 vs Birmingham City
12.03.06 vs Charlton Athletic
18.03.06 vs Blackburn Rovers
26.03.06 vs Bolton Wanderers
02.04.06 vs Manchester City

Newcastle matches:
01.04.06 vs Tottenham Hotspur
26.03.06 vs Charlton Athletic
19.03.06 vs Liverpool
12.03.06 vs Manchester United
04.03.06 vs Bolton Wanderers
25.02.06 vs Everton
22.02.06 vs Charlton Athletic

Goals
scored	3	2	1	1	2	4	1	3	1	1	0	3	2	0
conceded	0	0	0	2	3	3	0	1	3	3	2	1	0	0

Goal Statistics

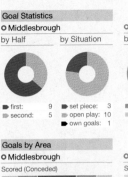

Middlesbrough

by Half
- first: 9
- second: 5

by Situation
- set piece: 3
- open play: 10
- own goals: 1

Newcastle United

by Half
- first: 7
- second: 3

by Situation
- set piece: 2
- open play: 8

Goals by Area

Middlesbrough
Scored (Conceded)
2 (4)
10 (3)
2 (1)

Newcastle United
Scored (Conceded)
3 (4)
5 (5)
2 (1)

Team Statistics

Starting Line-Ups

Queudrue
Taylor
Johnson
Viduka
Rochemback
Riggott
Schwarzer
Doriva
Yakubu
Shearer
Ehiogu
Boateng
Davies
Maccarone
Morrison

Solano
Dyer
Carr
Bowyer
Moore
Given
Ameobi
Emre
Faye
Bramble
N'Zogbia
Elliott

4/5/1
4/4/2

Unused Sub: Jones, Parnaby
Unused Sub: Harper, Ramage, Clark

Premiership Totals	Boro	Newcastle
Premiership Appearances	1,650	2,221
Team Appearances	1,005	1,498
Goals Scored	182	410
Assists	110	289
Clean Sheets (goalkeepers)	76	78
Yellow Cards	201	253
Red Cards	16	15
Full Internationals	8	9

Age/Height

Middlesbrough Age	Newcastle United Age
26 yrs, 5 mo	28 yrs, 5 mo
Middlesbrough Height	Newcastle United Height
6'	5'10"

Match Statistics

League Table after Fixture

		Played	Won	Drawn	Lost	For	Against	Pts
↑	10 Newcastle	33	13	6	14	36	40	45
↓	11 Everton	33	13	6	14	31	43	45
↓	12 Charlton	33	12	8	13	37	42	44
•	13 Man City	33	12	4	17	40	40	40
•	14 Middlesbrough	32	11	7	14	45	54	40
↑	15 Aston Villa	33	8	12	13	34	46	36
↓	16 Fulham	33	10	6	17	41	54	36
•	17 Birmingham	33	7	8	18	25	45	29
↑	18 West Brom	33	7	7	19	28	49	28

Statistics	Boro	Newcastle
Goals	1	2
Shots on Target	8	5
Shots off Target	5	9
Hit Woodwork	0	0
Possession %	47	53
Corners	6	5
Offsides	3	0
Fouls	14	21
Disciplinary Points	8	16

4-2

Middlesbrough ○
Charlton Athletic ○

► Fabio Rochemback fires in the opening goal

Event Line

11 ○ ⊕	Rochemback / RF / DFK / OA	
	Assist: Viduka	
13 ○ ⊕	Hughes / RF / OP / IA	
	Assist: Bartlett	
26 ○ ⊕	Morrison / RF / OP / IA	
Half time 2-1		
50 ○ ▨	Perry	
59 ○ ⇄	Thomas > Holland	
61 ○ ⇄	Bothroyd > Bartlett	
70 ○ ▨	Hasselbaink	
73 ○ ⊕	Hasselbaink / RF / OP / OA	
	Assist: Morrison	
76 ○ ⊕	Bothroyd / LF / IFK / 6Y	
	Assist: Perry	
77 ○ ⊕	Viduka / RF / OP / IA	
	Assist: Parnaby	
78 ○ ⇄	Euell > Kishishev	
80 ○ ⇄	Ehiogu > Hasselbaink	
Full time 4-2		

This was fantastic entertainment for a live TV audience. Less than a week after the nerve-tingling UEFA Cup heroics against Basel, the Boro boys kept us on the edge of their seats again with a thrilling victory over Charlton.

Steve McClaren made six changes from the side which lost at home to Newcastle the previous Sunday. Andrew Davies, Ugo Ehiogu, Doriva, Adam Johnson and Yakubu were left out while Franck Queudrue was injured. In came Stuart Parnaby, Gareth Southgate, Andrew Taylor, Stewart Downing, Mark Viduka and Jimmy Floyd Hasselbaink.

There's never a dull moment when Boro play in knockout competitions and this throwback to the FA Cup classics of old was no exception. Six goals shared by two fully-committed sides made for compulsive viewing.

The home side was in front after just 11 minutes. Fabio Rochemback bent a rasping, low free-kick around the Charlton wall from 35 yards. But the visitors were level within 75 seconds when Shaun Bartlett flicked on a hopeful long throw to Bryan Hughes, who found himself completely unmarked as he lashed home a first-time volley.

Boro regained the advantage after 26 minutes following a defensive scramble, James Morrison calmly converting from 12 yards. And they gave themselves more breathing space when Hasselbaink delivered a trademark strike midway through the second half.

Venue:	Riverside Stadium	Referee:	P.Dowd - 05/06		Middlesbrough
Attendance:	30,248	Matches:	42		Charlton Athletic
Capacity:	35,100	Yellow Cards:	165		
Occupancy:	86%	Red Cards:	7		

➤ James Morrison looks to make progress down the wing

Match Statistics

Starting Line-Ups

Taylor, Downing

Southgate, Rochemback

Hasselbaink (Ehiogu), Bent D

Schwarzer

Viduka, Bartlett (Bothroyd)

Riggott, Boateng

Parnaby, Morrison

➤ 4/4/2

Rommedahl, Spector

Holland (Thomas), Perry

Kishishev (Euell), Hreidarsson

Myhre

Hughes, Powell

➤ 4/4/2

Unused Sub: Jones, Doriva, Maccarone, Yakubu

Unused Sub: Andersen, Sorondo

Statistics	Boro	Charlton
Goals	4	2
Shots on Target	9	8
Shots off Target	6	2
Hit Woodwork	0	0
Possession %	54	46
Corners	5	2
Offsides	2	2
Fouls	12	14
Disciplinary Points	4	4

Age/Height

Middlesbrough Age
➤ **27 yrs, 9 mo**

Middlesbrough Height
➤ **6'**

Charlton Athletic Age
➤ **29 yrs, 2 mo**

Charlton Athletic Height
➤ **6'**

Morrison was the creator this time, pulling the ball back for Hasselbaink to drill in his 16th goal of the season. Game over? Hardly. There was more drama on the way when Southgate deflected the ball into his own net three minutes later.

There wasn't time to worry because shortly after the restart Mark Viduka produced one of the best goals the Riverside has seen. The big man performed a moment of pure ballet on the edge of the Charlton box as he beat two men before putting a rising drive past Thomas Myhre.

Boro had what looked sound appeals for a penalty turned down minutes later as Morrison fell under challenge from Jonathan Spector. Referee Phil Dowd, who had a good game, was well placed and turned it down.

Fans' Player of the Match

Mark Viduka

Quote

ⓕ **Steve McClaren**

The Basel game gave us so much belief and confidence. That's what we showed again tonight.

1-0 Portsmouth ○
Middlesbrough ○

➤ Matthew Bates clears the ball from danger

Event Line
Half time 0-0
46 ○ ⇄ Routledge > Davis
54 ○ ⊕ O'Neil / RF / OP / IA
Assist: Mwaruwari
59 ○ ⇄ Christie > Doriva
67 ○ ⇄ Karadas > Mwaruwari
77 ○ ⇄ Johnson > Morrison
78 ○ ⇄ Hughes > Todorov
85 ○ ⇄ Wheater > Bates
Full time 1-0

As an in-form Portsmouth fought for their Premiership lives, Boro came off second best in a fiercely competitive affair at Fratton Park.

Boro looked good going forward and their dynamic movement created gaps in the home defence. Portsmouth, whose fans sang the theme to 'The Great Escape', created chances but a combination of good defending and one great save from Brad Jones kept the scores all square at the break.

The second half was as open as the first. The game's only goal came after 54 minutes. After stretching the Boro defence, Benjani and Todorov combined to set up Gary O'Neill, who scored with a low shot from 12 yards out.

Boro made an immediate change, with injury-plagued striker Malcolm Christie introduced for his first Premiership appearance since February of the previous year. The high tempo continued to the end, both sides having chances but neither able to finish. The home team were roared on by their fans who endured a nervous finish as Boro won a last-minute corner. But Pompey held out for a win that took them out of the relegation zone for the first time since November.

Fans' Player of the Match

Brad Jones

Quote

🍎 **Steve McClaren**

I'm disappointed and frustrated that we weren't able to win this game.

Venue:	Fratton Park	Referee:	A.Marriner - 05/06		Portsmouth
Attendance:	20,204	Matches:	23		Middlesbrough
Capacity:	20,288	Yellow Cards:	71		
Occupancy:	100%	Red Cards:	7		

Form Coming into Fixture

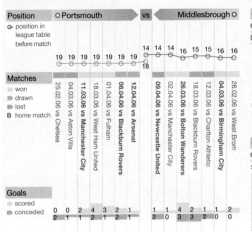

Position

O- position in league table before match

Portsmouth vs Middlesbrough

| | 19 | 19 | 19 | 19 | 19 | 19 | 19 | 18 | 14 | 14 | 14 | 16 | 15 | 15 | 16 | 16 |

Matches
- won
- drawn
- lost
- B home match

25.02.06 vs Chelsea
04.03.06 vs Aston Villa
11.03.06 vs Manchester City
18.03.06 vs West Ham United
01.04.06 vs Fulham
08.04.06 vs Blackburn Rovers
12.04.06 vs Arsenal
09.04.06 vs Newcastle United
02.04.06 vs Manchester City
26.03.06 vs Bolton Wanderers
18.03.06 vs Blackburn Rovers
12.03.06 vs Charlton Athletic
04.03.06 vs Birmingham City
26.02.06 vs West Brom

Goals
- scored
- conceded

| scored | 0 | 0 | 2 | 4 | 3 | 2 | 1 | | 1 | 1 | 4 | 2 | 1 | 1 | 2 |
| conceded | 2 | 1 | 1 | 2 | 1 | 2 | 1 | | 2 | 0 | 3 | 3 | 2 | 0 | 0 |

Goal Statistics

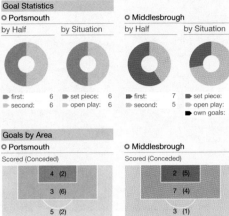

O Portsmouth

by Half | by Situation

- first: 6
- second: 6
- set piece: 6
- open play: 6

O Middlesbrough

by Half | by Situation

- first: 7
- second: 5
- set piece: 3
- open play: 8
- own goals: 1

Goals by Area

O Portsmouth

Scored (Conceded)

4 (2)
3 (6)
5 (2)

O Middlesbrough

Scored (Conceded)

2 (5)
7 (4)
3 (1)

Team Statistics

Starting Line-Ups

Taylor, D'Alessandro
Stefanovic, Mendes
Kiely
Todorov / Hughes
Primus, Davis / Routledge
Mwaruwari / Karadas
Priske, O'Neil

Morrison / Johnson, Parnaby
Boateng
Ehiogu
Yakubu, Doriva / Christie
Jones
Bates / Wheater
Rochemback
Downing, Taylor

4/4/2 **4/5/1**

Unused Sub: Ashdown, O'Brien
Unused Sub: Knight, Kennedy

Premiership Totals	O Portsmouth	Boro O
Premiership Appearances	903	1,141
Team Appearances	477	603
Goals Scored	40	114
Assists	56	86
Clean Sheets (goalkeepers)	52	3
Yellow Cards	92	143
Red Cards	4	7
Full Internationals	9	6

Age/Height

Portsmouth Age	Middlesbrough Age
27 yrs, 4 mo	**24 yrs, 3 mo**
Portsmouth Height	Middlesbrough Height
5'11"	**5'11"**

Match Statistics

League Table after Fixture

		Played	Won	Drawn	Lost	For	Against	Pts
↑ 9	Newcastle	34	14	6	14	39	41	48
↓ 10	Wigan	34	14	6	14	39	43	48
● 11	Everton	34	13	6	15	31	44	45
● 12	Charlton	34	12	8	14	38	44	44
● 13	Man City	34	12	4	18	40	41	40
● 14	Middlesbrough	33	11	7	15	45	55	40
↑ 15	Fulham	34	11	6	17	43	55	39
↓ 16	Aston Villa	33	8	12	13	34	46	36
↑ 17	Portsmouth	34	8	8	18	31	55	32

Statistics	O Portsmouth	Boro O
Goals	1	0
Shots on Target	11	9
Shots off Target	5	4
Hit Woodwork	0	0
Possession %	46	54
Corners	7	5
Offsides	1	0
Fouls	12	10
Disciplinary Points	0	0

2-0 Middlesbrough ○
West Ham United ○

▶ Jimmy Floyd Hasselbaink tries to make room for a shot

Event Line

14 ○ ▨	Sheringham
41 ○ ⊕	Hasselbaink / RF / OP / IA
	Assist: Bates
Half time 1-0	
46 ○ ⇄	Christie > Viduka
57 ○ ⊕	Maccarone / RF / P / IA
	Assist: Johnson
66 ○ ⇄	Ashton > Harewood
66 ○ ⇄	Zamora > Katan
66 ○ ⇄	Fletcher > Scaloni
72 ○ ⇄	Kennedy > Hasselbaink
76 ○ ⇄	Taylor > Johnson
Full time 2-0	

A goal in each half gave Boro all three points against West Ham at the Riverside.

Among the nine changes Steve McClaren made from the team that had lost at Portsmouth two days earlier was the introduction of teenage defender David Wheater for his first Premiership start.

Boro took the lead on 40 minutes. Massimo Maccarone picked out Matthew Bates, who raced to the by-line before cutting the ball back for Jimmy Floyd Hasselbaink to fire in from seven yards out.

Boro made one change at half-time, Malcolm Christie replacing Mark Viduka, whose injury would mean he would miss the crucial cup semi-finals with Steaua Bucharest and West Ham.

With 56 minutes played, Boro got their second of the game from the spot. Adam Johnson cut into the penalty area only to be pushed over by Shaun Newton. Maccarone stepped forward to strike a fine penalty past Hislop. The ineffective Hammers livened up towards the latter stages but their best chance fell to Dean Ashton, who blasted over the bar after Schwarzer failed to hold onto a cross.

Fans' Player of the Match	Quote	Premiership Milestone
David Wheater	🄺 **Steve McClaren**	▶ **125**
	It was important to win today as we move into the biggest week in the club's history.	Jimmy Floyd Hasselbaink netted his 125th Premiership goal.

Venue:	Riverside Stadium	Referee:	M.Atkinson - 05/06		Middlesbrough
Attendance:	27,658	Matches:	35		West Ham United
Capacity:	35,100	Yellow Cards:	72		
Occupancy:	79%	Red Cards:	2		

Form Coming into Fixture

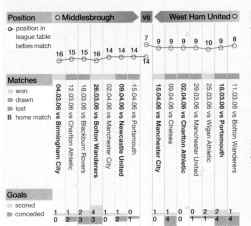

Position	○ Middlesbrough	vs	West Ham United ○

G- position in league table before match

16 15 15 16 14 14 14 / 14 — 7 9 9 9 9 10 9 8

Matches
- won
- drawn
- lost
- B home match

Middlesbrough:
04.03.06 vs Birmingham City
12.03.06 vs Charlton Athletic
18.03.06 vs Blackburn Rovers
26.03.06 vs Bolton Wanderers
02.04.06 vs Manchester City
09.04.06 vs Newcastle United
-15.04.06 vs Portsmouth

West Ham United:
15.04.06 vs Manchester City
09.04.06 vs Chelsea
02.04.06 vs Charlton Athletic
29.03.06 vs Manchester United
25.03.06 vs Wigan Athletic
18.03.06 vs Portsmouth
11.03.06 vs Bolton Wanderers

Goals
- scored
- conceded

| scored | 1 | 1 | 2 | 4 | 1 | 1 | 0 | | 1 | 1 | 0 | 0 | 2 | 2 | 1 |
| conceded | 0 | 2 | 3 | 3 | 0 | 2 | 1 | | 0 | 4 | 0 | 1 | 1 | 4 | 4 |

Goal Statistics

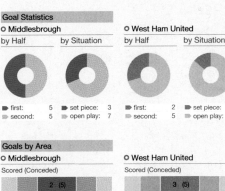

○ Middlesbrough

by Half | by Situation

- first: 5
- second: 5
- set piece: 3
- open play: 7

○ West Ham United

by Half | by Situation

- first: 2
- second: 5
- set piece: 1
- open play: 6

Goals by Area

○ Middlesbrough
Scored (Conceded)

2 (5)
6 (5)
2 (1)

○ West Ham United
Scored (Conceded)

3 (5)
4 (6)
0 (3)

Team Statistics

Starting Line-Ups

Middlesbrough:
Schwarzer
Queudrue, Johnson (Taylor)
Wheater, Doriva, Hasselbaink (Kennedy), Sheringham
Riggott, Parlour, Viduka (Christie), Harewood
Bates, Maccarone

▶ 4/4/2

Unused Sub: Knight, Parnaby

West Ham United:
Hislop
Newton, Scaloni (Fletcher)
Reo-Coker, Collins
Mullins, Gabbidon
Katan (Zamora), Konchesky
Ashton

▶ 4/4/2

Unused Sub: Walker, Reid

Premiership Totals	○ Boro	West Ham ○
Premiership Appearances	1,649	1,125
Team Appearances	820	392
Goals Scored	278	188
Assists	183	133
Clean Sheets (goalkeepers)	76	57
Yellow Cards	205	89
Red Cards	15	5
Full Internationals	6	8

Age/Height

Middlesbrough Age	West Ham United Age
▶ 26 yrs, 4 mo	▶ 27 yrs, 6 mo
Middlesbrough Height	West Ham United Height
▶ 6'	▶ 6'

Match Statistics

League Table after Fixture

		Played	Won	Drawn	Lost	For	Against	Pts
↓ 9	West Ham	35	14	7	14	48	52	49
● 10	Wigan	34	14	6	14	39	43	48
↑ 11	Charlton	35	13	8	14	40	45	47
↓ 12	Everton	35	13	6	16	31	47	45
↑ 13	Middlesbrough	34	12	7	15	47	55	43
↓ 14	Man City	34	12	4	18	40	41	40
● 15	Aston Villa	34	9	12	13	37	47	39
● 16	Fulham	34	11	6	17	43	55	39
● 17	Portsmouth	35	8	8	19	32	57	32

Statistics	○ Boro	West Ham ○
Goals	2	0
Shots on Target	9	6
Shots off Target	4	9
Hit Woodwork	0	0
Possession %	49	51
Corners	4	7
Offsides	2	4
Fouls	6	12
Disciplinary Points	0	4

1-0

Steaua Bucharest ○
Middlesbrough ○

▶ Ray Parlour fights for midfield supremacy

Event Line

30 ○	◻	Dica
30 ○	⊕	Dica / RF / OP / IA
		Assist: Radoi
33 ○	◻	Paraschiv
38 ○	◻	Goian
41 ○	◻	Nicolita
Half time 1-0		
70 ○	⇄	Parlour > Morrison
70 ○	⇄	Maccarone > Yakubu
75 ○	◻	Schwarzer
86 ○	⇄	Lovin > Paraschiv
89 ○	◻	Marin
89 ○	⇄	Cristea > Oprita
90 ○	◻	Parlour
Full time 1-0		

A resolute defensive display saw Boro withstand constant pressure and a few goalmouth scares to return from Bucharest with only a one-goal deficit to overturn seven days later.

Steaua Bucharest proved to be talented opponents, taking a 1-0 lead and setting up a grandstand finish to Boro's first ever European semi-final.

In front of a passionate crowd, Steaua's Nicolae Dica attempted the spectacular in order to break the deadlock but his overhead kick from seven yards out was always going wide. It took a fine tackle from Matthew Bates to block another chance on the edge of the penalty area as the game began to open up.

The Romanian champions took the lead after 29 minutes courtesy of the impressive Dica. A cross into the Boro box was flicked on to the Romanian international striker who, unchallenged, hit a fierce shot on the turn from 16 yards that was well out of Mark Schwarzer's reach.

Despite going a goal down, Boro remained composed and continued to keep their shape. They looked dangerous on the attack and Steaua were far from solid in defence. A cross intended for Yakubu was intercepted by George Ogararu and the defender narrowly missed hitting the net himself as his header hit the bar. From the resulting corner, James Morrison forced a flying block from defender Sorin Ghionea after hitting a low shot.

Boro found themselves under pressure early in the second half with Schwarzer making two quick saves. The first was a tame cross from Daniel Oprita but the second was an outstanding one-handed save to push Dorin Goian's effort over.

Venue:	Lia Manoliu Stadium	Referee:	A.Hamer (LUX)

Attendance: 41,000
Capacity: 60,120
Occupancy: 68%

▶ Stewart Downing skips away from a challenge

Match Statistics

Starting Line-Ups

Marin Bostina

Morrison Parnaby
Parlour

Ghionea Radoi
Dica Hasselbaink
Boateng Ehiogu

Fernandes

Schwarzer

Goian Paraschiv
Lovin
Oprita Yakubu
Cristea Maccarone Rochemback Bates

Ogararu Nicolita

Downing Queudrue

▶ 4/4/2   ▶ 4/4/2

Unused Sub: Cernea, Balan, Nesu, Baciu, Cristocea

Unused Sub: Jones, Taylor, Wheater, Doriva, Christie

Statistics	Steaua	Boro
Goals	1	0
Shots on Target	3	2
Shots off Target	8	2
Hit Woodwork	0	1
Possession %	54	46
Corners	7	2
Offsides	3	0
Fouls	13	21
Disciplinary Points	20	8

The visitors rode their luck a little and were relieved at not going go further behind. Stuart Parnaby misjudged a cross that dropped to Dica, who forced another fine save from Schwarzer. Then Ugo Ehiogu and Schwarzer collided, the loose ball dropping to Goian. Thankfully, Bates was on hand to hook the ball away to safety.

Both teams had chances to score in the dying minutes but, at half-time in the two-legged tie, Steaua settled with a narrow lead. Boro had created little in the second half but could take confidence from restricting Steaua to a single goal despite coming under increasing pressure.

Fans' Player of the Match

Mark Schwarzer

Quote

❝ **Ugo Ehiogu**

We knew they'd make it difficult for us and, to be honest, they came out more than we expected.

0-1 Middlesbrough ○
West Ham United ○

FA Cup
23.04.06

▶ Ayegbeni Yakubu threatens Shaka Hislop's goal

Event Line

19 ○ ▢	Reo-Coker	
42 ○ ⇄	Jones > Schwarzer	
Half time 0-0		
47 ○ ▢	Rochemback	
68 ○ ▢	Ashton	
75 ○ ⇄	Parlour > Rochemback	
78 ○ ⊕	Harewood / LF / OP / IA	
	Assist: Ashton	
80 ○ ⇄	Maccarone > Taylor	
80 ○ ⇄	Harewood	
82 ○	Maccarone	
83 ○	Collins	
85 ○ ⇄	Zamora > Ashton	
89 ○ ⇄	Newton > Etherington	
Full time 0-1		

Boro suffered FA Cup heartache and a second semi-final defeat in three days following the long trip back from UEFA Cup action in Romania. Despite dominating the first half, Steve McClaren's side lacked a cutting edge and were eventually beaten by a fine strike from Hammers forward Marlon Harewood.

Boro started brightly, despite the continued absence of injured talisman Mark Viduka. They were unable to capitalise on their possession, however. Jimmy Floyd Hasselbaink, Fabio Rochemback and Stewart Downing all had chances during the early stages without fully testing West Ham keeper Shaka Hislop. Then Gareth Southgate fired a cross through the box, which was put out for a corner, Franck Queudrue eventually heading just over.

Possibly the tie's defining moment came towards the end of the opening period. Mark Schwarzer suffered an elbow in the face following a collision with Hammers striker Dean Ashton. After lengthy treatment, he was forced to leave the field with a suspected fractured cheek-bone, Brad Jones coming on to replace him.

West Ham were a revived team after the break. The physical Harewood made his presence known early on, forcing his way past Southgate on the edge of the box before failing to hit the target. With Boro no longer in control, Ashton headed the ball against the bar following a cross from the left but the warning signs were ignored.

It was Ashton's strike partner Harewood who finally made Boro pay for their

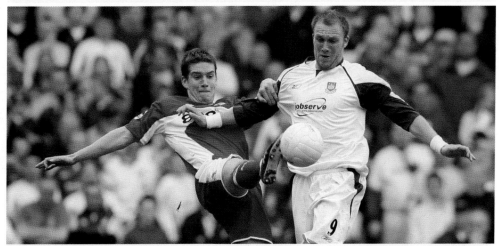

► Chris Riggott beats Dean Ashton to the ball

Match Statistics

Starting Line-Ups

5/3/2

Unused Sub: Bates, Ehiogu

4/4/2

Unused Sub: Walker, Scaloni, Sheringham

Statistics	○ Boro	West Ham ○
Goals	0	1
Shots on Target	9	5
Shots off Target	11	5
Hit Woodwork	0	1
Possession %	55	45
Corners	4	8
Offsides	4	1
Fouls	16	18
Disciplinary Points	8	16

Age/Height

Middlesbrough Age	West Ham United Age
► **27 yrs, 5 mo**	► **26 yrs**
Middlesbrough Height	West Ham United Height
► **6'**	► **5'11"**

missed opportunities. With 12 minutes left he out-muscled Southgate to hit a rocket-like shot past Jones from 10 yards.

With just over 10 minutes left, Boro piled forward with Massimo Maccarone replacing Andrew Taylor to add firepower up front. Jimmy Floyd Hasselbaink powered his way goalbound before being brought down on the edge of the box, Queudrue's resulting free kick forcing a save from Hislop.

Chris Riggott was pushed forward in a final attempt to snatch an equaliser – but, when the chance came, he failed to hit the target. The game's final chance fell to the defender but he hit his shot wide from 10 yards. As he sank to his knees, head in hands, the Boro fans knew that the FA Cup dream was over.

Fans' Player of the Match

Franck Queudrue

Quote

❝ **Steve McClaren**

It's not endeavour or character that has let us down – it is finishing. Our name was not on the cup.

4-2 Middlesbrough ○ Steaua Bucharest ○

UEFA Cup
27.04.06

► Jimmy Floyd Hasselbaink holds off his man

Event Line

16 ○ ⊕	Dica / RF / OP / IA
	Assist: Marin
24 ○ ⊕	Goian / RF / C / IA
26 ○ ⇄	Maccarone > Southgate
33 ○ ⊕	Maccarone / RF / OP / IA
	Assist: Viduka
Half time 1-2	
55 ○ ⇄	Yakubu > Taylor
60 ○ ☐	Boateng
62 ○ ☐	Hasselbaink
64 ○ ⊕	Viduka / H / OP / IA
	Assist: Downing
65 ○ ⇄	Balan > Iacob
68 ○ ☐	Dica
73 ○ ⊕	Riggott / RF / OP / 6Y
	Assist: Downing
74 ○ ☐	Balan
74 ○ ☐	Lovin
81 ○ ⇄	Baciu > Oprita
86 ○ ⇄	Nesu > Bostina
89 ○ ⊕	Maccarone / H / OP / IA
	Assist: Downing
90 ○ ⇄	Ehiogu > Hasselbaink
Full time 4-2	

So lightening does strike twice! For the second time in a month, Boro produced a comeback of titanic proportions, once again overturning a three-goal deficit to win 4-3 on aggregate and secure a place in the UEFA Cup final.

A late, great Massimo Maccarone goal from the outstanding Stewart Downing's left-wing cross saw Boro snatch victory from the jaws of defeat and send the Riverside faithful into delirium. Boro were in a European final!

The home side had known an early goal would swing the tie their way but, instead, the Romanians extended their aggregate lead on 16 minutes. Petre Marin's well-struck shot was fumbled by Brad Jones into the path of Nicolae Dica, who kept his cool to strike from 10 yards. All seemed lost when Boro conceded again after 23 minutes. A Steaua corner fell to Dorian Goian, whose initial header was saved by Jones. But the defender was first to the rebound, smashing the ball into the back of the net.

Steve McClaren responded by replacing the injured Southgate with another forward, Maccarone, and it was the Italian who gave Boro hope with a fine strike on 33 minutes.

Boro emerged from the break with purpose and determination, while Steaua appeared content to sit back and defend their lead. With just over an hour played, Downing struck a superb cross from the left wing, Viduka heading in from the edge of the six-yard box. Downing persistently tortured the Steaua defenders and it was no surprise when, on 72 minutes, he cut in from the left and fired a blistering shot at goal, Chris Riggott sliding in to score when the keeper saved.

➧ Massimo Maccarone starts manic celebrations after scoring his late, late winner

Match Statistics

Starting Line-Ups

➧ 5/3/2   ➧ 4/4/2

Unused Sub: Knight, Bates, Cattermole, Parlour

Unused Sub: Cernea, Cristocea, Simion, Cristea

Statistics	○ Boro	Steaua ○
Goals	4	2
Shots on Target	8	5
Shots off Target	11	2
Hit Woodwork	0	0
Possession %	64	36
Corners	3	4
Offsides	1	1
Fouls	21	14
Disciplinary Points	8	12

Belief coursed through the Boro side and visibly drained from the Steaua players, who were pegged back ever deeper in their own half. But time appeared to be running out for Steve McClaren's side.

The crucial fourth goal came with less than a minute of normal time to play. And, once again, it was that man Maccarone who took the glory, meeting Stewart Downing's pin-point cross with a fine header that gave Carlos Alberto no chance.

Soon after came the final whistle, the cue for delirious scenes as the comeback kings celebrated reaching the UEFA Cup final.

Fans' Player of the Match

Massimo Maccarone

Quote

🔊 **Steve McClaren**

I said lightning couldn't strike twice in the same place, but it has done tonight. Let's go one step further and win the final.

0-1

Middlesbrough ○
Everton ○

▶ Yakubu spins away from Gary Naysmith

Event Line

43 ○ ▢	Parlour	
45 ○ ▢	Naysmith	
Half time 0-0		
46 ○ ⇄	Kilbane > van der Meyde	
54 ○ ⇄	Turner > Wright	
72 ○ ⇄	Graham > Christie	
72 ○ ⇄	Cattermole > Doriva	
76 ○ ▢	Yobo	
89 ○ ⊕	McFadden / LF / OP / OA	
	Assist: Osman	
90 ○ ▢	Cattermole	
Full time 0-1		

Less than two days after qualifying for the UEFA Cup final in dramatic style against Steaua Bucharest, Boro were felled by a late goal from James McFadden in the season's final home game.

Only Andrew Taylor and Brad Jones remained in the starting line-up from the Euro heroics, with Tony McMahon making his first home start of an injury-ravaged season. In all, Boro began with six Academy recruits, with a further five on the bench.

Everton came into the game having failed to score in 424 minutes - and it showed. Boro dominated and had several chances to take the lead, all either narrowly missed or defended well by Everton.

After the break, the visitors were a little more lively but Boro still edged it in the quality stakes, Yakubu going closest to opening the scoring but firing narrowly wide. Everton, however, were going for a big finish and both McFadden and Kevin Kilbane went close before the former hit the winner with three minutes left. Jones raced well out of his area to meet a long ball that had dropped midway inside the Boro half and was well beaten by McFadden's clinical lob.

Fans' Player of the Match	Quote	Premiership Milestone
David Wheater	❝ **Steve McClaren**	▶ **100**

	We finished the game with eight Academy players on the park. The lads showed great potential and are gaining experience.	Yakubu made his 100th Premiership appearance.

Venue:	Riverside Stadium	Referee:	L.Mason - 05/06		Middlesbrough
Attendance:	29,224	Matches:	32		Everton
Capacity:	35,100	Yellow Cards:	77		
Occupancy:	83%	Red Cards:	2		

Form Coming into Fixture

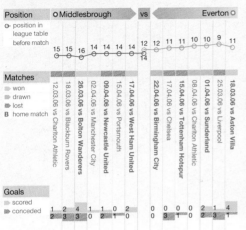

Position
- position in league table before match

Matches
- won
- drawn
- lost
- B home match

Goals
- scored
- conceded

Goal Statistics

○ Middlesbrough

by Half — first: 5, second: 6
by Situation — set piece: 4, open play: 7

○ Everton

by Half — first: 5, second: 2
by Situation — set piece: 3, open play: 4

Goals by Area

○ Middlesbrough — Scored (Conceded)

1 (5)
8 (5)
2 (1)

○ Everton — Scored (Conceded)

4 (2)
2 (6)
1 (2)

Team Statistics

Starting Line-Ups

Middlesbrough: Jones; Taylor, Johnson, Wheater, Doriva (Cattermole), Ehiogu, Parlour, Christie (Graham), Yakubu, McMahon, Morrison

○ 4/4/2

Unused Sub: Knight, Bates, Davies

Everton: van der Meyde (Kilbane), Yobo, Davies, Weir, Osman, Beattie, Neville, Stubbs, Naysmith, McFadden; Wright, Turner

○ 4/4/1/1

Unused Sub: Valente, Vidarsson, Anichebe

Premiership Totals	○ Boro	Everton ○
Premiership Appearances	1,130	1,786
Team Appearances	409	1,001
Goals Scored	113	151
Assists	82	131
Clean Sheets (goalkeepers)	3	30
Yellow Cards	136	167
Red Cards	9	16
Full Internationals	4	10

Age/Height

Middlesbrough Age — ○ **24 yrs**

Everton Age — ○ **27 yrs, 10 mo**

Middlesbrough Height — ○ **6'**

Everton Height — ○ **6'**

Match Statistics

League Table after Fixture

		Played	Won	Drawn	Lost	For	Against	Pts
↑	11 Everton	37	14	7	16	32	47	49
↓	12 Charlton	37	13	8	16	41	51	47
↑	13 Fulham	36	13	6	17	46	56	45
↓	14 Man City	36	13	4	19	42	43	43
↓	15 Middlesbrough	35	12	7	16	47	56	43
●	16 Aston Villa	37	9	12	16	40	54	39
●	17 Portsmouth	37	10	8	19	36	59	38
●	18 Birmingham	37	8	10	19	28	49	34
●	19 West Brom	36	7	8	21	29	55	29

Statistics	○ Boro	Everton ○
Goals	0	1
Shots on Target	3	4
Shots off Target	8	4
Hit Woodwork	0	0
Possession %	51	49
Corners	4	6
Offsides	2	1
Fouls	13	17
Disciplinary Points	8	8

0-0

Manchester United ○
Middlesbrough ○

▶ Ray Parlour demonstrates his commitment to the cause

Event Line

14 ○	▮	Bates
Half time 0-0		
56 ○	⇄	Richardson > Evra
56 ○	⇄	Ronaldo > Park
64 ○	⇄	Taylor > Queudrue
72 ○	⇄	Christie > Morrison
75 ○	▮	Rochemback
76 ○	▮	Neville
80 ○	⇄	Parlour > Maccarone
81 ○	⇄	Rossi > Saha
85 ○	▮	Silvestre
Full time 0-0		

Steve McClaren made yet another impressive Old Trafford return, guiding a team that included nine changes to a highly creditable draw.

The game was played at a pedestrian pace and only seemed to gather speed when Massimo Maccarone twice went close within two minutes. With 19 minutes played, a weighted pass from Rochemback took the Italian by surprise but he adapted well and shrugged off Rio Ferdinand before forcing a full-length save from Edwin van der Sar.

With an hour played, all Boro's hard work was in danger of being wasted when Lee Cattermole inexplicably handled the ball in the area and United were awarded a penalty at the Stretford end. But Brad Jones guessed correctly and made a great save to his right to deny Ruud van Nistelrooy.

The miss spurred on United but their relentless attacks were well dealt with by a young defence, led by stand-in captain Chris Riggott. After four agonising minutes of stoppage time, Boro's young team earned a valuable point and a big confidence boost.

Fans' Player of the Match

Brad Jones

Quote

🍑 **Steve McClaren**

The team is maturing. We are a young side, but are gaining experience and growing in belief.

Venue:	Old Trafford	Referee:	C.J.Foy - 05/06		Manchester United
Attendance:	69,531	Matches:	40		Middlesbrough
Capacity:	73,006	Yellow Cards:	93		
Occupancy:	95%	Red Cards:	10		

Form Coming into Fixture

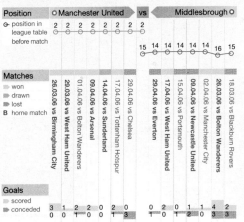

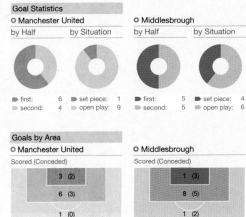

Position — Manchester United vs Middlesbrough

position in league table before match

Man Utd: 2 2 2 2 2 2 2 2
Boro: 15 14 14 14 14 14 16 15

Matches
- won
- drawn
- lost
- B home match

26.03.06 vs Birmingham City
29.03.06 vs West Ham United
01.04.06 vs Bolton Wanderers
09.04.06 vs Arsenal
14.04.06 vs Sunderland
17.04.06 vs Tottenham Hotspur
29.04.06 vs Chelsea

29.04.06 vs Everton
17.04.06 vs West Ham United
15.04.06 vs Portsmouth
09.04.06 vs Newcastle United
02.04.06 vs Manchester City
26.03.06 vs Bolton Wanderers
18.03.06 vs Blackburn Rovers

Goals
- scored: 3 1 2 2 0 2 0 | 0 2 0 1 1 4 2
- conceded: 0 0 1 0 0 1 3 | 1 0 1 2 0 3 3

Goal Statistics

Manchester United

by Half — first: 6, second: 4
by Situation — set piece: 1, open play: 9

Middlesbrough

by Half — first: 5, second: 5
by Situation — set piece: 4, open play: 6

Goals by Area

Manchester United — Scored (Conceded)

3 (2)
6 (3)
1 (0)

Middlesbrough — Scored (Conceded)

1 (3)
8 (5)
1 (2)

Team Statistics

Starting Line-Ups

Manchester United: van der Sar; Silvestre, Brown, Ferdinand, Neville (Park/Ronaldo); Evra (Richardson), Giggs, O'Shea; Saha (Rossi), van Nistelrooy

4/4/2

Unused Sub: Howard, Vidic

Middlesbrough: Jones; Parnaby, Riggott, Bates, Queudrue (Taylor); Morrison (Christie), Cattermole, Boateng, Downing; Maccarone (Parlour), Rochemback

4/5/1

Unused Sub: Knight, Wheater

Premiership Totals	Man Utd	Boro
Premiership Appearances	2,176	1,364
Team Appearances	1,772	720
Goals Scored	271	110
Assists	311	122
Clean Sheets (goalkeepers)	58	3
Yellow Cards	166	206
Red Cards	7	10
Full Internationals	13	5

Age/Height

Manchester United Age: **26 yrs, 11 mo**

Middlesbrough Age: **24 yrs, 6 mo**

Manchester United Height: **6'**

Middlesbrough Height: **5'11"**

Match Statistics

League Table after Fixture

		Played	Won	Drawn	Lost	For	Against	Pts
●	2 Man Utd	37	24	8	5	68	34	80
...	...	...	...	...	...	...	...	...
↑	14 Middlesbrough	36	12	8	16	47	56	44
↓	15 Man City	36	13	4	19	42	43	43
●	16 Aston Villa	37	9	12	16	40	54	39
●	17 Portsmouth	37	10	8	19	36	59	38
●	18 Birmingham	37	8	10	19	28	49	34
●	19 West Brom	37	7	8	22	29	56	29
●	20 Sunderland	36	2	6	28	23	66	12

Statistics	Man Utd	Boro
Goals	0	0
Shots on Target	7	7
Shots off Target	11	4
Hit Woodwork	0	0
Possession %	51	49
Corners	10	2
Offsides	3	3
Fouls	11	10
Disciplinary Points	8	8

1-1

Bolton Wanderers ○
Middlesbrough ○

▶ Adam Johnson celebrates the first goal of his senior career

Event Line

14 ○ ▢	Vaz Te	
45 ○ ▢	Cattermole	
Half time 0-0		
47 ○ ⊕	Johnson / RF / OP / IA	
	Assist: Wheater	
51 ○ ⊕	Vaz Te / H / OP / IA	
	Assist: Okocha	
59 ○ ⇄	Davies > McMahon	
64 ○ ⇄	Maccarone > Christie	
66 ○ ⇄	Giannakopoulos > Nolan	
73 ○ ⇄	Taylor > Johnson	
75 ○ ⇄	Speed > Nakata	
86 ○ ⇄	Borgetti > Campo	
Full time 1-1		

Two days after grabbing an unlikely point at Old Trafford, another young Boro side featuring few of the players expected to appear in the UEFA Cup final gave another excellent account of themselves.

Goalkeeper Ross Turnbull made his Boro debut after spending the majority of the season on loan at Crewe Alexandra. He barely had time to settle his nerves before he was called into action. Jay Jay Okacha broke free of the Boro defence after just 85 seconds to go one-on-one with Turnbull. But the keeper held his nerve well to produce an excellent one-handed save. Shortly afterwards Bolton had another chance well saved, Kevin Nolan's shot blocked by the legs of Turnbull.

Boro made the breakthrough after half-time. Adam Johnson went on a solo run down the left before cutting into the penalty area and curling a superb shot – assisted by a deflection - out of the reach of Jaaskelainen and into the net.

Bolton were level within five minutes, as Ricardo Vaz Te headed home from six yards out. But Boro should still have won it, Ugo Ehiogu missing a late sitter when Jaaskelainen fumbled a long-range free-kick at his feet.

Fans' Player of the Match

Ross Turnbull

Quote

❝ Steve Round

Once we got into our stride, I thought we played some great stuff, particularly in the second half.

Premiership Milestone

▶ Debut

Ross Turnbull made his Premiership debut.

Venue:	Reebok Stadium	Referee:	H.M.Webb - 05/06		Bolton Wanderers
Attendance:	22,733	Matches:	42		Middlesbrough
Capacity:	28,723	Yellow Cards:	106		
Occupancy:	79%	Red Cards:	6		

Form Coming into Fixture

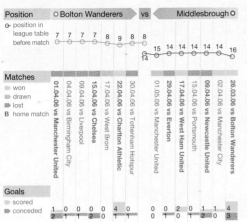

Position	Bolton Wanderers	vs	Middlesbrough
position in league table before match	7 7 7 7 8 9 8 8		15 14 14 14 14 14 16 / 14

Matches
- won
- drawn
- lost
- B home match

01.04.06 vs Manchester United
04.04.06 vs Birmingham City
09.04.06 vs Liverpool
15.04.06 vs Chelsea
17.04.06 vs West Brom
22.04.06 vs Charlton Athletic
30.04.06 vs Tottenham Hotspur
01.05.06 vs Manchester United
29.04.06 vs Everton
17.04.06 vs West Ham United
15.04.06 vs Portsmouth
09.04.06 vs Newcastle United
02.04.06 vs Manchester City
26.03.06 vs Bolton Wanderers

Goals

	scored	1 0 0 0 0 4 0	0 0 2 0 1 1 4
	conceded	2 1 1 2 0 1 1	0 1 0 1 2 0 3

Goal Statistics

○ Bolton Wanderers

by Half — by Situation

first:	4	set piece:	2
second:	1	open play:	3

○ Middlesbrough

by Half — by Situation

first:	4	set piece:	4
second:	4	open play:	4

Goals by Area

○ Bolton Wanderers

Scored (Conceded)

2 (2)
3 (5)
0 (1)

○ Middlesbrough

Scored (Conceded)

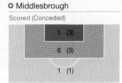

1 (3)
6 (3)
1 (1)

Team Statistics

Starting Line-Ups

Pedersen — Vaz Te — Christie / Maccarone — McMahon / Davies
Nakata / Speed — Parlour
Faye — Ehiogu
Jaaskelainen — Campo / Borgetti — Davies — Yakubu — Doriva — Turnbull
Ben Haim — Wheater
Okocha — Cattermole
Hunt — Nolan / Stelios — Johnson / Taylor — Queudrue

4/5/1 — **4/5/1**

Unused Sub: Walker, Jaidi — Unused Sub: Knight, Kennedy

Premiership Totals	○ Bolton	Boro ○
Premiership Appearances	1,747	1,329
Team Appearances	1,205	608
Goals Scored	215	139
Assists	161	104
Clean Sheets (goalkeepers)	49	0
Yellow Cards	236	174
Red Cards	8	14
Full Internationals	10	5

Age/Height

Bolton Wanderers Age	Middlesbrough Age
28 yrs, 11 mo	**24 yrs, 7 mo**
Bolton Wanderers Height	Middlesbrough Height
6'	**6'**

Match Statistics

League Table after Fixture

		Played	Won	Drawn	Lost	For	Against	Pts
● 8	Bolton	37	14	11	12	48	41	53
● 9	West Ham	37	15	7	15	50	54	52
● 10	Wigan	37	15	6	16	43	48	51
● 11	Everton	37	14	7	16	32	47	49
● 12	Charlton	37	13	8	16	41	51	47
↑ 13	Middlesbrough	37	12	9	16	48	57	45
↓ 14	Fulham	36	13	6	17	46	56	45
● 15	Man City	36	13	4	19	42	43	43
● 16	Aston Villa	37	9	12	16	40	54	39

Statistics	○ Bolton	Boro ○
Goals	1	1
Shots on Target	9	3
Shots off Target	8	2
Hit Woodwork	0	0
Possession %	50	50
Corners	6	1
Offsides	1	5
Fouls	9	10
Disciplinary Points	4	4

1-0

Fulham ○
Middlesbrough ○

▶ Danny Graham tries to get away from Moritz Volz

Event Line

Half time 0-0

51 ○ ▪	Graham
56 ○ ⇄	Helguson > John
62 ○ ⇄	Walker > Christie
70 ○ ⇄	Radzinski > McBride
81 ○ ⇄	Craddock > Graham
84 ○ ⊕	Helguson / RF / P / IA
	Assist: Helguson
85 ○ ⇄	Cooper > Kennedy

Full time 1-0

Steve McClaren marked his final league game as Boro manager by naming the youngest ever Premiership team on a proud day for the club's Academy. An all-English line-up included 15 home-produced players, with Malcolm Christie the only one born more than 25 miles from the Riverside.

18-year-old Lee Cattermole became Boro's youngest ever captain before 39-year-old Colin Cooper took the skipper's armband late on to beat his own record as Boro's oldest captain.

Boro had 11 locally-born players on the pitch when Christie made way to allow 17-year-old midfielder Josh Walker to make his first team debut, while striker Tom Craddock also made his debut late in the game.

But Fulham clinched a win with six minutes remaining. Boro conceded a penalty when Brian McBride was brought down by David Wheater and Heidar Helguson sent Turnbull the wrong way from the spot.

Fans' Player of the Match	Quote	Premiership Milestone
Ross Turnbull	❝ **Steve McClaren**	▶ **Debut**
	The way the young players performed augurs well for the future of the club. They have put on a display today that has made me proud.	Both Josh Walker and Tom Craddock made their Premiership debuts.

Venue:	Craven Cottage	Referee:	M.R.Halsey - 05/06
Attendance:	22,434	Matches:	36
Capacity:	22,646	Yellow Cards:	54
Occupancy:	99%	Red Cards:	6

Fulham
Middlesbrough

Form Coming into Fixture

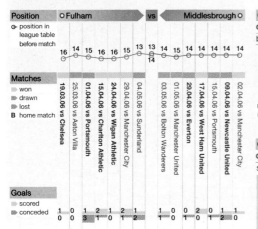

Position	O Fulham	vs	Middlesbrough O
position in league table before match	16 14 15 16 16 15 13 13/14 14 15 14 14 14 14 14		

Matches
- won
- drawn
- lost
- B home match

	19.03.06 vs Chelsea	25.03.06 vs Aston Villa	01.04.06 vs Portsmouth	15.04.06 vs Charlton Athletic	24.04.06 vs Wigan Athletic	29.04.06 vs Manchester City	04.05.06 vs Sunderland	03.05.06 vs Bolton Wanderers	01.05.06 vs Manchester United	29.04.06 vs Everton	17.04.06 vs West Ham United	15.04.06 vs Portsmouth	09.04.06 vs Newcastle United	02.04.06 vs Manchester City

Goals
- scored
- conceded

scored	1	0	1	2	1	2	1		1	0	0	2	0	1
conceded	0	0	3	1	0	1	2		1	0	1	0	2	0

Goal Statistics

O Fulham

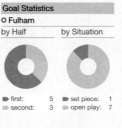

by Half		by Situation	
first:	5	set piece:	1
second:	3	open play:	7

O Middlesbrough

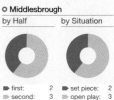

by Half		by Situation	
first:	2	set piece:	2
second:	3	open play:	3

Goals by Area

O Fulham
Scored (Conceded)

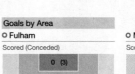

0 (3)
6 (3)
2 (1)

O Middlesbrough
Scored (Conceded)

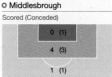

0 (1)
4 (3)
1 (1)

Team Statistics

Starting Line-Ups

Fulham (left): Niemi; Rosenior, Bocanegra, Christanval, Volz; Bridge, Diop, Brown, Malbranque; McBride Radzinski, Christie Walker; John Helguson, Graham Craddock

Middlesbrough (right): Turnbull; Morrison, Davies; Kennedy Cooper, Bates; Cattermole, Wheater; Johnson, Taylor

4/4/2   **4/4/2**

Unused Sub: Crossley, Goma, Elliott   Unused Sub: Knight, McMahon

Premiership Totals	O Fulham	Boro O
Premiership Appearances	1,161	525
Team Appearances	695	325
Goals Scored	135	45
Assists	118	30
Clean Sheets (goalkeepers)	25	0
Yellow Cards	115	64
Red Cards	6	0
Full Internationals	9	1

Age/Height

Fulham Age	Middlesbrough Age
27 yrs, 6 mo	**21 yrs, 6 mo**
Fulham Height	Middlesbrough Height
5'10"	**6'**

Match Statistics

League Table after Fixture

	Played	Won	Drawn	Lost	For	Against	Pts
↑ 12 Fulham	38	14	6	18	48	58	48
↓ 13 Charlton	38	13	8	17	41	55	47
↓ 14 Middlesbrough	38	12	9	17	48	58	45
● 15 Man City	38	13	4	21	43	48	43
● 16 Aston Villa	38	10	12	16	42	55	42
● 17 Portsmouth	38	10	8	20	37	62	38
● 18 Birmingham	38	8	10	20	28	50	34
● 19 West Brom	38	7	9	22	31	58	30
● 20 Sunderland	38	3	6	29	26	69	15

Statistics	O Fulham	Boro O
Goals	1	0
Shots on Target	4	3
Shots off Target	5	3
Hit Woodwork	0	0
Possession %	51	49
Corners	8	4
Offsides	2	5
Fouls	8	12
Disciplinary Points	0	4

0-4

Middlesbrough ○
Sevilla ○

➧ Gareth Southgate and Chris Riggott attempt to snuff out the danger

Event Line

27 ○	⊕ Fabiano / H / OP / IA	
	Assist: Alves	
Half time 0-1		
46 ○	⇄ Maccarone > Morrison	
46 ○	⇄ Kanoute > Saviola	
53 ○	▢ Alves	
70 ○	⇄ Yakubu > Queudrue	
72 ○	⇄ Renato > Fabiano	
78 ○	⊕ Maresca / RF / OP / 6Y	
	Assist: Kanoute	
81 ○	▢ Escude	
83 ○	▢ Rochemback	
84 ○	⊕ Maresca / LF / C / OA	
85 ○	▢ Maresca	
86 ○	⇄ Cattermole > Viduka	
86 ○	⇄ Puerta > Adriano	
89 ○	⊕ Kanoute / RF / OP / IA	
	Assist: Maresca	
Full time 0-4		

Boro's UEFA Cup dreams ended in tears as three late goals from a slick Sevilla side resulted in a drubbing in a game dubbed the biggest in the club's long history.

In his 250th and final match as Boro manager, England-bound Steve McClaren saw his side well beaten, but the game tipped Sevilla's way thanks to two defining moments – both involving Mark Viduka. Both went against Boro and Sevilla ended worthy winners. It had been a wonderful 15-game trip around Europe, taking in some of the club's greatest ever games, but Gareth Southgate and co had fallen one game short of winning the UEFA Cup.

Amid a fantastic atmosphere at the Philips Stadion, Sevilla created the first chance of note, Brazilian wing-back Daniel Alves flashing a shot through the Boro box, narrowly wide of Mark Schwarzer's right-hand post. Boro hit back when Fabio Rochemback fired in a thunderous free-kick that was parried by keeper Palop before the ball was scrambled clear. Another Brazilian, striker Adriano then caused problems, racing down Boro's right, his cross intercepted by Chris Riggott.

Sevilla opened the scoring on 26 minutes, Riggott losing Adriano, whose fine header gave Schwarzer no chance for a fine finish following an inch-perfect cross from the ever-dangerous Alves. It could have been worse had Adriano not fired inches over but Boro survived to regroup at half-time, with semi-final super-sub Massimo Maccarone introduced to the fray in place of James Morrison.

Adriano swerved a shot inches wide before Boro came agonisingly close to an equaliser. Riggott headed Rochemback's free-kick into Viduka's path. Sadly, with only the keeper to beat, the striker struck Palop's legs and the chance was lost.

Venue:	Philips Stadium	Referee:	H.Fandel (GER)		**Middlesbrough**
Attendance:	36,500				**Sevilla**
Capacity:	36,500				
Occupancy:	100%				

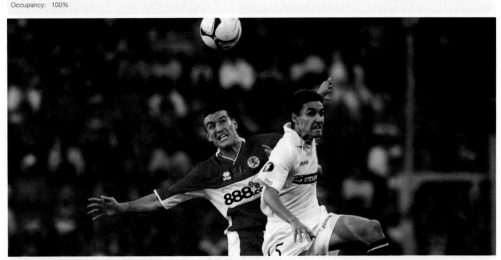

▶ Franck Queudrue focuses on the ball

Match Statistics

Starting Line-Ups

▶ 4/4/2   ▶ 4/4/2

Unused Sub: Jones, Ehiogu, Bates, Parlour

Unused Sub: Notario, Ocio, Sales, Kepa

Statistics	○ Boro	Sevilla ○
Goals	0	4
Shots on Target	2	11
Shots off Target	3	7
Hit Woodwork	0	0
Possession %	47	53
Corners	5	6
Offsides	3	1
Fouls	21	12
Disciplinary Points	4	12

Boro were more impressive in the second period but struggled to create clear-cut openings even after a fourth striker, Yakubu, was introduced. Perhaps Boro's last chance disappeared when referee Herbert Fandel dismissed claims for a penalty when Navarro clumsily challenged Viduka from behind.

Within minutes, Sevilla took a two-goal lead, Enzo Maresca firing home after Schwarzer could only parry a shot from sub Freddie Kanoute. And the game was over when Maresca fired home his second and his side's third six minutes from time. To rub salt into the wound, Sevilla scored an undeserved fourth in the final minute, Schwarzer failing to hold a shot from Jesus Navas and Kanoute scoring from the rebound.

Fans' Player of the Match

Fabio Rochemback

Quote

🔘 **Steve McClaren**

We had our moments, but it just wasn't our night. Maybe in the end it was a game too far, but it has been a fantastic run.

1

Mark Schwarzer
Goalkeeper

It's now nearly a decade since Mark Schwarzer joined Boro but few of his 10 years have been as dramatic as his 2005–06 campaign that culminated in his appearance for Australia at the World Cup finals in Germany, his parents' homeland. Boro's all-time most-capped player enjoyed a see-saw season that took in the lows of being dropped, having a transfer request accepted and suffering a fractured cheekbone during the FA Cup semi-final defeat to West Ham – and the highs of stunning UEFA Cup performances in Rome and Bucharest. That he should play such a big part in helping Boro reach their first European final was fitting because it was his last-minute penalty save at Manchester City on the last day of the 2004–05 season that sent Boro into a second successive UEFA Cup.

Player Details:

Date of Birth:	06.10.1972
Place of Birth:	Sydney
Nationality:	Australian
Height:	6'5"
Weight:	15st 1lb
Foot:	Right

Player Performance 05/06

League Performance

Percentage of total possible time player was on pitch   ⊕ position in league table at end of month

Month:	Aug	Sep	Oct	Nov	Dec	Jan	Feb	Mar	Apr	May	Total
	100%	67%	75%	67%	100%	50%	100%	100%	40%	0%	71%
	12	11	11	10	14	16	16	14	15	14	
Team Pts:	4/12	4/9	7/12	4/9	2/15	4/12	6/9	6/12	6/15	2/9	45/114
Team Gls F:	3	3	9	5	3	7	5	8	4	1	48
Team Gls A:	5	4	6	5	8	12	4	8	4	2	58
Total mins:	360	180	270	180	450	180	270	360	180	0	2,430
Starts (sub):	4	2	3	2	5	2	3	4	2	0	27
Goals:	0	0	0	0	0	0	0	0	0	0	0
Assists:	0	0	0	0	0	0	1	0	0	0	1
Clean sheets:	2	0	0	1	1	2	1	1	0	8
Cards (Y/R):	0	0	0	0	0	0	0	0	0	0	0

League Performance Totals

Clean Sheets

- Schwarzer: 8
- Team-mates: 2
- **Total: 10**

Assists

- Schwarzer: 1
- Team-mates: 41
- **Total: 42**

Cards

- Schwarzer: 0
- Team-mates: 54
- **Total: 54**

Cup Games

	Apps	CS	Cards
UEFA Cup	11	4	1
FA Cup	6	3	0
Carling Cup	3	1	0
Total	**20**	**8**	**1**

Career History

Career Milestones

Club Debut:

vs Stockport C (A), W 0-2, League Cup

 26.02.97

Time Spent at the Club:

▶ **9.5 Seasons**

First Goal Scored for the Club:

—

▶ —

Full International:

 **Australia**

Premiership Totals

92-06

Appearances	262
Clean Sheets	77
Assists	1
Yellow Cards	3
Red Cards	1

Clubs

Year	Club	Apps	CS
97-06	Middlesbrough	354	118
96-97	Bradford	16	5
95-96	Kaiserslautern		
94-95	Dynamo Dresden		
90-94	Marconi		

Off the Pitch

Age:

- Schwarzer: 33 years, 7 months
- Team: 26 years, 1 month
- League: 26 years, 11 months

Height:

- Schwarzer: 6'5"
- Team: 5'11"
- League: 5'11"

Weight:

- Schwarzer: 15st 1lb
- Team: 12st 2lb
- League: 12st

22 Brad Jones
Goalkeeper

Player Details:

Date of Birth:	19.03.1982
Place of Birth:	Armadale
Nationality:	Australian
Height:	6'3"
Weight:	12st 1lb
Foot:	Right

Season Review 05/06

Jones emerged as an able understudy to Mark Schwarzer in 2005-06 as the former Academy graduate enjoyed his best season yet. The Aussie built on the European experience he had gained during the previous campaign with impressive clean sheets in the early stages of last season's UEFA Cup, culminating in an appearance in the semi-final showdown with Steaua Bucharest. He also deputised for Schwarzer when his fellow Aussie suffered a fractured cheekbone during the FA Cup semi-final with West Ham at Villa Park. 2006-07 promises to be his biggest season yet as he looks to press Schwarzer for the 'keeper's shirt.

League Performance Totals

Clean Sheets

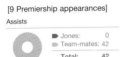

- Jones: 2
- Team-mates: 8
- **Total: 10**

[9 Premiership appearances]

Assists

- Jones: 0
- Team-mates: 42
- **Total: 42**

Cards

- Jones: 0
- Team-mates: 54
- **Total: 54**

Cup Games

	Apps	CS	Cards
UEFA Cup	4	3	1
FA Cup	3	0	0
Carling Cup	0	0	0
Total	**7**	**3**	**1**

33 Andrew Taylor
Defence

Player Details:

Date of Birth:	01.08.1986
Place of Birth:	Hartlepool
Nationality:	English
Height:	5'10"
Weight:	10st 12lb
Foot:	Left

Season Review 05/06

The talented youngster is yet another of the Boro Academy graduates who featured in the first team over the course of the season. A member of the Youth Cup winning team, the left-back spent the early part of the season on loan at Bradford City in League One. He was recalled in January and made his first team debut in the 7-0 thrashing at Arsenal. However, he went on to play a key role in several big games, showing his ability for link-up play during the FA Cup semi-final against West Ham as he and Stewart Downing put on an impressive first half display.

League Performance Totals

Goals

- Taylor: 0
- Team-mates: 47
- **Total: 47**
- own goals: 1

[13 Premiership appearances]

Assists

- Taylor: 0
- Team-mates: 42
- **Total: 42**

Cards

- Taylor: 0
- Team-mates: 54
- **Total: 54**

Cup Games

	Apps	Goals	Cards
UEFA Cup	3	0	0
FA Cup	4	0	1
Carling Cup	0	0	0
Total	**7**	**0**	**1**

3

Franck Queudrue
Defence

Season Review 05/06

The French left-back continued to be a fans' favourite in the 2005-2006 season, but was forced to fight for his place following the arrival of Emanuel Pogatetz. However, he showed his versatility with a series of excellent performances as part of a three-man central defence and hardly missed a game during the run-in as Boro came so close to cup glory. Surprisingly uncapped at full level, Queudrue has impressed fans with his ability on the ball and willingness to get forward to support attacks.

Player Details:

Date of Birth:	25.08.1978
Place of Birth:	Paris
Nationality:	French
Height:	6'1"
Weight:	12st 7lb
Foot:	Left

Player Performance 05/06

League Performance

Percentage of total possible time player was on pitch   ⊖- position in league table at end of month

Month:	Aug	Sep	Oct	Nov	Dec	Jan	Feb	Mar	Apr	May	Total
% on pitch	88%	100%	63%	84%	82%	0%	33%	100%	32%	57%	63%
League position	12	11	11	10	14	16	16	14	15	14	
Team Pts:	4/12	4/9	7/12	4/9	2/15	4/12	6/9	6/12	6/15	2/9	45/114
Team Gls F:	3	3	9	5	3	7	5	8	4	1	48
Team Gls A:	5	4	6	5	8	12	4	8	4	2	58
Total mins:	316	270	226	226	369	0	90	360	145	154	2,156
Starts (sub):	4	3	2 (2)	3	4 (1)	0	1	4	3	2	26 (3)
Goals:	1	0	1	0	1	0	0	0	0	0	3
Assists:	0	0	0	0	0	0	0	1	0	0	1
Clean sheets:	2	0	0	0	1	0	1	1	1	0	6
Cards (Y/R):	1	2	0	0	1	0	0	1	0	0	5

League Performance Totals

Goals
- Queudrue: 3
- Team-mates: 44
- **Total: 47**
- own goals: 1

Assists
- Queudrue: 1
- Team-mates: 41
- **Total: 42**

Cards
- Queudrue: 5
- Team-mates: 49
- **Total: 54**

Cup Games

	Apps	Goals	Cards
UEFA Cup	14	0	1
FA Cup	3	0	1
Carling Cup	3	0	0
Total	**20**	**0**	**2**

Career History

Career Milestones

Club Debut:
vs Charlton (A), D 0-0, Premiership

 **13.10.01**

First Goal Scored for the Club:
vs Sunderland (H), W 2-0, Premiership

▶ **22.10.01**

Time Spent at the Club:
▶ **5 Seasons**

Full International:
▶ —

Premiership Totals

92-06

Appearances	150
Goals	11
Assists	15
Yellow Cards	28
Red Cards	5

Clubs

Year	Club	Apps	Gls
01-06	Middlesbrough	197	11
99-01	RC Lens		

Off the Pitch

Age:

- Queudrue: 27 years, 9 months
- Team: 26 years, 1 month
- League: 26 years, 11 months

Height:

- Queudrue: 6'1"
- Team: 5'11"
- League: 5'11"

Weight:

- Queudrue: 12st 7lb
- Team: 12st 2lb
- League: 12st

4 Ugo Ehiogu
Defence

Player Details:

Date of Birth:	03.11.1972
Place of Birth:	Hackney
Nationality:	English
Height:	6'2"
Weight:	14st 10lb
Foot:	Right

Player Performance 05/06

League Performance

Percentage of total possible time player was on pitch   ○ position in league table at end of month

Month:	Aug	Sep	Oct	Nov	Dec	Jan	Feb	Mar	Apr	May	Total
% on pitch	71%	80%	0%	30%	21%	18%	0%	75%	80%	33%	42%
League position	12	11	11	10	14	16	16	14	15	14	
Team Pts:	4/12	4/9	7/12	4/9	2/15	4/12	6/9	6/12	6/15	2/9	45/114
Team Gls F:	3	3	9	5	3	7	5	8	4	1	48
Team Gls A:	5	4	6	5	8	12	4	8	4	2	58
Total mins:	254	217	0	81	94	63	0	270	360	90	1,429
Starts (sub):	3	3	0	1	1 (1)	0 (1)	0	3	4	1	16 (2)
Goals:	0	0	0	0	0	0	0	0	0	0	0
Assists:	0	0	0	0	0	0	0	0	0	0	0
Clean sheets:	2	0	0	0	0	0	0	0	1	0	3
Cards (Y/R):	0/1	0	0	0	0	0	0	0	0	0	0/1

League Performance Totals

Goals

▶ Ehiogu:	0
▷ Team-mates:	47
Total:	**47**
● own goals:	1

Assists

▶ Ehiogu:	0
▷ Team-mates:	42
Total:	**42**

Cards

▶ Ehiogu:	1
▷ Team-mates:	53
Total:	**54**

Cup Games

	Apps	Goals	Cards
UEFA Cup	7	0	0
FA Cup	3	0	0
Carling Cup	2	0	0
Total	**12**	**0**	**0**

Career History

Career Milestones

Club Debut:
vs Charlton (A), L 1-0, Premiership

▶ **21.10.00**

Time Spent at the Club:

▶ **6 Seasons**

First Goal Scored for the Club:
vs Bradford (H), D 2-2, Premiership

▶ **25.11.00**

Full International:

▶ **England**

Premiership Totals

92-06

Appearances	355
Goals	19
Assists	6
Yellow Cards	42
Red Cards	5

Clubs

Year	Club	Apps	Gls
00-06	Middlesbrough	151	8
91-00	Aston Villa	303	15
89-91	West Brom	2	0

Off the Pitch

Age:

▶ Ehiogu: 33 years, 6 months
▷ Team: 26 years, 1 month
| League: 26 years, 11 months

Height:

▶ Ehiogu: 6'2"
▷ Team: 5'11"
| League: 5'11"

Weight:

▶ Ehiogu: 14st 10lb
▷ Team: 12st 2lb
| League: 12st

5

Chris Riggott
Defence

Player Details:

Date of Birth:	01.09.1980
Place of Birth:	Derby
Nationality:	English
Height:	6'
Weight:	12st 5lb
Foot:	Right

Season Review 05/06

After joining Boro as a central defender of potential, Riggott has developed into a leader on the pitch, deputising for Gareth Southgate as captain several times over the course of the 2005-06 season. His impressive performances in nailing down a regular place at the heart of the Boro defence earned him the accolade of being the club's Players' Player of the Season. After missing the beginning of the season with a knee injury, the former Derby defender established an automatic place in the starting 11. Bounced back from the heart-break of missing a late chance in the FA Cup semi-final to get on the scoresheet in the UEFA Cup win over Steaua three days later

Player Performance 05/06

League Performance

Percentage of total possible time player was on pitch   ⊙ position in league table at end of month

Month:	Aug	Sep	Oct	Nov	Dec	Jan	Feb	Mar	Apr	May	Total
			100%	100%	79%	58%	67%	38%	60%	33%	55%
	0%	0%									
(position)	12	11	11	10	14	16	16	14	15	14	
Team Pts:	4/12	4/9	7/12	4/9	2/15	4/12	6/9	6/12	6/15	2/9	45/114
Team Gls F:	3	3	9	5	3	7	5	8	4	1	48
Team Gls A:	5	4	6	5	8	12	4	8	4	2	58
Total mins:	0	0	360	270	354	207	180	136	270	90	1,867
Starts (sub):	0	0	4	3	4	3	2	2	3	1	22
Goals:	0	0	0	0	0	0	0	0	0	0	0
Assists:	0	0	0	0	0	0	0	0	0	0	0
Clean sheets:	0	0	0	0	1	0	2	1	2	1	7
Cards (Y/R):	0	0	1	0	1/1	0	0	0	0	0	2/1

League Performance Totals

Goals
- ▶ Riggott: 0
- ▷ Team-mates: 47
- **Total: 47**
- ▶ own goals: 1

Assists
- ▶ Riggott: 0
- ▷ Team-mates: 42
- **Total: 42**

Cards
- ▶ Riggott: 3
- ▷ Team-mates: 51
- **Total: 54**

Cup Games

	Apps	Goals	Cards
UEFA Cup	13	1	3
FA Cup	5	1	0
Carling Cup	2	0	0
Total	**20**	**2**	**3**

Career History

Career Milestones

Club Debut:
vs Liverpool (A), D 1-1, Premiership

 08.02.03

Time Spent at the Club:

▶ **3.5 Seasons**

First Goal Scored for the Club:
vs Sunderland (A), W 1-3, Premiership

 22.02.03

Full International:

▶ —

Premiership Totals

92-06

Appearances	134
Goals	7
Assists	1
Yellow Cards	21
Red Cards	1

Clubs

Year	Club	Apps	Gls
03-06	Middlesbrough	103	7
99-03	Derby	100	7

Off the Pitch

Age:

- ▶ Riggott: 25 years, 8 months
- ▷ Team: 26 years, 1 month
- | League: 26 years, 11 months

Height:
- ▶ Riggott: 6'
- ▷ Team: 5'11"
- | League: 5'11"

Weight:
- ▶ Riggott: 12st 5lb
- ▷ Team: 12st 2lb
- | League: 12st

6 Gareth Southgate
Defence

Boro's Captain led the team through a rollercoaster ride of a season. Always a great leader on the pitch, he was also needed to lead the team through the disappointment of heavy league defeats to Arsenal and Aston Villa in the league before the highs of reaching two cup semi-finals and finally a trip to Eindhoven for the UEFA Cup final.

Niggling injuries throughout the season limited the former England defender's playing appearances, the worst of which forced him into leaving the pitch after just 20 minutes of the UEFA Cup semi-final win over Steaua. Recovered in time to captain the side in the final. Succeeded Steve McClaren as Boro manager in June 2006.

Player Details:

Date of Birth:	03.09.1970
Place of Birth:	Watford
Nationality:	English
Height:	6'
Weight:	12st 6lb
Foot:	Right

Player Performance 05/06

League Performance

Percentage of total possible time player was on pitch   ○⊷ position in league table at end of month

Month:	Aug	Sep	Oct	Nov	Dec	Jan	Feb	Mar	Apr	May	Total
	100%	100%	57%	67%	100%	75%	100%	25%	0%	0%	61%
	12	11	11	10	14	16	16	14	15	14	
Team Pts:	4/12	4/9	7/12	4/9	2/15	4/12	6/9	6/12	6/15	2/9	45/114
Team Gls F:	3	3	9	5	3	7	5	8	4	1	48
Team Gls A:	5	4	6	5	8	12	4	8	4	2	58
Total mins:	360	270	205	180	450	270	270	90	0	0	2,095
Starts (sub):	4	3	3	2	5	3	3	1	0	0	24
Goals:	0	0	0	0	0	0	0	0	0	0	0
Assists:	0	0	0	0	1	1	0	0	0	0	2
Clean sheets:	2	0	0	0	1	1	2	1	0	0	7
Cards (Y/R):	1	1	0	0	0	0	1	0	0	0	3

League Performance Totals

Goals
- Southgate: 0
- Team-mates: 47
- **Total: 47**
- own goals: 1

Assists
- Southgate: 2
- Team-mates: 40
- **Total: 42**

Cards
- Southgate: 3
- Team-mates: 51
- **Total: 54**

Cup Games

	Apps	Goals	Cards
UEFA Cup	9	0	0
FA Cup	7	0	0
Carling Cup	2	0	1
Total	**18**	**0**	**1**

Career History

Career Milestones

Club Debut:
vs Arsenal (H), L 0-4, Premiership
▶ **18.08.01**

Time Spent at the Club:
▶ **5 Seasons**

First Goal Scored for the Club:
vs Liverpool (H), L 1-2, Premiership
▶ **16.03.02**

Full International:
▶ **England**

Premiership Totals

92-06
Appearances	426
Goals	17
Assists	20
Yellow Cards	33
Red Cards	1

Clubs

Year	Club	Apps	Gls
01-06	Middlesbrough	204	4
95-01	Aston Villa	244	9
89-95	Crystal Palace	191	22

Off the Pitch

Age:
- Southgate: 35 years, 8 months
- Team: 26 years, 1 month
- League: 26 years, 11 months

Height:
- Southgate: 6'
- Team: 5'11"
- League: 5'11"

Weight:
- Southgate: 12st 6lb
- Team: 12st 2lb
- League: 12st

12 Emanuel Pogatetz
Defence

Season Review 05/06

The Austrian left-back won over Boro supporters with his hard-working and full-blooded displays as he ousted fans' favourite Franck Queudrue from his favoured position. Signed from German side Bayer Leverkusen, Pogatetz had impressed when facing Boro while on loan to Grazer AK in the previous season's UEFA Cup campaign. Often asked to play at left wing-back during the early part to the season, he also displayed great versatility when standing in as a central defender, most notably when scoring his first Boro goal in the memorable 3-0 win at Sunderland. Had his season cut short when suffering a fractured cheekbone in the UEFA Cup quarter-final with Basel.

Player Details:

Date of Birth:	16.01.1983
Place of Birth:	Steinbock
Nationality:	Austrian
Height:	6'2"
Weight:	12st 13lb
Foot:	Left

Player Performance 05/06

League Performance

Percentage of total possible time player was on pitch   G position in league table at end of month

Month:	Aug	Sep	Oct	Nov	Dec	Jan	Feb	Mar	Apr	May	Total
	12%	76%	100%	84%	59%	75%	100%	87%	0%	0%	57%
	12	11	11	10	14	16	16	14	15	14	
Team Pts:	4/12	4/9	7/12	4/9	2/15	4/12	6/9	6/12	6/15	2/9	45/114
Team Gls F:	3	3	9	5	3	7	5	8	4	1	48
Team Gls A:	5	4	6	5	8	12	4	8	4	2	58
Total mins:	44	205	360	226	265	270	270	314	0	0	1,954
Starts (sub):	0 (1)	2 (1)	4	3	3	3	3	3 (1)	0	0	21 (3)
Goals:	0	0	0	0	0	1	0	0	0	0	1
Assists:	0	0	2	0	0	0	0	0	0	0	2
Clean sheets:	0	0	0	0	1	1	2	1	0	0	5
Cards (Y/R):	0	1	2	0	0	0	0	2	0	0	5

League Performance Totals

Goals

- Pogatetz: 1
- Team-mates: 46
- **Total: 47**
- own goals: 1

Assists

- Pogatetz: 2
- Team-mates: 40
- **Total: 42**

Cards

- Pogatetz: 5
- Team-mates: 49
- **Total: 54**

Cup Games

	Apps	Goals	Cards
UEFA Cup	9	0	4
FA Cup	5	0	2
Carling Cup	3	0	0
Total	**17**	**0**	**6**

Career History

Career Milestones

Club Debut:
vs Charlton (H), L 0-3, Premiership

 **28.08.05**

Time Spent at the Club:

 **1 Season**

First Goal Scored for the Club:
vs Sunderland (A), W 0-3, Premiership

31.01.06

Full International:

Austria

Premiership Totals

92-06

Appearances	24
Goals	1
Assists	2
Yellow Cards	5
Red Cards	0

Clubs

Year	Club	Apps	Gls
05-06	Middlesbrough	41	1
05-05	Spartak Moscow		
03-05	Grazer AK		
02-03	Aarau		
01-05	B Leverkusen		
00-01	Karnten		
99-00	Sturm Graz		

Off the Pitch

Age:

- Pogatetz: 23 years, 4 months
- Team: 26 years, 1 month
- League: 26 years, 11 months

Height:

- Pogatetz: 6'2"
- Team: 5'11"
- League: 5'11"

Weight:

- Pogatetz: 12st 13lb
- Team: 12st 2lb
- League: 12st

24

Andrew Davies
Defence

Season Review 05/06

Like several of Boro's young players, Davies spent the early part of the season on loan. His spell in the Championship with Derby County was cut short when he was recalled in January to help cover Boro's minor injury crisis. The former youth team captain went directly from playing at Pride Park to UEFA Cup action as Boro recorded famous wins over Stuttgart and Roma. Originally a centre-back, Davies has displayed great versatility in adapting to a regular first-team role as a right-back and will be looking to challenge Stuart Parnaby for a starting place in 2006-07.

Player Details:

Date of Birth:	17.12.1984
Place of Birth:	Stockton-on-Tees
Nationality:	English
Height:	6'2"
Weight:	14st 8lb
Foot:	Right

League Performance Totals

Goals

Davies: 0
Team-mates: 47
Total: 47
own goals: 1

[12 Premiership appearances]

Assists

Davies: 0
Team-mates: 42
Total: 42

Cards

Davies: 0
Team-mates: 54
Total: 54

Cup Games

	Apps	Goals	Cards
UEFA Cup	4	0	1
FA Cup	0	0	0
Carling Cup	0	0	0
Total	**4**	**0**	**1**

31

David Wheater
Defence

Season Review 05/06

Another of Boro's 2004 FA Youth Cup heroes, Wheater impressed when given his first-team chance on return from a successful loan spell with League One side Doncaster Rovers. He won't forget his debut in a hurry, as he made a substitute appearance in the 7-0 mauling at Arsenal, but the tall central defender grew in stature with several composed displays during the end-of-season run-in as first-choice stars were rested from Premier League action. Was one of 12 Academy scholars who took part in the season's final league game at Fulham.

Player Details:

Date of Birth:	14.02.1987
Place of Birth:	Redcar
Nationality:	English
Height:	6'5"
Weight:	12st 12lb
Foot:	Right

League Performance Totals

Goals

Wheater: 0
Team-mates: 47
Total: 47
own goals: 1

[6 Premiership appearances]

Assists

Wheater: 1
Team-mates: 41
Total: 42

Cards

Wheater: 0
Team-mates: 54
Total: 54

Cup Games

	Apps	Goals	Cards
UEFA Cup	0	0	0
FA Cup	0	0	0
Carling Cup	0	0	0
Total	**0**	**0**	**0**

21 Stuart Parnaby
Defence

Season Review 05/06

Parnaby put many of his former injury problems behind him in 2005-06, playing more than 40 games in a dramatic league and cup campaign. Missed the early part of the season as first Michael Reiziger and then Abel Xavier enjoyed short runs at right-back, but established himself as first choice as the season progressed with a series of mature performances topped by four goals – the first of his career. Those strikes included a crucial UEFA Cup goal in Stuttgart and a last-minute winner in the dramatic 4-3 league success over Bolton.

Player Details:

Date of Birth:	19.07.1982
Place of Birth:	Durham
Nationality:	English
Height:	5'10"
Weight:	11st
Foot:	Right

Player Performance 05/06

League Performance

Percentage of total possible time player was on pitch   ⊖ position in league table at end of month

Month:	Aug	Sep	Oct	Nov	Dec	Jan	Feb	Mar	Apr	May	Total
				100%		100%	100%				
	12	11	56% 11	10	38% 14	16	16	14 31%	40% 15	14 33%	48%
	0%	0%									
Team Pts:	4/12	4/9	7/12	4/9	2/15	4/12	6/9	6/12	6/15	2/9	45/114
Team Gls F:	3	3	9	5	3	7	5	8	4	1	48
Team Gls A:	5	4	6	5	8	12	4	8	4	2	58
Total mins:	0	0	201	270	169	360	270	110	180	90	1,650
Starts (sub):	0	0	2 (1)	3	2	4	3	2	2	1	19 (1)
Goals:	0	0	0	0	0	1	0	1	0	0	2
Assists:	0	0	1	0	0	0	0	0	0	0	1
Clean sheets:	0	0	0	0	1	1	2	0	1	1	6
Cards (Y/R):	0	0	0	1	0	0	0	0	0	0	1

League Performance Totals

Goals

▶ Parnaby:	2
▷ Team-mates:	45
Total:	**47**
▶ own goals:	1

Assists

▶ Parnaby:	1
▷ Team-mates:	41
Total:	**42**

Cards

▶ Parnaby:	1
▷ Team-mates:	53
Total:	**54**

Cup Games

	Apps	Goals	Cards
UEFA Cup	11	1	0
FA Cup	8	1	1
Carling Cup	3	0	1
Total	**22**	**2**	**2**

Career History

Career Milestones

Club Debut:

vs Macclesfield (H), W 2-1, League Cup

▶ **19.09.00**

Time Spent at the Club:

▶ **6 Seasons**

First Goal Scored for the Club:

vs Nuneaton (H), W 5-2, FA Cup

▶ **17.01.06**

Full International:

▶ **—**

Premiership Totals

92-06

Appearances	73
Goals	2
Assists	4
Yellow Cards	3
Red Cards	0

Clubs

Year	Club	Apps	Gls
00-00	Halifax T	6	0
00-06	Middlesbrough	106	4

Off the Pitch

Age:

▶ Parnaby:	23 years, 10 months
▷ Team:	26 years, 1 month
∣ League:	26 years, 11 months

Height:

▶ Parnaby:	5'10"
▷ Team:	5'11"
∣ League:	5'11"

Weight:

▶ Parnaby:	11st
▷ Team:	12st 2lb
∣ League:	12st

26 Matthew Bates
Defence

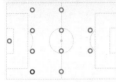

Player Details:

Date of Birth:	10.12.1986
Place of Birth:	Stockton-on-Tees
Nationality:	English
Height:	5'10"
Weight:	12st 3lb
Foot:	Right/Left

Season Review 05/06

After a loan spell at Darlington in 2004-05, Bates was keen to establish himself in the first team last season. He duly made great progress, making 18 starts over the course of the season together with eight substitute appearances. Predominantly a centre-back, Bates displayed an excellent attitude in filling in at right-back when required. In the season's final Premier League game, at Fulham, he partnered his 2004 FA Youth Cup team-mate David Wheater in central defence. However, the season's highlight was a first class performance as stand-in for Gareth Southgate in the UEFA Cup semi-final in Bucharest.

Player Performance 05/06

League Performance

Percentage of total possible time player was on pitch   ⊖ position in league table at end of month

Month:	Aug	Sep	Oct	Nov	Dec	Jan	Feb	Mar	Apr	May	Total
	25%	0%	50%	0%	62%	40%	0%	0%	39%	67%	31%
(position)	12	11	11	10	14	16	16	14	15	14	
Team Pts:	4/12	4/9	7/12	4/9	2/15	4/12	6/9	6/12	6/15	2/9	45/114
Team Gls F:	3	3	9	5	3	7	5	8	4	1	48
Team Gls A:	5	4	6	5	8	12	4	8	4	2	58
Total mins:	89	0	180	0	281	143	0	0	175	180	1,048
Starts (sub):	1 (2)	0	2	0	3 (1)	2 (1)	0	0	2	2	12 (4)
Goals:	0	0	0	0	0	0	0	0	0	0	0
Assists:	0	0	0	0	0	0	0	0	1	0	1
Clean sheets:	0	0	0	0	0	0	0	0	1	1	2
Cards (Y/R):	0	0	0	0	2	1	0	0	0	1	4

League Performance Totals

Goals

▶ Bates:	0
▷ Team-mates:	47
Total:	**47**
● own goals:	1

Assists

▶ Bates:	1
▷ Team-mates:	41
Total:	**42**

Cards

▶ Bates:	4
▷ Team-mates:	50
Total:	**54**

Cup Games

	Apps	Goals	Cards
UEFA Cup	5	0	1
FA Cup	4	0	1
Carling Cup	3	0	0
Total	**12**	**0**	**2**

Career History

Career Milestones

Club Debut:
vs Man City (H), W 3-2, Premiership

 **06.12.04**

Time Spent at the Club:

▶ **2.5 Seasons**

First Goal Scored for the Club:
—

▶ —

Full International:

▶ —

Premiership Totals

92-06

Appearances	18
Goals	0
Assists	1
Yellow Cards	4
Red Cards	0

Clubs

Year	Club	Apps	Gls
05-05	Darlington	4	0
04-06	Middlesbrough	30	0

Off the Pitch

Age:

▶ Bates: 19 years, 5 months
▷ Team: 26 years, 1 month
| League: 26 years, 11 months

Height:

▶ Bates: 5'10"
▷ Team: 5'11"
| League: 5'11"

Weight:

▶ Bates: 12st 3lb
▷ Team: 12st 2lb
| League: 12st

29 Tony McMahon
Defence

Season Review 05/06

Voted Boro's young player of the year in 2004-05, McMahon's heady progress ground to a halt last season as the result of a dislocated shoulder suffered in the season's opening reserve team game. It was February before the talented right-back played again, making his comeback in the 2-0 FA Cup win at Preston. His second – and final – appearance of the season came in a Premier League game at Charlton in March when his misfortune continued, suffering ankle ligament damage that forced his substitution in the 12th minute. The captain of Boro's 2004 FA Youth Cup winners will be hoping for more luck in 2006-07.

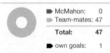

Player Details:

Date of Birth:	24.03.1986
Place of Birth:	Bishop Auckland
Nationality:	English
Height:	5'11"
Weight:	11st 4lb
Foot:	Right

League Performance Totals

Goals

- McMahon: 0
- Team-mates: 47

Total: 47

- own goals: 1

[3 Premiership appearances]

Assists

- McMahon: 0
- Team-mates: 42

Total: 42

Cards

- McMahon: 0
- Team-mates: 54

Total: 54

Cup Games

	Apps	Goals	Cards
UEFA Cup	0	0	0
FA Cup	1	0	1
Carling Cup	0	0	0
Total	**1**	**0**	**1**

37 Adam Johnson
Midfield

Season Review 05/06

Yet another product of Boro's Academy, the teenager made his first team debut in September's 2-1 win over Arsenal at the Riverside. The tricky left-winger went on to play in several league games as well as making appearances in all three cup competitions, including the UEFA Cup win in Stuttgart. Like many of his former Academy teammates, Stewart Downing's understudy benefited from the fixture congestion at the business end of the season and took his opportunities well. After a season of hard work, he got his reward with his first Boro goal in the penultimate Premier League game, at Bolton.

Player Details:

Date of Birth:	14.07.1987
Place of Birth:	Sunderland
Nationality:	English
Height:	5'9"
Weight:	9st 11lb
Foot:	Left

League Performance Totals

Goals

- Johnson: 1
- Team-mates: 46

Total: 47

- own goals: 1

[13 Premiership appearances]

Assists

- Johnson: 1
- Team-mates: 41

Total: 42

Cards

- Johnson: 0
- Team-mates: 54

Total: 54

Cup Games

	Apps	Goals	Cards
UEFA Cup	3	0	0
FA Cup	1	0	0
Carling Cup	1	0	0
Total	**5**	**0**	**0**

7 George Boateng
Midfield

Player Details:

Date of Birth:	09.05.1975
Place of Birth:	Nkawkaw, Ghana
Nationality:	Dutch
Height:	5'9"
Weight:	10st 12lb
Foot:	Right

Season Review 05/06

The high-energy, all-action midfielder was as vibrant as ever in the Boro midfield last season, regularly acting as the driving force behind the team's best displays. An ankle injury forced Boateng out of action over the Christmas period and much of January. For a second successive season, his high-tempo displays were sorely missed and it was little surprise that the team experienced an upturn in results following his return to action. Played crucial roles in helping Boro reach both the UEFA Cup final and FA Cup's last four, but suffered the heartbreak of missing out on a place in the Dutch World Cup squad.

Player Performance 05/06

League Performance

Percentage of total possible time player was on pitch   ⊖ position in league table at end of month

Month:	Aug	Sep	Oct	Nov	Dec	Jan	Feb	Mar	Apr	May	Total
	100%	100%	100%	100%	60%	0%	52%	75%	60%	33%	67%
	12	11	11	10	14	16	16	14	15	14	
Team Pts:	4/12	4/9	7/12	4/9	2/15	4/12	6/9	6/12	6/15	2/9	45/114
Team Gls F:	3	3	9	5	3	7	5	8	4	1	48
Team Gls A:	5	4	6	5	8	12	4	8	4	2	58
Total mins:	360	270	360	270	270	0	141	270	270	90	2,301
Starts (sub):	4	3	4	3	3	0	1 (1)	3	3	1	25 (1)
Goals:	0	0	1	0	0	0	0	0	1	0	2
Assists:	0	1	1	0	0	0	0	0	0	0	2
Clean sheets:	2	0	0	0	0	0	1	1	1	1	6
Cards (Y/R):	1	1	2	0	0	0	0	1	0	0	5

League Performance Totals

Goals

- Boateng: 2
- Team-mates: 45

Total: 47

- own goals: 1

Assists

- Boateng: 2
- Team-mates: 40

Total: 42

Cards

- Boateng: 5
- Team-mates: 49

Total: 54

Cup Games

	Apps	Goals	Cards
UEFA Cup	12	1	4
FA Cup	4	0	0
Carling Cup	2	0	0
Total	**18**	**1**	**4**

Career History

Career Milestones

Club Debut:

vs Southampton (A), D 0-0, Premiership

▶ **17.08.02**

Time Spent at the Club:

▶ **4 Seasons**

First Goal Scored for the Club:

vs Blackburn (A), W 0-4, Premiership

▶ **16.10.04**

Full International:

▶ **Netherlands**

Premiership Totals

92-06	
Appearances	264
Goals	14
Assists	14
Yellow Cards	62
Red Cards	1

Clubs

Year	Club	Apps	Gls
02-06	Middlesbrough	144	6
99-02	Aston Villa	135	5
97-99	Coventry	57	7
95-97	Feyenoord		
94-95	Excelsior		

Off the Pitch

Age:

- Boateng: 31 years
- Team: 26 years, 1 month
- League: 26 years, 11 months

Height:

- Boateng: 5'9"
- Team: 5'11"
- League: 5'11"

Weight:

- Boateng: 10st 12lb
- Team: 12st 2lb
- League: 12st

10
Fabio Rochemback
Midfield

Season Review 05/06

The Brazilian international took time to adapt to the changes in playing style and culture following his early season move from Sporting Lisbon, but he was one of Boro's star performers as Steve McClaren's side bid for glory on two fronts as the season came to a close. Despite a fine debut in a 2-1 win over Arsenal, Rochemback initially struggled to stamp his authority in the Boro engine room. The turning point was his rather fortuitous second-minute strike against Chelsea that began a 3-0 rout of the champions. The creative midfielder was one of the stars as Boro overcame Basel and Steaua to reach the UEFA Cup final.

Player Details:

Date of Birth:	10.12.1981
Place of Birth:	Soledade
Nationality:	Brazilian
Height:	6'
Weight:	13st 1lb
Foot:	Right/Left

Player Performance 05/06

League Performance

Percentage of total possible time player was on pitch   ⊖ position in league table at end of month

Month:	Aug	Sep	Oct	Nov	Dec	Jan	Feb	Mar	Apr	May	Total
	0%	100%	83%	95%	74%	19%	33%	48%	60%	33%	54%
	12	11	11	10	14	16	16	14	15	14	
Team Pts:	4/12	4/9	7/12	4/9	2/15	4/12	6/9	6/12	6/15	2/9	45/114
Team Gls F:	3	3	9	5	3	7	5	8	4	1	48
Team Gls A:	5	4	6	5	8	12	4	8	4	2	58
Total mins:	0	270	299	256	331	70	90	173	270	90	1,849
Starts (sub):	0	3	4	3	4	1	1	2	3	1	22
Goals:	0	0	0	0	0	0	1	1	0	0	2
Assists:	0	0	2	0	1	0	0	0	0	0	3
Clean sheets:	0	0	0	0	0	0	1	0	1	1	3
Cards (Y/R):	0	1	0	1	0	0	0	0	1	1	4

League Performance Totals

Goals
- Rochemback: 2
- Team-mates: 45
- **Total: 47**
- own goals: 1

Assists
- Rochemback: 3
- Team-mates: 39
- **Total: 42**

Cards
- Rochemback: 4
- Team-mates: 50
- **Total: 54**

Cup Games

	Apps	Goals	Cards
UEFA Cup	6	0	1
FA Cup	5	1	1
Carling Cup	3	0	1
Total	**14**	**1**	**3**

Career History

Career Milestones

Club Debut:
vs Arsenal (H), W 2-1, Premiership
➡ 10.09.05

First Goal Scored for the Club:
vs Chelsea (H), W 3-0, Premiership
➡ 11.02.06

Time Spent at the Club:
➡ 1 Season

Full International:
➡ Brazil

Premiership Totals
92-06

Appearances	22
Goals	2
Assists	3
Yellow Cards	4
Red Cards	0

Clubs

Year	Club	Apps	Gls
05-06	Middlesbrough	36	3
03-05	Sporting Lisbon		
01-05	Barcelona		
00-01	Internacional		

Off the Pitch

Age:

- Rochemback: 24 years, 5 months
- Team: 26 years, 1 month
- League: 26 years, 11 months

Height:
- Rochemback: 6'
- Team: 5'11"
- League: 5'11"

Weight:

- Rochemback: 13st 1lb
- Team: 12st 2lb
- League: 12st

14 Gaizka Mendieta
Midfield

Season Review 05/06

The Spanish midfielder will be looking to put behind him two injury-ravaged seasons in 2006-07. Mendieta had missed most of the 2004-05 season after damaging his cruciate ligaments. However, he fought back from injury and looked to have recaptured the form that once earned him a reputation as Europe's finest midfielder with a scintillating performance, capped by two goals, in October's 4-1 Premier League humbling of Manchester United. Sadly, the season would not have a happy ending. A training ground accident left him with a broken foot, bringing a premature end to his season and forcing him to sit out Boro's charge to the UEFA Cup final.

Player Performance 05/06

League Performance

Percentage of total possible time player was on pitch   ⊙ position in league table at end of month

Month:	Aug	Sep	Oct	Nov	Dec	Jan	Feb	Mar	Apr	May	Total
	43%	0%	79%	33%	37%	69%	88%	19%	0%	0%	37%
	12	11	11	10	14	16	16	14	15	14	
Team Pts:	4/12	4/9	7/12	4/9	2/15	4/12	6/9	6/12	6/15	2/9	45/114
Team Gls F:	3	3	9	5	3	7	5	8	4	1	48
Team Gls A:	5	4	6	5	8	12	4	8	4	2	58
Total mins:	155	0	286	90	168	249	238	68	0	0	1,254
Starts (sub):	2 (1)	0	3 (1)	1	2	3	3	1	0	0	15 (2)
Goals:	0	0	2	0	0	0	0	0	0	0	2
Assists:	0	0	1	0	0	1	0	0	0	0	2
Clean sheets:	0	0	0	0	1	1	2	0	0	0	4
Cards (Y/R):	0	0	0	0	1	0	1	0	0	0	2

League Performance Totals

Goals

- Mendieta: 2
- Team-mates: 45
- **Total: 47**
- own goals: 1

Assists

- Mendieta: 2
- Team-mates: 40
- **Total: 42**

Cards

- Mendieta: 2
- Team-mates: 52
- **Total: 54**

Cup Games

	Apps	Goals	Cards
UEFA Cup	6	0	1
FA Cup	6	1	0
Carling Cup	0	0	0
Total	**12**	**1**	**1**

Career History

Career Milestones

Club Debut:
vs Leicester (A), D 0-0, Premiership
▶ **26.08.03**

First Goal Scored for the Club:
vs Wigan (A), W 1-2, League Cup
▶ **29.10.03**

Time Spent at the Club:
▶ **3 Seasons**

Full International:
▶ **Spain**

Premiership Totals

92-06

Appearances	55
Goals	4
Assists	12
Yellow Cards	6
Red Cards	0

Clubs

Year	Club	Apps	Gls
03-06	Middlesbrough	75	6
02-03	Barcelona		
01-03	Lazio		
92-01	Valencia		
91-92	Castellon		

Off the Pitch

Age:

- Mendieta: 32 years, 2 months
- Team: 26 years, 1 month
- League: 26 years, 11 months

Height:
- Mendieta: 5'8"
- Team: 5'11"
- League: 5'11"

Weight:
- Mendieta: 10st 12lb
- Team: 12st 2lb
- League: 12st

17
Doriva
Midfield

Season Review 05/06

The evergreen Brazilian enjoyed another fine season as one of the Boro squad's unsung heroes, playing more games than in any of his previous three years with the club. Regularly called into action when Boro were forced to deal with injuries and fixture overloads, Doriva was the model of consistency, further enhancing his reputation as a players' player with his tough-tackling midfield displays. Although he was not called upon for the big end-of-season cup ties, he played his part in helping Boro navigate their way through the UEFA Cup's early stages, appearing in all of the group games. Released in July 2006 as Gareth Southgate looked to develop Boro's young stars.

Player Details:

Date of Birth:	28.05.1972
Place of Birth:	Sao Paulo
Nationality:	Brazilian
Height:	5'9"
Weight:	11st 7lb
Foot:	Right

Player Performance 05/06

League Performance

Percentage of total possible time player was on pitch   ⊙ position in league table at end of month

Month:	Aug	Sep	Oct	Nov	Dec	Jan	Feb	Mar	Apr	May	Total
	5%	21%	79%	9%	97%	70%	67%	31%	69%	33%	52%
	12	11	11	10	14	16	16	14	15	14	
Team Pts:	4/12	4/9	7/12	4/9	2/15	4/12	6/9	6/12	6/15	2/9	45/114
Team Gls F:	3	3	9	5	3	7	5	8	4	1	48
Team Gls A:	5	4	6	5	8	12	4	8	4	2	58
Total mins:	17	57	284	24	438	253	180	112	311	90	1,766
Starts (sub):	0 (1)	0 (2)	3 (1)	0 (3)	5	3	2	1 (1)	4	1	19 (8)
Goals:	0	0	0	0	0	0	0	0	0	0	0
Assists:	0	0	0	0	0	0	0	0	0	0	0
Clean sheets:	0	0	0	0	1	1	1	0	1	0	4
Cards (Y/R):	0	0	1	0	1	1/1	1	0	0	0	4/1

League Performance Totals

Goals

Doriva:	0
Team-mates:	47
Total:	**47**
own goals:	1

Assists

Doriva:	0
Team-mates:	42
Total:	**42**

Cards

Doriva:	5
Team-mates:	49
Total:	**54**

Cup Games

	Apps	Goals	Cards
UEFA Cup	8	0	0
FA Cup	3	0	0
Carling Cup	3	0	0
Total	**14**	**0**	**0**

Career History

Career Milestones

Club Debut:
vs West Brom (H), W 3-0, Premiership

05.04.03

First Goal Scored for the Club:
vs Notts County (A), W 1-2, FA Cup

08.01.05

Time Spent at the Club:

▶ **3.5 Seasons**

Full International:

▶ **Brazil**

Premiership Totals

92-06

Appearances	79
Goals	0
Assists	2
Yellow Cards	14
Red Cards	1

Clubs

Year	Club	Apps	Gls
03-06	Middlesbrough	110	1
00-03	Celta Vigo		
98-00	Sampdoria		
97-98	FC Porto		
95-97	Atletico MG		
93-94	Sao Paulo		

Off the Pitch

Age:

▶ Doriva: 34 years
▷ Team: 26 years, 1 month
| League: 26 years, 11 months

Height:

▶ Doriva: 5'9"
▷ Team: 5'11"
| League: 5'11"

Weight:

▶ Doriva: 11st 7lb
▷ Team: 12st 2lb
| League: 12st

19 Stewart Downing
Midfield

Player Details:

Date of Birth:	22.07.1984
Place of Birth:	Middlesbrough
Nationality:	English
Height:	5'11"
Weight:	11st
Foot:	Left

Season Review 05/06

Yet another comeback hero in a team that earned itself a reputation as the comeback kings in 2005-06. Downing bounced back from serious cruciate ligament damage to force his way into England's 2006 World Cup squad. The early-season injury threatened to wreck his hopes of building on his lone international cap, but the Park End-born left winger proved he could provide a valuable outlet for England thanks to his superb crossing ability. Memorably scored in the 3-0 win over Chelsea, but it was his crucial crosses against Roma and, decisively, Steaua Bucharest that clinched his place in Sven-Goran Eriksson's final squad.

Player Performance 05/06

League Performance

Percentage of total possible time player was on pitch   ⟳ position in league table at end of month

Month:	Aug	Sep	Oct	Nov	Dec	Jan	Feb	Mar	Apr	May	Total
	100%						67%				
	12	11	11	10	14	46% 16	16	14	40% 15	33% 14	29%
	0%	0%	0%	0%			2%				
Team Pts:	4/12	4/9	7/12	4/9	2/15	4/12	6/9	6/12	6/15	2/9	45/114
Team Gls F:	3	3	9	5	3	7	5	8	4	1	48
Team Gls A:	5	4	6	5	8	12	4	8	4	2	58
Total mins:	360	0	0	0	0	167	180	7	180	90	984
Starts (sub):	4	0	0	0	0	2	2	0 (1)	2	1	11 (1)
Goals:	0	0	0	0	0	0	1	0	0	0	1
Assists:	1	0	0	0	0	2	0	0	1	0	4
Clean sheets:	2	0	0	0	0	1	1	0	1	1	6
Cards (Y/R):	0	0	0	0	0	0	0	0	0	0	0

League Performance Totals

Goals
- Downing: 1
- Team-mates: 46
- Total: 47
- own goals: 1

Assists
- Downing: 4
- Team-mates: 38
- Total: 42

Cards
- Downing: 0
- Team-mates: 54
- Total: 54

Cup Games

	Apps	Goals	Cards
UEFA Cup	9	0	1
FA Cup	5	0	0
Carling Cup	0	0	0
Total	**14**	**0**	**1**

Career History

Career Milestones

Club Debut:
vs Ipswich (A), L 1-0, Premiership

 24.04.02

Time Spent at the Club:

5 Seasons

First Goal Scored for the Club:
vs Brentford (A), W 1-4, League Cup

 01.10.02

Full International:

England

Premiership Totals
92-06

Appearances	72
Goals	6
Assists	19
Yellow Cards	1
Red Cards	0

Clubs

Year	Club	Apps	Gls
03-03	Sunderland	7	3
01-06	Middlesbrough	104	8

Off the Pitch

Age:
- Downing: 21 years, 10 months
- Team: 26 years, 1 month
- League: 26 years, 11 months

Height:
- Downing: 5'11"
- Team: 5'11"
- League: 5'11"

Weight:

- Downing: 11st
- Team: 12st 2lb
- League: 12st

25 James Morrison
Midfield

Season Review 05/06

The U-20 England International started the season looking to secure a regular place in the first 11 – and ended it with a start in the UEFA Cup final. The talented young midfielder became a regular name on the teamsheet, his pace offering Boro a speedy outlet down the right side of midfield and causing opposition defenders countless problems. Scored in the 4-2 FA Cup quarter-final success over Charlton and played his part in many of the big end-of-season fixtures. The two-goal hero in the 2004 FA Youth Cup final, Morrison was joined in the first team by many of his former Academy team-mates as the season progressed.

Player Details:

Date of Birth:	25.05.1986
Place of Birth:	Darlington
Nationality:	English
Height:	5'10"
Weight:	10st 1lb
Foot:	Right

Player Performance 05/06

League Performance

Percentage of total possible time player was on pitch   ⊙ position in league table at end of month

Month:	Aug	Sep	Oct	Nov	Dec	Jan	Feb	Mar	Apr	May	Total
	50% 12	40% 11	11 / 1%	68% 10	74% 14	50% 16	14% 16	42% 14	77% 15	60% 14	49%
Team Pts:	4/12	4/9	7/12	4/9	2/15	4/12	6/9	6/12	6/15	2/9	45/114
Team Gls F:	3	3	9	5	3	7	5	8	4	1	48
Team Gls A:	5	4	6	5	8	12	4	8	4	2	58
Total mins:	179	108	3	183	335	180	39	152	346	162	1,687
Starts (sub):	2 (1)	2	0 (1)	2 (1)	4	2	1	2	4	2	21 (3)
Goals:	0	0	0	1	0	0	0	0	0	0	1
Assists:	1	0	0	0	1	1	0	2	0	0	5
Clean sheets:	1	0	0	0	1	0	0	0	1	0	3
Cards (Y/R):	0	0	0	0	0	0	0	0	0	0	0

League Performance Totals

Goals

▶ Morrison:	1
▷ Team-mates:	46
Total:	**47**
▶ own goals:	1

Assists

▶ Morrison:	5
▷ Team-mates:	37
Total:	**42**

Cards

▶ Morrison:	0
▷ Team-mates:	54
Total:	**54**

Cup Games

	Apps	Goals	Cards
UEFA Cup	9	0	0
FA Cup	3	1	0
Carling Cup	1	0	0
Total	**13**	**1**	**0**

Career History

Career Milestones

Club Debut:
vs Notts County (H), W 2-0, FA Cup

 03.01.04

Time Spent at the Club:

▶ **3 Seasons**

First Goal Scored for the Club:
vs Banik (A), D 1-1, UEFA Cup

▶ **30.09.04**

Full International:

▶ —

Premiership Totals

92-06

Appearances	39
Goals	1
Assists	6
Yellow Cards	1
Red Cards	0

Clubs

Year	Club	Apps	Gls
04-06	Middlesbrough	62	6

Off the Pitch

Age:

▶ Morrison: 20 years
▷ Team: 26 years, 1 month
❘ League: 26 years, 11 months

Height:

▶ Morrison: 5'10"
▷ Team: 5'11"
❘ League: 5'11"

Weight:

▶ Morrison: 10st 1lb
▷ Team: 12st 2lb
❘ League: 12st

15

Ray Parlour
Midfield

Season Review 05/06

Parlour has brought valuable experience to the Boro squad since ending a trophy-laden career with Arsenal to move north as Steve McClaren planned for Europe in 2004-05. Snapped up on a free transfer, the former England international was a regular choice in the Boro starting line-up in his first season, often playing along the right side of midfield, but also able to slot into a more central role. However, a knee ligament injury suffered early in 2005-06 sidelined him until January and he was unable to force his way back into the side on a regular basis.

Player Details:

Date of Birth:	07.03.1973
Place of Birth:	Romford
Nationality:	English
Height:	5'10"
Weight:	11st 12lb
Foot:	Right

Player Performance 05/06

League Performance

Percentage of total possible time player was on pitch   ○— position in league table at end of month

Month:	Aug	Sep	Oct	Nov	Dec	Jan	Feb	Mar	Apr	May	Total
	100%	43%	0%	0%	0%	25%	0%	32%	40%	37%	28%
Team Pts:	4/12	4/9	7/12	4/9	2/15	4/12	6/9	6/12	6/15	2/9	45/114
Team Gls F:	3	3	9	5	3	7	5	8	4	1	48
Team Gls A:	5	4	6	5	8	12	4	8	4	2	58
Total mins:	360	116	0	0	0	90	0	115	180	100	961
Starts (sub):	4	1 (1)	0	0	0	1	0	2	2	1 (1)	11 (2)
Goals:	0	0	0	0	0	0	0	0	0	0	0
Assists:	0	0	0	0	0	0	0	0	0	0	0
Clean sheets:	2	0	0	0	0	0	0	0	1	0	3
Cards (Y/R):	1	0	0	0	0	0	0	1	1	0	3

(Monthly league positions: Aug 12, Sep 11, Oct 11, Nov 10, Dec 14, Jan 16, Feb 16, Mar 14, Apr 15, May 14)

League Performance Totals

Goals
- ▶ Parlour: 0
- ▷ Team-mates: 47
- **Total:** 47
- ■ own goals: 1

Assists
- ▶ Parlour: 0
- ▷ Team-mates: 42
- **Total:** 42

Cards
- ▶ Parlour: 3
- ▷ Team-mates: 51
- **Total:** 54

Cup Games

	Apps	Goals	Cards
UEFA Cup	4	0	1
FA Cup	2	0	0
Carling Cup	0	0	0
Total	**6**	**0**	**1**

Career History

Career Milestones

Club Debut:
vs Newcastle (H), D 2-2, Premiership
▶ **14.08.04**

First Goal Scored for the Club:
—
▶ **—**

Time Spent at the Club:
▶ **2 Seasons**

Full International:
▶ **England**

Premiership Totals
92-06

Appearances	379
Goals	21
Assists	34
Yellow Cards	62
Red Cards	3

Clubs

Year	Club	Apps	Gls
04-06	Middlesbrough	60	0
91-04	Arsenal	468	32

Off the Pitch

Age:

- ▶ Parlour: 33 years, 2 months
- ▷ Team: 26 years, 1 month
- | League: 26 years, 11 months

Height:
- ▶ Parlour: 5'10"
- ▷ Team: 5'11"
- | League: 5'11"

Weight:

- ▶ Parlour: 11st 12lb
- ▷ Team: 12st 2lb
- | League: 12st

159

39 Lee Cattermole
Midfield

Player Details:

Date of Birth:	21.03.1988
Place of Birth:	Stockton-on-Tees
Nationality:	English
Height:	5'10"
Weight:	12st
Foot:	Right

Season Review 05/06

A season that began with the satisfaction of earning a regular place in the Boro reserves side ended with a substitute appearance in the UEFA Cup final for the Fairfield teenager. As the 2005-06 campaign got underway, 17-year-old Cattermole was delighted to be handed the captaincy of the young second-string side, but his performances – allied to a growing injury list – were rewarded with a first-team debut as substitute against Litex Lovech and a full debut in the pulsating atmosphere of a Tyne-Tees derby at Newcastle. His energetic, full-throttle midfield displays earned him cult status among the Riverside faithful and, at 18, he became Boro's youngest ever captain in the final league game at Fulham.

Player Performance 05/06

League Performance

Percentage of total possible time player was on pitch

position in league table at end of month

Month:	Aug	Sep	Oct	Nov	Dec	Jan	Feb	Mar	Apr	May	Total
	12	11	11	10	14	81% / 16	67% / 16	39% 14	15 / 24%	100% / 14	29%
	0%	0%	0%	0%	0%						
Team Pts:	4/12	4/9	7/12	4/9	2/15	4/12	6/9	6/12	6/15	2/9	45/114
Team Gls F:	3	3	9	5	3	7	5	8	4	1	48
Team Gls A:	5	4	6	5	8	12	4	8	4	2	58
Total mins:	0	0	0	0	0	290	180	139	108	270	987
Starts (sub):	0	0	0	0	0	3 (1)	2	1 (2)	1 (1)	3	10 (4)
Goals:	0	0	0	0	0	0	0	0	1	0	1
Assists:	0	0	0	0	0	0	0	1	0	0	1
Clean sheets:	0	0	0	0	0	1	1	1	1	1	5
Cards (Y/R):	0	0	0	0	0	1	1	0	1	1	4

League Performance Totals

Goals

- Cattermole: 1
- Team-mates: 46
- **Total: 47**
- own goals: 1

Assists

- Cattermole: 1
- Team-mates: 41
- **Total: 42**

Cards

- Cattermole: 4
- Team-mates: 50
- **Total: 54**

Cup Games

	Apps	Goals	Cards
UEFA Cup	5	0	3
FA Cup	5	0	1
Carling Cup	0	0	0
Total	**10**	**0**	**4**

Career History

Career Milestones

Club Debut:
vs Litex (H), W 2-0, UEFA Cup
15.12.05

Time Spent at the Club:
1 Season

First Goal Scored for the Club:
vs Man City (A), W 0-1, Premiership
02.04.06

Full International:
—

Premiership Totals

92-06

Appearances	14
Goals	1
Assists	1
Yellow Cards	4
Red Cards	0

Clubs

Year	Club	Apps	Gls
05-06	Middlesbrough	24	1

Off the Pitch

Age:

- Cattermole: 18 years, 2 months
- Team: 26 years, 1 month
- League: 26 years, 11 months

Height:

- Cattermole: 5'10"
- Team: 5'11"
- League: 5'11"

Weight:

- Cattermole: 12st
- Team: 12st 2lb
- League: 12st

34 Jason Kennedy
Midfield

Season Review 05/06

Hard-working midfielder Kennedy made his first Premiership start in the Academy-dominated team that took on Fulham in the last league game of the season. He had previously made his full first-team debut in the 2-0 UEFA Cup group win over Litex Lovech, while also enjoying further European experience with substitute appearances against Dnipro and Stuttgart. A goalscoring hero in Boro's 2004 FA Youth Cup success, Kennedy has adapted from striker to midfield role, displaying a first class attitude in his bid for ongoing progress.

Player Details:

Date of Birth:	11.09.1986
Place of Birth:	Roseworth
Nationality:	English
Height:	6'1"
Weight:	11st 10lb
Foot:	Right

League Performance Totals

[3 Premiership appearances]

Goals
- Kennedy: 0
- Team-mates: 47
- Total: 47
- own goals: 1

Assists
- Kennedy: 0
- Team-mates: 42
- Total: 42

Cards
- Kennedy: 0
- Team-mates: 54
- Total: 54

Cup Games

	Apps	Goals	Cards
UEFA Cup	3	0	0
FA Cup	0	0	0
Carling Cup	0	0	0
Total	3	0	0

11 Malcolm Christie
Forward

Season Review 05/06

The former Derby County striker has been plagued by injuries during his time with Boro but has proved he is full of bouncebackability. After countless setbacks in his bid to overcome double foot and leg fractures, Christie finally made his comeback in the latter stages of last season. He made a shock return as substitute away to Portsmouth in April before playing 45 minutes in the home win over West Ham, his first appearance at the Riverside for 14 months. From there he continued in his quest for full match fitness, playing in several league games, though he was unable to get back on the goals trail.

Player Details:

Date of Birth:	11.04.1979
Place of Birth:	Peterborough
Nationality:	English
Height:	6'
Weight:	11st
Foot:	Right

League Performance Totals

[6 Premiership appearances]

Goals
- Christie: 0
- Team-mates: 47
- Total: 47
- own goals: 1

Assists
- Christie: 0
- Team-mates: 42
- Total: 42

Cards
- Christie: 0
- Team-mates: 54
- Total: 54

Cup Games

	Apps	Goals	Cards
UEFA Cup	0	0	0
FA Cup	0	0	0
Carling Cup	0	0	0
Total	0	0	0

18 Massimo Maccarone
Forward

Player Details:

Date of Birth:	06.09.1979
Place of Birth:	luogo Galliate
Nationality:	Italian
Height:	5'11"
Weight:	11st 9lb
Foot:	Right

Season Review 05/06

The Italian striker ensured his place as a Riverside cult hero with his last-gasp, super-sub goalscoring heroics in Boro's dramatic UEFA Cup comebacks against Basel and Steaua Bucharest. Having spent most of the season in the shadows – or more accurately, on the bench – Boro's £8.15m record signing grabbed the glory with his unforgettable Euro performances. His 89th minute header against Steaua means he will be forever remembered as the man who sent Boro to the UEFA Cup final. And yet, Maccarone will no doubt look back on the season with some frustration, as he was unable to win a regular place and was often played on the right side of midfield.

Player Performance 05/06

League Performance

Percentage of total possible time player was on pitch   G position in league table at end of month

Month:	Aug	Sep	Oct	Nov	Dec	Jan	Feb	Mar	Apr	May	Total
	12 / 13%	60% 11 / 32%	11 / 0%	10 / 1%	14 / 0%	16	16 / 23%	14 / 27%	15 / 26%	39% 14	21%
Team Pts:	4/12	4/9	7/12	4/9	2/15	4/12	6/9	6/12	6/15	2/9	45/114
Team Gls F:	3	3	9	5	3	7	5	8	4	1	48
Team Gls A:	5	4	6	5	8	12	4	8	4	2	58
Total mins:	48	161	115	0	6	0	62	98	118	106	714
Starts (sub):	0 (2)	1 (2)	2	0	0 (2)	0	0 (2)	1 (1)	1 (1)	1 (1)	6 (11)
Goals:	0	1	0	0	0	0	0	0	1	0	2
Assists:	0	0	0	0	0	0	0	0	0	0	0
Clean sheets:	0	0	0	0	0	0	0	0	1	1	2
Cards (Y/R):	0	1	0	0	0	0	1	0	1	0	3

League Performance Totals

Goals
- Maccarone: 2
- Team-mates: 45
- **Total: 47**
- own goals: 1

Assists
- Maccarone: 0
- Team-mates: 42
- **Total: 42**

Cards
- Maccarone: 3
- Team-mates: 51
- **Total: 54**

Cup Games

	Apps	Goals	Cards
UEFA Cup	8	5	2
FA Cup	3	0	1
Carling Cup	2	0	0
Total	**13**	**5**	**3**

Career History

Career Milestones

Club Debut:
vs Southampton (A), D 0-0, Premiership
➡ 17.08.02

First Goal Scored for the Club:
vs Fulham (H), D 2-2, Premiership
➡ 24.08.02

Time Spent at the Club:
➡ 4 Seasons

Full International:
➡ Italy

Premiership Totals
92-06

Appearances	74
Goals	17
Assists	13
Yellow Cards	9
Red Cards	0

Clubs

Year	Club	Apps	Gls
05-05	Siena	18	8
04-04	Parma	12	2
02-06	Middlesbrough	94	23
00-02	Empoli		
99-99	Varese		
98-00	Prato		
98-98	Modena		
97-98	AC Milan		

Off the Pitch

Age:

- Maccarone: 26 years, 8 months
- Team: 26 years, 1 month
- League: 26 years, 11 months

Height:
- Maccarone: 5'11"
- Team: 5'11"
- League: 5'11"

Weight:
- Maccarone: 11st 9lb
- Team: 12st 2lb
- League: 12st

20 Aiyegbeni Yakubu
Forward

Player Details:

Date of Birth:	22.11.1982
Place of Birth:	Benin City
Nationality:	Nigerian
Height:	6'
Weight:	13st 1lb
Foot:	Right/Left

Season Review 05/06

The £7.5m signing from Portsmouth enjoyed a dramatic first season with the club, finishing the campaign as Boro's 19-goal top scorer and voted Player of the Year by the club and fans. He opened his scoring account with a great goal in the 2-1 home win over Arsenal and recorded memorable strikes against champions Chelsea and, crucially, from the spot in the UEFA Cup success over Roma. But Yakubu will feel he can do even better in 2006-07. The goals dried up in the latter stages of the season and he will have been frustrated to have lost out to Hasselbaink and Viduka for a starting place in the UEFA Cup final.

Player Performance 05/06

League Performance

Percentage of total possible time player was on pitch   ⊙ position in league table at end of month

Month:	Aug	Sep	Oct	Nov	Dec	Jan	Feb	Mar	Apr	May	Total
	59%	90%	100%	87%	97%	74%	82%	46%	80%	33%	76%
	12	11	11	10	14	16	16	14	15	14	
Team Pts:	4/12	4/9	7/12	4/9	2/15	4/12	6/9	6/12	6/15	2/9	45/114
Team Gls F:	3	3	9	5	3	7	5	8	4	1	48
Team Gls A:	5	4	6	5	8	12	4	8	4	2	58
Total mins:	211	244	360	234	435	265	222	165	360	90	2,586
Starts (sub):	3	3	4	3	5	3 (1)	2 (1)	1 (3)	4	1	29 (5)
Goals:	0	2	4	2	2	2	1	0	0	0	13
Assists:	0	1	1	1	0	0	2	1	0	0	6
Clean sheets:	1	0	0	0	1	0	2	1	1	0	6
Cards (Y/R):	0	0	0	0	0	0	0	0	0	0	0

League Performance Totals

Goals
- ▶ Yakubu: 13
- ▷ Team-mates: 34
- **Total: 47**
- ● own goals: 1

Assists
- ▶ Yakubu: 6
- ▷ Team-mates: 36
- **Total: 42**

Cards
- ▶ Yakubu: 0
- ▷ Team-mates: 54
- **Total: 54**

Cup Games

	Apps	Goals	Cards
UEFA Cup	14	2	0
FA Cup	7	4	1
Carling Cup	2	0	0
Total	**23**	**6**	**1**

Career History

Career Milestones

Club Debut:
vs Liverpool (H), D 0-0, Premiership
▶ **13.08.05**

Time Spent at the Club:
▶ **1 Season**

First Goal Scored for the Club:
vs Arsenal (H), W 2-1, Premiership
▶ **10.09.05**

Full International:
▶ **Nigeria**

Premiership Totals

92-06

Appearances	101
Goals	42
Assists	21
Yellow Cards	4
Red Cards	0

Clubs

Year	Club	Apps	Gls
05-06	Middlesbrough	57	19
03-05	Portsmouth	92	43
00-03	Maccabi Haifa		
99-00	Hapoel Kfar-Saba		
99-00	Gil Vicente		
98-99	Julius Berger		

Off the Pitch

Age:
- ▶ Yakubu: 23 years, 6 months
- ▷ Team: 26 years, 1 month
- | League: 26 years, 11 months

Height:
- ▶ Yakubu: 6'
- ▷ Team: 5'11"
- | League: 5'11"

Weight:
- ▶ Yakubu: 13st 1lb
- ▷ Team: 12st 2lb
- | League: 12st

9 Jimmy Floyd Hasselbaink
Forward

Season Review 05/06

A stunning second half to the season saw Hasselbaink at his lethal best, defying his years with a prolific goalscoring average. Often forced to sit it out on the bench during the early months, the previous season's top scorer was clearly unhappy to play second fiddle to Yakubu and Mark Viduka. But suggestions that he could be set to leave the club in January provided the springboard to a transformation in his fortunes. A stunning long-range strike against Basel in the UEFA Cup quarter-final was probably the pick of his 17 goals, a tally that topped his impressive 16-goal total in his first season with Boro. Released by new manager Gareth Southgate, he joined Charlton in July 2006.

Player Details:

Date of Birth:	27.03.1972
Place of Birth:	Paramaribo, Surinam
Nationality:	Dutch
Height:	6'
Weight:	13st 10lb
Foot:	Right

Player Performance 05/06

League Performance

Percentage of total possible time player was on pitch   ⊖ position in league table at end of month

Month:	Aug	Sep	Oct	Nov	Dec	Jan	Feb	Mar	Apr	May	Total
	64%	11	11	69%	14	39% 16	44% 16	14	15	14	
	12	10%	40%	10	24%			20%	16%	0%	32%
Team Pts:	4/12	4/9	7/12	4/9	2/15	4/12	6/9	6/12	6/15	2/9	45/114
Team Gls F:	3	3	9	5	3	7	5	8	4	1	48
Team Gls A:	5	4	6	5	8	12	4	8	4	2	58
Total mins:	231	26	144	187	110	139	118	73	72	0	1,100
Starts (sub):	3	0 (1)	1 (2)	2 (1)	1 (3)	1 (2)	2 (1)	1	1	0	12 (10)
Goals:	0	0	1	1	0	3	1	2	1	0	9
Assists:	0	0	0	1	0	0	1	1	0	0	3
Clean sheets:	0	0	0	0	0	1	0	0	0	0	1
Cards (Y/R):	1	0	0	0	1	1	0	1	0	0	4

League Performance Totals

Goals
- Hasselbaink: 9
- Team-mates: 38
- **Total: 47**
- own goals: 1

Assists
- Hasselbaink: 3
- Team-mates: 39
- **Total: 42**

Cards
- Hasselbaink: 4
- Team-mates: 50
- **Total: 54**

Cup Games

	Apps	Goals	Cards
UEFA Cup	13	4	2
FA Cup	6	3	2
Carling Cup	3	1	0
Total	**22**	**8**	**4**

Career History

Career Milestones

Club Debut:
vs Newcastle (H), D 2-2, Premiership

 **14.08.04**

Time Spent at the Club:

2 Seasons

First Goal Scored for the Club:
vs Newcastle (H), D 2-2, Premiership

 **14.08.04**

Full International:

Netherlands

Premiership Totals
92-06

Appearances	263
Goals	125
Assists	77
Yellow Cards	40
Red Cards	2

Clubs

Year	Club	Apps	Gls
04-06	Middlesbrough	89	33
00-04	Chelsea	177	88
99-00	Atletico Madrid		
97-99	Leeds	87	42
96-97	Boavista		
92-96	Campomaiorense		
90-92	AZ Alkmaar		
90-90	Telstar		

Off the Pitch

Age:

- Hasselbaink: 34 years, 2 months
- Team: 26 years, 1 month
- League: 26 years, 11 months

Height:
- Hasselbaink: 6'
- Team: 5'11"
- League: 5'11"

Weight:
- Hasselbaink: 13st 10lb
- Team: 12st 2lb
- League: 12st

36

Mark Viduka
Forward

Season Review 05/06

The Australian international enjoyed a rollercoaster season of mixed fortunes but ended it as Boro's talismanic striker, acting as the driving force in many of Boro's finest wins in a truly dramatic campaign. His total of 16 goals does not do justice to the quality of some of his strikes, most notably long-range bullets at Birmingham and Charlton, together with crucial strikes against Charlton again in the FA Cup and against Basel and Steaua in Europe. Injury hampered Viduka in the latter stages of the season and he was a big miss in the FA Cup semi-final against West Ham. Capped a dramatic campaign by captaining Australia in the World Cup finals during summer 2006.

Player Details:

Date of Birth:	09.10.1975
Place of Birth:	Melbourne
Nationality:	Australian
Height:	6'2"
Weight:	14st 4lb
Foot:	Right/Left

Player Performance 05/06

League Performance

Percentage of total possible time player was on pitch   ○ position in league table at end of month

Month:	Aug	Sep	Oct	Nov	Dec	Jan	Feb	Mar	Apr	May	Total
	65%	56%	13%	43% 10%	84%	75%	18%	94%	20%	0%	49%
	12	11	11	14	14	16	16	14	15	14	
Team Pts:	4/12	4/9	7/12	4/9	2/15	4/12	6/9	6/12	6/15	2/9	45/114
Team Gls F:	3	3	9	5	3	7	5	8	4	1	48
Team Gls A:	5	4	6	5	8	12	4	8	4	2	58
Total mins:	235	151	47	115	378	270	48	338	90	0	1,672
Starts (sub):	2 (2)	2	0 (2)	1 (1)	4 (1)	4	1 (1)	4	1 (1)	0	19 (8)
Goals:	2	0	0	1	0	0	0	4	0	0	7
Assists:	0	1	0	0	0	2	0	0	1	0	4
Clean sheets:	1	0	0	0	1	0	0	0	0	0	2
Cards (Y/R):	0	0	0	0	0	0	0	0	0	0	0

League Performance Totals

Goals
- ▶ Viduka: 7
- ▧ Team-mates: 40
- **Total:** 47
- ▪ own goals: 1

Assists
- ▶ Viduka: 4
- ▧ Team-mates: 38
- **Total:** 42

Cards
- ▶ Viduka: 0
- ▧ Team-mates: 54
- **Total:** 54

Cup Games

	Apps	Goal
UEFA Cup	9	6
FA Cup	5	2
Carling Cup	2	1
Total	**16**	**9**

Career History

Career Milestones

Club Debut:
vs Fulham (A), W 0-2, Premiership

▶ **25.08.04**

Time Spent at the Club:

▶ **2 Seasons**

First Goal Scored for the Club:
vs Fulham (A), W 0-2, Premiership

▶ **25.08.04**

Full International:

▶ **Australia**

Premiership Totals

92-06
Appearances	173
Goals	71
Assists	29
Yellow Cards	16
Red Cards	2

Clubs

Year	Club	Apps	Gls
04-06	Middlesbrough	64	23
00-04	Leeds	166	72
98-00	Celtic	46	31
95-98	Croatia Zagreb		
94-95	Melbourne K		

Off the Pitch

Age:

- ▶ Viduka: 30 years, 7 months
- ▧ Team: 26 years, 1 month
- | League: 26 years, 11 months

Height:

- ▶ Viduka: 6'2"
- ▧ Team: 5'11"
- | League: 5'11"

Weight:

- ▶ Viduka: 14st 4lb
- ▧ Team: 12st 2lb
- | League: 12st

Fame Academy

Boro have jobs for the boys

Boro were football's unofficial Academy award-winners last season as a steady of stream of locally-born players broke into the first-team squad.

In fact, the Teessiders left their rivals standing when it came to giving local youngsters the opportunity to shine in the Premier League.

While World Cup winger Stewart Downing and right-back Stuart Parnaby had already established themselves in the first-team squad, they were followed into Premiership action by no fewer than 14 more home-produced starlets during the 2005-06 campaign.

It culminated in Boro fielding an all-English 16 at Fulham on the final day of the Premier League season, with all but one of them – Malcolm Christie – born within 25 miles of the Riverside Stadium.

Incredibly, the average age of Boro's starting line-up on a proud day for the club's Academy was just 21, making them easily the youngest ever Premier League team. That average age duly dropped even further, to just 19, when 17-year-old Josh Walker and striker Tom Craddock, 19, replaced Jason Kennedy and Malcolm Christie.

On an occasion that saw club records re-written, Lee Cattermole became Boro's youngest captain of all-time, just six weeks after his 18th birthday.

Until then, Colin Cooper held the distinction of having been Boro's youngest and oldest skipper, having captained the side aged 21 and 38. So it was particularly fitting that on the day he lost his proud record as youngest captain he should make a late substitute appearance, receive the captain's armband from Cattermole and so, at the age of 39, extend his record as the oldest player to skipper a Boro side.

Indeed, eight of Cooper's team-mates at Craven Cottage weren't even born when he made his Boro debut back in November 1985.

Boro's ability to give youth a chance stems from the outstanding Academy under the guidance of David Parnaby, Ron Bone and Stephen Pears.

It first came to the fore in 2003 when Boro were FA Youth Cup finalists. Just 12 months later, they were back in the final, this time beating Aston Villa by a 4-0 aggregate.

No fewer than eight of the 2004 Youth Cup winners have gone on to play first-team football for Boro. Defenders Tony McMahon, Andrew Taylor, David Wheater and Matthew Bates have been joined in the Premiership by midfielders James Morrison, Jason Kennedy and Adam Johnson plus striker Tom Craddock.

In addition, Andrew Davies and Ross Turnbull from the 2003 final have made their mark in the first-team squad.

Incredibly, no fewer than 10 Boro teenagers appeared in Premier League action during 2005-06, a figure far higher than any other club.

And the MFC first team weren't the only beneficiaries of this commitment to young talent, as Boro supplied England's teams from U-16 to full level with more players than any other club.

Boro's team v Fulham, May 2006: Ross Turnbull, aged 21, born Bishop Auckland; Andrew Davies, 21, Stockton; Andrew Taylor, 19, Hartlepool; Matthew Bates, 19, Stockton; David Wheater, 19, Redcar; Lee Cattermole, 18, Stockton; Jason Kennedy, 19, Stockton; James Morrison, 19, Darlington; Adam Johnson, 18, Sunderland; Danny Graham, 20, Gateshead; Malcolm Christie, 27, Peterborough. Subs: Tom Craddock, 19; Josh Walker, 17; Colin Cooper, 39, Sedgefield; Tony McMahon, 20, Bishop Auckland; David Knight, 19, Sunderland.

▶ Lee Cattermole, became Boro's youngest captain of all-time just six weeks after his 18th birthday.

Pride of England

Boro's England youth representatives

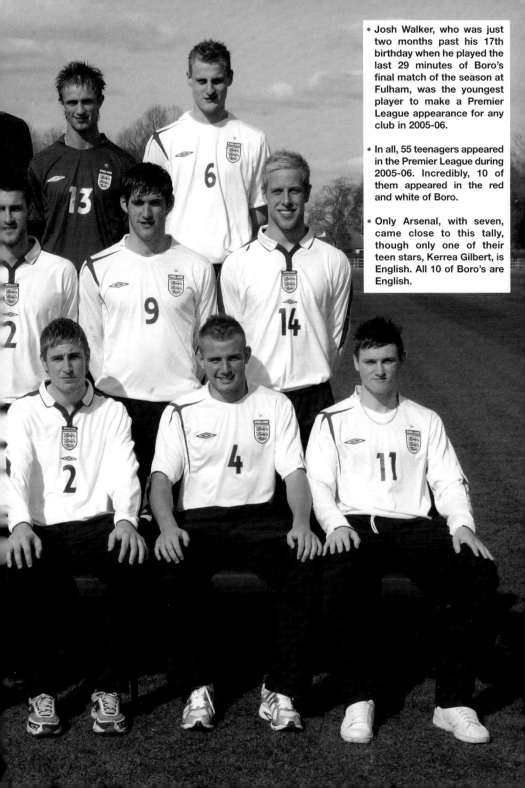

- Josh Walker, who was just two months past his 17th birthday when he played the last 29 minutes of Boro's final match of the season at Fulham, was the youngest player to make a Premier League appearance for any club in 2005-06.

- In all, 55 teenagers appeared in the Premier League during 2005-06. Incredibly, 10 of them appeared in the red and white of Boro.

- Only Arsenal, with seven, came close to this tally, though only one of their teen stars, Kerrea Gilbert, is English. All 10 of Boro's are English.

Arsenal °

Nickname:	The Gunners	Telephone:	020 7704 4000
Manager:	Arsène Wenger	Ticket Office:	020 7704 4040
Chairman:	Peter Hill-Wood	Club Shop:	020 7704 4120
Website:	www.arsenal.com		

Season Review 05/06

It was a season of mixed fortunes for an Arsenal side that grew up enormously over the course of the campaign.

Reaching the Champions League Final was a terrific achievement, with defeat to Barcelona tempered by Thierry Henry's decision to stay at the club. Prior to that, the Gunners said goodbye to Highbury by clinching fourth place at the expense of Tottenham.

Points / Position

won drawn lost H home A away

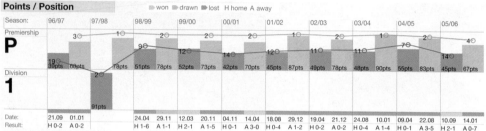

Season:	96/97	97/98	98/99	99/00	00/01	01/02	02/03	03/04	04/05	05/06
Premiership **P**	3	1	2	2	2	1	2	1	2	4
	19 39pts	68pts	9 78pts	12 51pts 78pts	14 52pts 73pts	12 42pts 70pts	11 45pts 87pts	11 49pts 78pts	7 48pts 90pts	14 55pts 83pts 45pts 67pts
Division **1**		2 91pts								

Date:	21.09	01.01	24.04	29.11	12.03	20.11	04.11	14.04	18.08	29.12	19.04	21.12	24.08	10.01	09.04	22.08	10.09	14.01
Result:	H 0-2	A 0-2	H 1-6	A 1-1	H 2-1	A 1-5	H 0-1	A 3-0	H 0-4	A 1-2	H 0-2	A 0-2	H 0-4	A 1-4	H 0-1	A 3-5	H 2-1	A 0-7

Recent Meetings

22.08.04	09.04.05	10.09.05	14.01.06
OO **5-3** Attendance: 37,415	OO **0-1** Attendance: 33,874	OO **2-1** Attendance: 28,075	OO **7-0** Attendance: 38,186
Referee: S.W.Dunn	Referee: P.Dowd	Referee: M.A.Riley	Referee: R.Styles
O 25 Henry O 43 Job	O 73 Pires	O 40 Yakubu O 90 Reyes	O 20 Henry O 59 Gilberto Silva
O 54 Bergkamp O 50 Hasselbaink		O 59 Maccarone	O 22 Senderos O 68 Henry
O 65 Reyes O 53 Queudrue			O 30 Henry O 84 Hleb
O 65 Pires			O 45 Pires
O 90 Henry			

Prem. Head-to-Head

Facts	O Boro	Arsenal O
Games		
Points	15	48
Won	4	15
Drawn	3	3
Goals		
For	20	55
Clean Sheets	2	9
Shots on Target	79	190
Disciplinary		
Fouls (5 years)	146	121
Yellow Cards	37	29
Red Cards	5	2

Goals by Area

O Middlesbrough   O Arsenal

	3	8	
16			39
1			8

Goals Scored by Period

1	1	8	6	2	2
0	15	30	45	60	75	90
6	8	10	10	8	13

Goals by Position

O Middlesbrough   O Arsenal

	forward:	13		forward:	32
	midfield:	3		midfield:	19
	defence:	1		defence:	3
	own goals:	3		own goals:	1

Average Attendance

▶ **29,801**

▶ **36,524**

All-Time Records

Total Premiership Record	O Boro	Arsenal O
Played	422	544
Points	516	1,013
Won	131	289
Drawn	123	146
Lost	168	109
For	506	911
Against	582	481
Players Used	132	113

All-Time Record vs Boro

Competition	Played	Won	Drawn	Lost	For	Against
League	112	57	27	28	221	131
FA Cup	8	5	1	2	16	12
League Cup	3	0	1	2	3	5
Other	0	0	0	0	0	0
Total	123	62	29	32	240	148

Aston Villa ○

Nickname:	The Villans	Telephone:	0121 327 2299
Manager:	David O'Leary	Ticket Office:	0121 327 5353
Chairman:	Doug Ellis	Club Shop:	0121 326 1559
Website:	www.avfc.co.uk		

Season Review 05/06

It was a season of frustration at Villa Park, with many disillusioned fans calling for the heads of Manager David O'Leary and Chairman Doug Ellis.

A 3-0 Carling Cup hammering at League One side Doncaster was the low point of a campaign in which Villa finished just eight points and two places away from relegation to the Championship.

Points / Position

won ▬ drawn ▬ lost H home A away

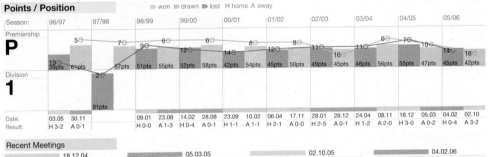

Season:	96/97	97/98	98/99	99/00	00/01	01/02	02/03	03/04	04/05	05/06
Premiership P	19○ 39pts	5○ 7○ 61pts	9○ 57pts 6○ 51pts	6○ 55pts	12○ 52pts 14○ 58pts	8○ 42pts 12○ 54pts	8○ 45pts 11○ 50pts	16○ 49pts 11○ 45pts	6○ 48pts 7○ 56pts	10○ 55pts 14○ 47pts	16○ 45pts 42pts
Division 1		2○ 91pts								
Date:	03.05 H 3-2	30.11 A 0-1	09.01 H 0-0	23.08 A 1-3	14.02 H 0-4	28.08 A 0-1	23.09 H 1-1	10.02 A 1-1	06.04 H 2-1	17.11 A 0-0	28.01 H 2-5	28.12 A 0-1	24.04 H 1-2	08.11 A 2-0	18.12 H 3-0	05.03 A 0-2	04.02 H 0-4	02.10 A 3-2
Result:										

Recent Meetings

○○○ 3-0 18.12.04 Attendance: 31,338
Referee: A.P.D'Urso
- ○ 20 Hasselbaink
- ○ 68 Job
- ○ 88 Reiziger

○○ 2-0 05.03.05 Attendance: 34,201
Referee: R.Styles
- ○ 64 Laursen
- ○ 79 Moore

○○ 2-3 02.10.05 Attendance: 29,719
Referee: M.L.Dean
- ○ 50 Moore
- ○ 90 Davis
- ○ 33 Yakubu
- ○ 64 Boateng
- ○ 88 Yakubu

○○ 0-4 04.02.06 Attendance: 27,299
Referee: L.Mason
- ○ 18 Moore
- ○ 24 Phillips
- ○ 62 Moore
- ○ 64 Moore

Prem. Head-to-Head

Facts	○ Boro	Aston Villa ○
Games		
Points	20	41
Won	5	12
Drawn	5	5
Goals		
For	22	40
Clean Sheets	5	10
Shots on Target	106	121
Disciplinary		
Fouls (5 years)	111	145
Yellow Cards	35	24
Red Cards	1	2

Goals by Area
○ Middlesbrough ○ Aston Villa

	3	9
19		28
0		3

Goals by Position
○ Middlesbrough ○ Aston Villa

Middlesbrough		Aston Villa	
▬ forward:	13	▬ forward:	26
▬ midfield:	4	▬ midfield:	7
▬ defence:	3	▬ defence:	6
▬ own goals:	2	▬ own goals:	1

Goals Scored by Period

0	3	6	2	5	6	
0	15	30	45	60	75	90
4	6	7	6	10	7	

Average Attendance

▶ **28,799**

▶ **30,276**

All-Time Records

Total Premiership Record	○ Boro	Aston Villa ○
Played	422	544
Points	516	767
Won	131	203
Drawn	123	158
Lost	168	183
For	506	668
Against	582	632
Players Used	132	120

All-Time Record vs Boro

Competition	Played	Won	Drawn	Lost	For	Against
League	122	56	28	38	218	156
FA Cup	5	2	2	1	10	8
League Cup	4	4	0	0	6	2
Other	0	0	0	0	0	0
Total	131	62	30	39	234	166

Blackburn Rovers ○

Nickname: Rovers
Manager: Mark Hughes
Chairman: John Williams
Website: www.rovers.co.uk

Telephone: 08701 113 232
Ticket Office: 08701 123 456
Club Shop: 0870 042 3875

Season Review 05/06

Mark Hughes guided Blackburn to sixth place and UEFA Cup qualification in his first full season in charge. Despite operating with a relatively small squad, the Ewood Park outfit also reached the last four in the Carling Cup.

Craig Bellamy proved to be a shrewd acquisition, whilst the likes of Steven Reid and Morten Gamst Pedersen really shone.

Points / Position

■ won ■ drawn ■ lost H home A away

Season:	96/97	97/98	98/99	99/00	00/01	01/02	02/03	03/04	04/05	05/06
Premiership **P**	19⊖ 39pts / 13⊖ 42pts	6⊖ 58pts	9⊖ 51pts / 19⊖ 35pts	12⊖ 52pts	14⊖ 42pts	12⊖ 45pts	10⊖ 46pts / 11⊖ 49pts	6⊖ 60pts / 11⊖ 48pts	15⊖ 44pts / 7⊖ 55pts	15⊖ 42pts / 14⊖ 45pts / 6⊖ 63pts
Division **1**		2⊖ 91pts		11⊖ 62pts	2⊖ 91pts					

Date:	19.03	08.05		17.10	03.04		20.04	01.12	31.08	01.01	07.02	26.12	05.02	16.10	26.12	18.03
Result:	H 2-1	A 0-0		H 2-1	A 0-0		H 1-3	A 1-0	H 1-0	A 0-1	H 0-1	A 2-2	H 1-0	A 4-0	H 0-2	A 2-3

Recent Meetings

16.10.04
○○ **0-4** Attendance: 20,385
Referee: M.A.Riley
- ○ 46 Hasselbaink
- ○ 50 Boateng
- ○ 57 Hasselbaink
- ○ 90 Hasselbaink

05.02.05
○○ **1-0** Attendance: 30,564
Referee: M.A.Riley
- ○ 35 Queudrue

26.12.05
○○ **0-2** Attendance: 29,881
Referee: U.D.Rennie
- ○ 38 Kuqi
- ○ 79 Kuqi

18.03.06
○○ **3-2** Attendance: 18,681
Referee: C.J.Foy
- ○ 11 Bellamy
- ○ 28 Pedersen
- ○ 68 Bellamy
- ○ 16 Viduka
- ○ 62 Rochemback

Prem. Head-to-Head

Facts	○ Boro	Blackburn ○
Games		
Points	28	22
Won	8	6
Drawn	4	4
Goals		
For	22	18
Clean Sheets	7	6
Shots on Target	97	89
Disciplinary		
Fouls (5 years)	122	140
Yellow Cards	32	33
Red Cards	3	2

Goals by Area
○ Middlesbrough ○ Blackburn

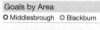

	4	6	
	15		9
3			3

Goals by Position
○ Middlesbrough ○ Blackburn

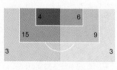 

	Middlesbrough	Blackburn
■ forward:	14	10
■ midfield:	6	5
■ defence:	2	2
■ own goals:		1

Goals Scored by Period

	0	1	6	6	4	5
0	15	30	45	60	75	90
	2	2	5	2	4	3

Average Attendance

▶ **28,646**
▶ **23,190**

All-Time Records

Total Premiership Record	○ Boro	Blackburn ○
Played	422	468
Points	516	695
Won	131	190
Drawn	123	125
Lost	168	153
For	506	650
Against	582	553
Players Used	132	124

All-Time Record vs Boro

Competition	Played	Won	Drawn	Lost	For	Against
League	106	46	26	34	180	147
FA Cup	8	4	2	2	12	7
League Cup	3	3	0	0	6	3
Other	0	0	0	0	0	0
Total	117	53	28	36	198	157

Bolton Wanderers °

Nickname: **The Trotters**
Manager: **Sam Allardyce**
Chairman: **Phil Gartside**
Website: **www.bwfc.co.uk**

Telephone: **01204 673 673**
Ticket Office: **0871 871 2932**
Club Shop: **01204 673 650**

Season Review 05/06

It was another encouraging season for Bolton, with a top-half finish and European adventure to boot. Games against the likes of eventual winners Sevilla in the UEFA Cup only served to raise the profile of the club.

A disappointing end to the campaign was attributed in many quarters to the incessant speculation linking boss Sam Allardyce to the England job.

Points / Position

■ won ■ drawn ■ lost H home A away

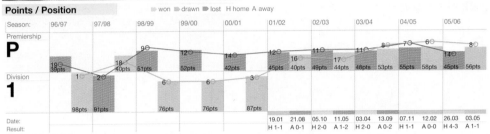

Season:	96/97	97/98	98/99	99/00	00/01	01/02	02/03	03/04	04/05	05/06
Premiership P			9○	12○	14○	12○ 45pts	11○ 49pts	11○ 48pts	8○ 55pts	6○ 8○ 56pts
	19○ 39pts	18○ 40pts	51pts	52pts	42pts	16 40pts	17○ 44pts	53pts	58pts	14○ 45pts
Division 1	1○	2○	6○	6○	3○					
	98pts	91pts	76pts	76pts	87pts					

Date:						19.01 H 1-1	21.08 A 0-1	05.10 H 2-0	11.05 A 1-2	03.04 H 2-0	13.09 A 0-2	07.11 H 1-1	12.02 A 0-0	26.03 H 4-3	03.05 A 1-1

Recent Meetings

○○ 1-1 07.11.04
Attendance: 29,656
Referee: P.Walton
○ 90 Boateng ○ 72 Pedersen

○○ 0-0 12.02.05
Attendance: 24,322
Referee: A.G.Wiley

○○ 4-3 26.03.06
Attendance: 25,971
Referee: H.M.Webb
○ 8 Hasselbaink ○ 3 Giannakopoulos
○ 30 Viduka ○ 58 Okocha
○ 47 Hasselbaink ○ 81 Jaidi
○ 90 Parnaby

○○ 1-1 03.05.06
Attendance: 22,733
Referee: H.M.Webb
○ 51 Vaz Te ○ 47 Johnson

Prem. Head-to-Head

Facts	○ Boro	Bolton ○
Games		
Points	14	17
Won	3	4
Drawn	5	5
Goals		
For	14	16
Clean Sheets	3	3
Shots on Target	63	69
Disciplinary		
Fouls (5 years)	139	145
Yellow Cards	23	25
Red Cards	1	1

Goals by Area
○ Middlesbrough ○ Bolton

	2	5	
12			7
0			4

Goals by Position
○ Middlesbrough ○ Bolton

	Middlesbrough	Bolton
▶ forward:	5	7
▶ midfield:	6	6
▶ defence:	2	3
▶ own goals:	1	

Goals Scored by Period

2	2	2	3	2	3
0	15	30	45	60	75	90
3	3	2	2	4	2

Average Attendance

▶ **28,700**
▶ **23,306**

All-Time Records

Total Premiership Record	○ Boro	Bolton ○
Played	422	266
Points	516	320
Won	131	81
Drawn	123	77
Lost	168	108
For	506	311
Against	582	386
Players Used	132	109

All-Time Record vs Boro						
Competition	Played	Won	Drawn	Lost	For	Against
League	102	46	25	31	171	150
FA Cup	7	1	3	3	2	7
League Cup	2	0	0	2	2	4
Other	0	0	0	0	0	0
Total	**111**	**47**	**28**	**36**	**175**	**161**

Charlton Athletic °

Nickname: The Addicks
Manager: Iain Dowie
Chairman: Richard Murray
Website: www.cafc.co.uk

Telephone: 020 8333 4000
Ticket Office: 020 8333 4010
Club Shop: 020 8333 4035

Season Review 05/06

The 2005-06 season will be remembered at Charlton as the last during Alan Curbishley's 15-year reign. A great start saw the Addicks win five of their first six league games, but they ultimately slipped to a respectable 13th-place.

Darren Bent arrived from Ipswich with a bang, firing in 18 goals to finish as the leading English marksman in the Premiership.

Points / Position

● won ● drawn ● lost H home A away

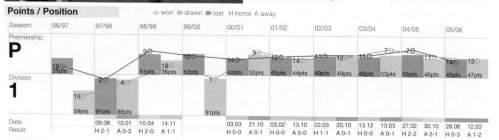

Season:	96/97	97/98	98/99	99/00	00/01	01/02	02/03	03/04	04/05	05/06
Premiership P			9	12	9	12	14	11	7	13
	19 39pts		51pts	52pts	42pts	52pts 45pts	14 44pts	49pts 49pts	11 48pts 53pts 55pts	14 46pts 45pts 47pts
Division 1	15	2 88pts	18 36pts		1					
	59pts	91pts		52pts	91pts					

Date:	09.08	10.01	10.04	14.11	03.03	21.10	03.02	13.10	22.03	20.10	13.12	13.03	27.02	30.10	28.08	12.03
Result:	H 2-1	A 0-3	H 2-0	A 1-1	H 0-0	A 0-1	H 0-0	A 0-0	H 1-1	A 0-1	H 0-0	A 0-1	H 2-2	A 2-1	H 0-3	A 1-2

Recent Meetings

	30.10.04		27.02.05		28.08.05		12.03.06
○○ 1-2	Attendance: 26,031	○○ 2-2	Attendance: 29,603	○○ 0-3	Attendance: 26,206	○○ 2-1	Attendance: 24,830

Referee: M.R.Halsey
○ 46 Johansson   ○ 21 El Karkouri (og)
○ 58 Zenden

Referee: M.A.Riley
○ 74 Riggott   ○ 14 Holland
○ 86 Graham   ○ 80 Bartlett

Referee: M.L.Dean
○ 38 Rommedahl
○ 81 Perry
○ 90 Bent D

Referee: A.G.Wiley
○ 73 Bent D   ○ 81 Viduka
○ 86 Bent D

Prem. Head-to-Head

Facts	○ Boro	Charlton ○
Games		
Points	13	22
Won	2	5
Drawn	7	7
Goals		
For	9	13
Clean Sheets	5	8
Shots on Target	76	57
Disciplinary		
Fouls (5 years)	131	138
Yellow Cards	14	23
Red Cards	0	0

Goals by Area

○ Middlesbrough ○ Charlton

	2	3	
6			7
1			3

Goals by Position

○ Middlesbrough   ○ Charlton

	Middlesbrough	Charlton
▶ forward:	4	▶ forward: 9
▶ midfield:	3	▶ midfield: 3
▶ defence:	1	▶ defence: 1
▶ own goals:	1	

Goals Scored by Period

	0	1	1	3	2	2
0	15	30	45	60	75	90
2	2	2	1	2	4	

Average Attendance

▶ **28,358**

▶ 23,420

All-Time Records

Total Premiership Record	○ Boro	Charlton ○
Played	422	266
Points	516	327
Won	131	85
Drawn	123	72
Lost	168	109
For	506	308
Against	582	382
Players Used	132	74

All-Time Record vs Boro

Competition	Played	Won	Drawn	Lost	For	Against
League	84	34	18	32	122	119
FA Cup	9	0	5	4	9	14
League Cup	1	1	0	0	2	1
Other	0	0	0	0	0	0
Total	94	35	23	36	133	134

Chelsea °

Nickname: The Blues
Manager: José Mourinho
Chairman: Bruce Buck
Website: www.chelseafc.com

Telephone: 0870 300 2322
Ticket Office: 0870 300 2322
Club Shop: 0870 300 1212

Season Review 05/06

Chelsea dominated the league season from start to finish, though they were less successful in cup competitions. Barcelona, Liverpool and Charlton ensured that Jose Mourinho had to content himself with the Premiership and Community Shield.

England internationals John Terry and Frank Lampard were once again star performers, whilst Joe Cole found the consistency to match his abundance of skill.

Points / Position

won drawn lost H home A away

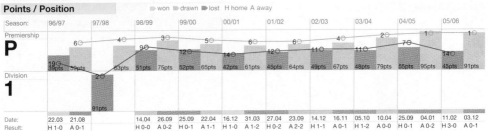

Season:	96/97	97/98	98/99	99/00	00/01	01/02	02/03	03/04	04/05	05/06
Premiership **P**	6	4	3	5	6	6	4	2	1	1
	19 59pts		9 63pts	12 51pts	14 75pts	12 52pts	6 65pts	11 42pts	11 61pts	7 45pts	14 64pts
Division **1**		2 91pts								
Date:	22.03 21.08		14.04 26.09	25.09 22.04	16.12 31.03	27.04 23.09	14.12 16.11	05.10 10.04	25.09 04.01	11.02 03.12
Result:	H 1-0 A 0-1		H 0-0 A 0-2	H 0-1 A 1-1	H 1-0 A 1-2	H 0-2 A 2-2	H 1-1 A 0-1	H 1-2 A 0-0	H 0-1 A 0-2	H 3-0 A 0-1

Recent Meetings

○○0-1 25.09.04
Attendance: 32,341
Referee: M.R.Halsey
○ 81 Drogba

○○2-0 04.01.05
Attendance: 40,982
Referee: S.G.Bennett
○ 15 Drogba
○ 17 Drogba

○○1-0 03.12.05
Attendance: 41,666
Referee: M.A.Riley
○ 62 Terry

○○3-0 11.02.06
Attendance: 31,037
Referee: S.G.Bennett
○ 2 Rochemback
○ 45 Downing
○ 68 Yakubu

Prem. Head-to-Head

Facts	○ Boro	Chelsea ○
Games		
Points	18	42
Won	4	12
Drawn	6	6
Goals		
For	13	28
Clean Sheets	7	13
Shots on Target	107	152
Disciplinary		
Fouls (5 years)	121	129
Yellow Cards	34	44
Red Cards	1	0

Goals by Area
○ Middlesbrough ○ Chelsea

	2	5	
9			16
2			3

Goals by Position
○ Middlesbrough ○ Chelsea

	Boro	Chelsea
▶ forward:	6	forward: 14
▶ midfield:	5	midfield: 7
▶ defence:	2	defence: 6
		▶ own goals: 1

Goals Scored by Period

1	0	4	3	3	2
0	15	30	45	60	75 90
3	3	7	6	4	5

Average Attendance

▶ **29,278**

▶ **33,267**

All-Time Records

Total Premiership Record	○ Boro	Chelsea ○
Played	422	544
Points	516	930
Won	131	261
Drawn	123	147
Lost	168	136
For	506	848
Against	582	556
Players Used	132	135

All-Time Record vs Boro

Competition	Played	Won	Drawn	Lost	For	Against
League	98	42	29	27	145	116
FA Cup	3	2	0	1	4	2
League Cup	3	2	0	1	6	4
Other	2	1	0	1	1	2
Total	**106**	**47**	**29**	**30**	**156**	**124**

Everton °

Nickname:	The Toffees	Telephone:	0870 442 1878
Manager:	David Moyes	Ticket Office:	0870 442 1878
Chairman:	Bill Kenwright	Club Shop:	0870 442 1878
Website:	www.evertonfc.com		

Season Review 05/06

Everton failed to follow up the amazing form of their previous campaign, but shrugged off a disappointing start to finish in mid-table. A return to European football brought only heartbreak, as the Toffees fell early in both the Champions League and UEFA Cup.

Nigel Martyn continued to defy his advancing years in goal, whilst James Beattie began to show what he could do at the other end.

Points / Position

won drawn lost H home A away

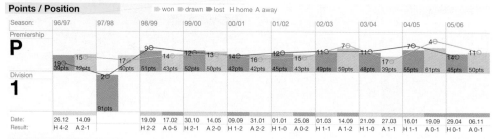

Season:	96/97	97/98	98/99	99/00	00/01	01/02	02/03	03/04	04/05	05/06
Premiership **P**	15 / 19 / 39pts	17 / 42pts	9 / 40pts	14 / 51pts / 43pts	12 / 13 / 52pts / 50pts	14 / 16 / 42pts / 42pts	12 / 15 / 45pts / 43pts	7 / 11 / 49pts / 59pts	17 / 11 / 48pts / 39pts	7 / 4 / 55pts / 61pts	14 / 45pts	11 / 50pts
Division **1**		2 / 91pts										
Date:	26.12	14.09		19.09	17.02	30.10	14.05	09.09	31.01	01.01	25.08	01.03	14.09	21.09	27.03	16.01	19.09	29.04	06.11
Result:	H 4-2	A 2-1		H 2-2	A 0-5	H 2-1	A 2-0	H 1-2	A 2-2	H 1-0	A 0-2	H 1-1	A 1-2	H 1-0	A 1-1	H 1-1	A 0-1	H 0-1	A 0-1

Recent Meetings

00 1-0 19.09.04 Attendance: 34,078
Referee: H.M.Webb
O 47 Bent M

00 1-1 16.01.05 Attendance: 31,794
Referee: D.J.Gallagher
O 26 Zenden   O 76 Cahill

00 1-0 06.11.05 Attendance: 34,349
Referee: M.A.Riley
O 16 Beattie

00 0-1 29.04.06 Attendance: 29,224
Referee: L.Mason
O 89 McFadden

Prem. Head-to-Head

Facts	O Boro	Everton O
Games		
Points	24	36
Won	6	10
Drawn	6	6
Goals		
For	24	35
Clean Sheets	3	7
Shots on Target	138	151
Disciplinary		
Fouls (5 years)	142	156
Yellow Cards	44	37
Red Cards	1	1

Goals by Area
O Middlesbrough O Everton

9	14
11	17
4	4

Goals by Position
O Middlesbrough O Everton

Middlesbrough		Everton	
forward:	9	forward:	16
midfield:	10	midfield:	9
defence:	3	defence:	10
own goals:	2		

Goals Scored by Period

	6	3	2	3	6	4
	4	6	5	8	5	7

0 15 30 45 60 75 90

Average Attendance

▶ 29,503
▶ 34,171

All-Time Records

Total Premiership Record	O Boro	Everton O
Played	422	544
Points	516	677
Won	131	177
Drawn	123	146
Lost	168	221
For	506	651
Against	582	739
Players Used	132	132

All-Time Record vs Boro

Competition	Played	Won	Drawn	Lost	For	Against
League	106	51	26	29	182	139
FA Cup	11	4	5	2	18	15
League Cup	5	2	2	1	7	6
Other	0	0	0	0	0	0
Total	122	57	33	32	207	160

Fulham

Nickname: The Cottagers
Manager: Chris Coleman
Chairman: Mohamed Al Fayed
Website: www.fulhamfc.com

Telephone: 0870 442 1222
Ticket Office: 0870 442 1234
Club Shop: 0870 442 1223

Season Review 05/06

Fulham experienced a real Jekyll and Hyde campaign, with an abysmal away record undoing much of their good work at Craven Cottage. It took Chris Coleman's team until April to win on the road, whilst they claimed 13 Premiership victories on home soil.

Luis Boa Morte excelled in his role as captain, notably scoring the only goal in a memorable win against local rivals Chelsea.

Points / Position

● won ● drawn ● lost H home A away

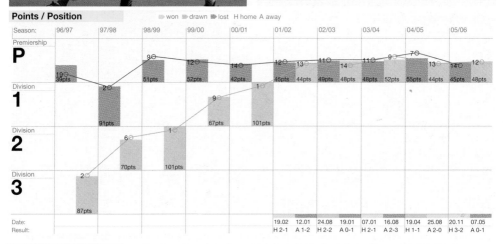

Season:	96/97	97/98	98/99	99/00	00/01	01/02	02/03	03/04	04/05	05/06
Premiership P			9○ 51pts	12○ 52pts	14○ 42pts	12○ 45pts	13 44pts	11○ 14 49pts	11○ 48pts	9○ 52pts	7○ 55pts	13○ 44pts	14○ 45pts	12○ 48pts
Division 1	19○ 39pts	2○ 91pts		9○ 67pts	1○ 101pts					
Division 2			6○ 70pts	1○ 101pts						
Division 3	2○ 87pts									
Date:						19.02	12.01	24.08	19.01	07.01	16.08	19.04	25.08	20.11	07.05
Result:						H 2-1	A 1-2	H 2-2	A 0-1	H 2-1	A 2-3	H 1-1	A 2-0	H 3-2	A 0-1

Prem. Head-to-Head

Facts	○ Boro	Fulham ○
Games		
Points	14	14
Won	4	4
Drawn	2	2
Goals		
For	15	14
Clean Sheets	1	2
Shots on Target	51	53
Disciplinary		
Fouls (5 years)	126	133
Yellow Cards	13	9
Red Cards	0	0

Goals by Area
● Middlesbrough ○ Fulham

	6	6
7		8
2		0

Goals Scored by Period

3	1	1	2	2	6
0	15	30	45	60	75	90
1	1	3	2	2	5

Goals by Position
● Middlesbrough ○ Fulham

● forward: 11   ● forward: 10
● midfield: 3   ● midfield: 4
● defence: 1   ● defence: 0

Average Attendance

▶ **28,188**

▶ **17,593**

All-Time Records

Total Premiership Record	○ Boro	Fulham ○
Played	422	190
Points	516	236
Won	131	63
Drawn	123	47
Lost	168	80
For	506	229
Against	582	258
Players Used	132	60

All-Time Record vs Boro

Competition	Played	Won	Drawn	Lost	For	Against
League	50	20	7	23	69	84
FA Cup	0	0	0	0	0	0
League Cup	0	0	0	0	0	0
Other	0	0	0	0	0	0
Total	**50**	**20**	**7**	**23**	**69**	**84**

Liverpool °

Nickname:	The Reds	Telephone:	0151 263 2361
Manager:	Rafael Benitez	Ticket Office:	0870 444 4949
Chairman:	David Moores	Club Shop:	0870 066 7036
Website:	www.liverpoolfc.tv		

Season Review 05/06

Liverpool added both the UEFA Super Cup and FA Cup to their collection, with captain Steven Gerrard winning the PFA Player of the Year award.

A clear improvement was also evident in the league, as Rafael Benitez's team finished 24 points better off than 12 months previously. In fact, only champions Chelsea could boast a better defensive record than the Merseysiders.

Points / Position

won   drawn   lost   H home   A away

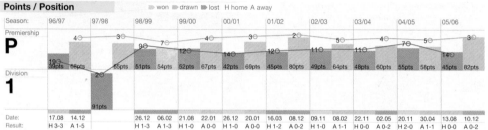

Season:	96/97	97/98	98/99	99/00	00/01	01/02	02/03	03/04	04/05	05/06
Premiership **P**	4	3	9 7	4	3	2	5	4	7 5	3
	19 39pts	68pts	65pts 51pts 54pts	52pts 67pts	42pts 69pts	45pts 80pts	49pts 64pts	48pts 60pts	55pts 58pts	14 45pts 82pts
Division **1**		2 91pts								
Date:	17.08 14.12		26.12 06.02	21.08 22.01	26.12 20.01	16.03 08.12	09.11 08.02	22.11 02.05	20.11 30.04	13.08 10.12
Result:	H 3-3 A 1-5		H 1-3 A 1-3	H 1-0 A 0-0	H 1-0 A 0-0	H 1-2 A 0-2	H 1-0 A 1-1	H 0-0 A 0-2	H 2-0 A 1-1	H 0-0 A 0-2

Recent Meetings

20.11.04	30.04.05	13.08.05	10.12.05
2-0 Attendance: 34,751	**1-1** Attendance: 43,250	**0-0** Attendance: 31,908	**2-0** Attendance: 43,510
Referee: S.G.Bennett	Referee: P.Dowd	Referee: M.R.Halsey	Referee: S.G.Bennett
O 36 Riggott	O 52 Gerrard O 4 Nemeth		O 72 Morientes
O 62 Zenden			O 77 Morientes

Prem. Head-to-Head

Facts	O Boro	Liverpool O
Games		
Points	22	37
Won	5	10
Drawn	7	7
Goals		
For	18	32
Clean Sheets	8	8
Shots on Target	86	166
Disciplinary		
Fouls (5 years)	141	111
Yellow Cards	40	29
Red Cards	2	1

Goals by Area
O Middlesbrough   O Liverpool

6	4
10	23
2	5

Goals by Position
O Middlesbrough   O Liverpool

forward:	8	forward:	16
midfield:	4	midfield:	8
defence:	5	defence:	8
own goals:	1		

Goals Scored by Period

3	1	6	1	3	4
0	15	30	45	60	75 90
5	4	8	3	5	7

Average Attendance

32,084

41,974

All-Time Records

Total Premiership Record	O Boro	Liverpool
Played	422	544
Points	516	931
Won	131	265
Drawn	123	136
Lost	168	143
For	506	868
Against	582	552
Players Used	132	108

All-Time Record vs Boro

Competition	Played	Won	Drawn	Lost	For	Against
League	128	54	37	37	222	166
FA Cup	1	1	0	0	2	0
League Cup	6	3	0	3	9	7
Other	0	0	0	0	0	0
Total	135	58	37	40	233	173

Manchester City ○

Nickname: The Citizens
Manager: Stuart Pearce
Chairman: John Wardle
Website: www.mcfc.co.uk

Telephone: 0870 062 1894
Ticket Office: 0870 062 1894
Club Shop: 0870 062 1894

Season Review 05/06

It was largely a season of disappointment for the blue half of Manchester. Stuart Pearce's team made an encouraging start to the campaign, but lost nine of their final ten games to slide down the table.

There was still reason for optimism, however, with the continued emergence of talented youngsters such as Micah Richards and Stephen Ireland.

Points / Position

won ▬ drawn ▬ lost H home A away

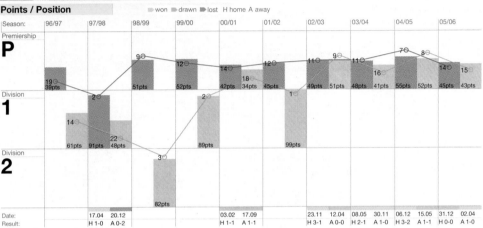

Season:	96/97	97/98	98/99	99/00	00/01	01/02	02/03	03/04	04/05	05/06
Premiership P	19 39pts	51pts	9	12 52pts	14 42pts	18 34pts 45pts	12 49pts	11 9 51pts 48pts	11 16 41pts	7 55pts	8 52pts	14 45pts	15 43pts
Division 1	14 61pts	2 91pts	22 48pts		2 89pts		1 99pts			
Division 2			3 82pts							
Date:		17.04 20.12			03.02 17.09		23.11 12.04	08.05 30.11	06.12 15.05	31.12 02.04
Result:		H 1-0 A 0-2			H 1-1 A 1-1		H 3-1 A 0-0	H 2-1 A 1-0	H 3-2 A 1-1	H 0-0 A 1-0

Prem. Head-to-Head

Facts	○ Boro	Man City ○
Games		
Points	32	5
Won	9	0
Drawn	5	5
Goals		
For	21	8
Clean Sheets	7	2
Shots on Target	67	66
Disciplinary		
Fouls (5 years)	89	112
Yellow Cards	21	21
Red Cards	1	2

Goals by Area
○ Middlesbrough ○ Man City

3	1
16	7
2	0

Goals Scored by Period

3 4 4 5 4 1
0 15 30 45 60 75 90
1 1 2 1 2 1

Goals by Position
○ Middlesbrough ○ Man City

	Middlesbrough	Man City
forward:	12	5
midfield:	4	2
defence:	3	0
own goals:	2	1

Average Attendance

▶ **28,669**

▷ **36,037**

All-Time Records

Total Premiership Record	○ Boro	Man City
Played	422	354
Points	516	410
Won	131	103
Drawn	123	101
Lost	168	150
For	506	413
Against	582	482
Players Used	132	126

All-Time Record vs Boro						
Competition	Played	Won	Drawn	Lost	For	Against
League	108	42	25	41	154	164
FA Cup	6	1	2	3	5	6
League Cup	3	1	0	2	5	3
Other	0	0	0	0	0	0
Total	**117**	**44**	**27**	**46**	**164**	**173**

Manchester United

Nickname:	The Red Devils	Telephone:	0870 442 1994
Manager:	Sir Alex Ferguson	Ticket Office:	0870 442 1994
Owner:	Malcolm Glazer	Club Shop:	0870 111 8107
Website:	www.manutd.com		

Season Review 05/06

A Carling Cup triumph and second place in the Premiership would be seen as success at most clubs, but not at Manchester United. In fact, Sir Alex Ferguson's charges never genuinely threatened Chelsea's grip on the title.

The performances of Wayne Rooney continued to win him admirers across the globe, with Edwin van der Sar providing calm assurance in goal.

Points / Position

won drawn lost H home A away

Season:	96/97	97/98	98/99	99/00	00/01	01/02	02/03	03/04	04/05	05/06
Premiership **P**	1	2	1	1	1	3	1	3	3	2
	19 39pts	9 75pts	9 77pts	12 51pts 79pts	14 52pts 91pts	12 42pts 80pts	11 45pts 77pts	11 49pts 83pts	7 48pts 75pts	14 55pts 77pts 45pts 83pts
Division **1**		2 91pts								

Date:	23.11	05.05	09.05	19.12	10.04	29.01	28.04	11.11	15.12	23.03	26.12	03.09	28.12	11.02	01.01	03.10	29.10	01.05
Result:	H 2-2	A 3-3	H 0-1	A 3-2	H 3-4	A 0-1	H 0-2	A 1-2	H 0-1	A 1-0	H 3-1	A 0-1	H 0-1	A 3-2	H 0-2	A 1-1	H 4-1	A 0-0

Recent Meetings

03.10.04	01.01.05	29.10.05	01.05.06
1-1 Attendance: 67,988	**0-2** Attendance: 34,199	**4-1** Attendance: 30,579	**0-0** Attendance: 69,531
Referee: R.Styles	Referee: A.G.Wiley	Referee: A.G.Wiley	Referee: C.J.Foy
O 81 Smith O 33 Downing	O 9 Fletcher O 79 Giggs	O 2 Mendieta O 90 Ronaldo O 25 Hasselbaink O 45 Yakubu O 78 Mendieta	

Prem. Head-to-Head

Facts	O Boro	Man Utd O
Games		
Points	20	41
Won	5	12
Drawn	5	5
Goals		
For	25	36
Clean Sheets	2	11
Shots on Target	96	159
Disciplinary		
Fouls (5 years)	126	129
Yellow Cards	35	40
Red Cards	1	2

Goals by Area
O Middlesbrough   O Man Utd

7	11
13	19
5	6

Goals Scored by Period

3	4	9	3	0	6
0	15	30	45	60	75	90
4	3	6	4	9	10

Goals by Position
O Middlesbrough   O Man Utd

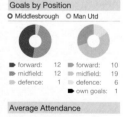

forward:	12	forward:	10
midfield:	12	midfield:	19
defence:	1	defence:	6
		own goals:	1

Average Attendance

▶ **32,415**

▶ **59,212**

All-Time Records

Total Premiership Record	O Boro	Man Utd O
Played	422	544
Points	516	1,143
Won	131	339
Drawn	123	126
Lost	168	79
For	506	1,057
Against	582	489
Players Used	132	99

All-Time Record vs Boro

Competition	Played	Won	Drawn	Lost	For	Against
League	96	47	20	29	169	145
FA Cup	12	6	3	3	21	11
League Cup	6	3	2	1	6	2
Other	0	0	0	0	0	0
Total	114	56	25	33	196	158

Newcastle United °

Nickname: The Magpies
Manager: Glenn Roeder
Chairman: Freddy Shepherd
Website: www.nufc.co.uk

Telephone: 0191 201 8400
Ticket Office: 0191 261 1571
Club Shop: 0191 201 8426

Season Review 05/06

Glenn Roeder was the toast of Tyneside as he led Newcastle from a position of adversity to Intertoto Cup qualification. The team collected 32 points from 15 games under the former West Ham boss, thus earning him the job on a permanent basis.

Alan Shearer finally hung up his boots, bowing out of competitive action with a goal in the 4-1 triumph at arch-rivals Sunderland.

Points / Position

■ won ■ drawn ■ lost H home A away

Season:	96/97	97/98	98/99	99/00	00/01	01/02	02/03	03/04	04/05	05/06
Premiership **P**	2○		9○	12○ 11○	11○	12○	4○ 3○	5○ 11○	7○ 14○	7○
	19○ 39pts 68pts	13○ 44pts	13○ 51pts 46pts	52pts 52pts	14○ 42pts 51pts	45pts 71pts	49pts 69pts	48pts 56pts	14○ 55pts 44pts	45pts 58pts
Division **1**		2○ 91pts								

Date:	22.02	03.11		06.12	01.05	02.05	03.10	16.10	17.03	08.09	26.12	05.03	04.11	18.10	21.02	14.08	27.04	09.04	02.01
Result:	H 0-1	A 1-3		H 2-2	A 1-1	H 2-2	A 1-2	H 1-3	A 2-1	H 1-4	A 0-3	H 1-0	A 0-2	H 0-1	A 1-2	H 2-2	A 0-0	H 1-2	A 2-2

Recent Meetings

■ 14.08.04	○○ **2-2** Attendance: 34,268	
Referee: S.G.Bennett		
○ 73 Downing	○ 14 Bellamy	
○ 90 Hasselbaink	○ 83 Shearer	

■ 27.04.05	○○○ **0-0** Attendance: 52,047	
Referee: M.R.Halsey		

■ 02.01.06	○○ **2-2** Attendance: 52,302	
Referee: S.G.Bennett		
○ 27 Solano	○ 54 Yakubu	
○ 90 Clark	○ 87 Hasselbaink	

■ 09.04.06	○○ **1-2** Attendance: 31,202	
Referee: A.G.Wiley		
○ 79 Boateng	○ 29 Boateng	
	○ 44 Ameobi	

Prem. Head-to-Head

Facts	○ Boro	Newcastle ○
Games		
Points	12	42
Won	2	12
Drawn	6	6
Goals		
For	19	36
Clean Sheets	2	6
Shots on Target	86	115
Disciplinary		
Fouls (5 years)	139	157
Yellow Cards	36	24
Red Cards	3	0

Goals by Area

○ Middlesbrough ○ Newcastle

Goals by Position

○ Middlesbrough ○ Newcastle

■ forward: 8	■ forward: 20
■ midfield: 7	■ midfield: 7
■ defence: 3	■ defence: 8
■ own goals: 1	■ own goals: 1

Goals Scored by Period

3	1	3	3	2	7
0	15	30	45	60	75 90
3	7	6	4	7	9

Average Attendance

▶ **32,525**

▶ **45,821**

All-Time Records

Total Premiership Record	○ Boro	Newcastle ○
Played	422	502
Points	516	786
Won	131	218
Drawn	123	132
Lost	168	152
For	506	761
Against	582	606
Players Used	132	125

All-Time Record vs Boro

Competition	Played	Won	Drawn	Lost	For	Against
League	108	43	31	34	158	132
FA Cup	2	0	0	2	3	6
League Cup	5	2	1	2	5	6
Other	0	0	0	0	0	0
Total	115	45	32	38	166	144

Portsmouth °

Nickname: **Pompey**
Manager: **Harry Redknapp**
Chairman: **Milan Mandaric**
Website: **www.pompeyfc.co.uk**

Telephone: 02392 731 204
Ticket Office: 0871 230 1898
Club Shop: 02392 778 552

Season Review 05/06

Portsmouth seemed destined to be relegated for much of the season, but were saved by a combination of Alexandre Gaydamak's millions and the nous of returning manager Harry Redknapp.

Having picked up just 18 points from their first 28 games, an astonishing turnaround in form saw the South Coast club collect a further 20 to beat the drop with a match to spare.

Points / Position

won ■ drawn ■ lost H home A away

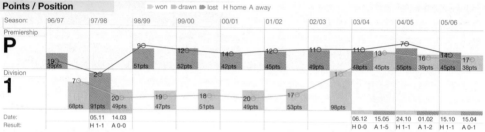

Season:	96/97	97/98	98/99	99/00	00/01	01/02	02/03	03/04	04/05	05/06
Premiership P			9○ 90	12○	14○	12○	11○	11○ 13○	7○ 16○	14○ 17○
	19○ 39pts		51pts	52pts	42pts	45pts	49pts	48pts 45pts	55pts 39pts	45pts 38pts
Division 1	7○	2○		19○	18○	20○	17○	1○		
	68pts	91pts	20○ 49pts	47pts	51pts	49pts	53pts	98pts		

| Date: | | | 05.11 | 14.03 | | | | | 06.12 | 15.05 | 24.10 | 01.02 | 15.10 | 15.04 |
| Result: | | | H 1-1 | A 0-0 | | | | | H 0-0 | A 1-5 | H 1-1 | A 1-2 | H 1-1 | A 0-1 |

Recent Meetings

24.10.04
○○ **1-1** Attendance: 30,964
Referee: M.Atkinson
○ 74 Downing ○ 5 Kamara

01.02.05
○○ **2-1** Attendance: 19,620
Referee: P.Crossley
○ 40 Taylor ○ 35 Christie
○ 58 Yakubu

15.10.05
○○ **1-1** Attendance: 26,551
Referee: C.J.Foy
○ 54 Yakubu ○ 46 O'Neil

15.04.06
○○ **1-0** Attendance: 20,204
Referee: A.Marriner
○ 54 O'Neil

Prem. Head-to-Head

Facts	○ Boro	Portsmouth ○
Games		
Points	3	12
Won	0	3
Drawn	3	3
Goals		
For	4	10
Clean Sheets	1	2
Shots on Target	34	31
Disciplinary		
Fouls (5 years)	68	68
Yellow Cards	6	8
Red Cards	0	1

Goals by Area
○ Middlesbrough ○ Portsmouth

Goals by Position
○ Middlesbrough ○ Portsmouth

	Middlesbrough	Portsmouth
■ forward:	2	7
■ midfield:	2	3
■ defence:	0	0

Goals Scored by Period

0	1	1	1	1	0
0	15	30	45	60	75	90
3	0	2	3	0	2

Average Attendance
▶ **28,515**
▶ **19,986**

All-Time Records

Total Premiership Record	○ Boro	Portsmouth ○
Played	422	114
Points	516	122
Won	131	32
Drawn	123	26
Lost	168	56
For	506	127
Against	582	175
Players Used	132	64

All-Time Record vs Boro						
Competition	Played	Won	Drawn	Lost	For	Against
League	94	34	23	37	134	153
FA Cup	6	2	3	1	10	8
League Cup	0	0	0	0	0	0
Other	0	0	0	0	0	0
Total	100	36	26	38	144	161

Reading

Nickname:	The Royals
Manager:	Steve Coppell
Chairman:	John Madejski
Website:	www.readingfc.co.uk

Telephone:	0118 968 1100
Ticket Office:	0870 999 1871
Club Shop:	0118 968 1234

Season Review 05/06

Reading were an unstoppable force as they blazed a trail towards promotion to the top-flight. The 106 points amassed by the Royals was a record for the second-tier of English football, whilst 99 goals were also scored along the way.

Manager Steve Coppell engendered a real spirit of togetherness amongst his troops, with no one player more important than the team.

Points / Position

won · drawn · lost H home A away

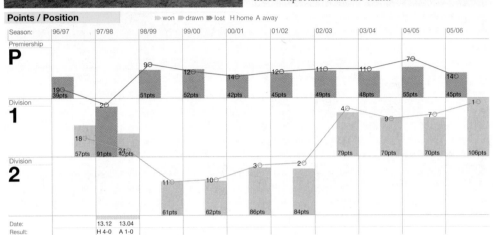

Season:	96/97	97/98	98/99	99/00	00/01	01/02	02/03	03/04	04/05	05/06
Premiership P	19 39pts		9 51pts	12 52pts	14 42pts	12 45pts	11 49pts	11 48pts	7 55pts	14 45pts
Division 1		18 57pts / 2 91pts	24 42pts				4 79pts	9 70pts	7 70pts	1 106pts
Division 2			11 61pts	10 62pts	3 86pts	2 84pts				

Date:	13.12	13.04
Result:	H 4-0	A 1-0

Prem. Head-to-Head

Facts	O Boro	Reading O
Games		
Points	0	0
Won	0	0
Drawn	0	0
Goals		
For	0	0
Clean Sheets	0	0
Shots on Target	0	0
Disciplinary		
Fouls (5 years)	0	0
Yellow Cards	0	0
Red Cards	0	0

Goals by Area
O Middlesbrough O Reading

	0	0
0		0
0		0

Goals Scored by Period

0	0	0	0	0	0	
0	15	30	45	60	75	90
0	0	0	0	0	0	

Goals by Position
O Middlesbrough O Reading

forward: 0	forward: 0
midfield: 0	midfield: 0
defence: 0	defence: 0

Average Attendance

All-Time Records

Total Premiership Record	O Boro	Reading O
Played	422	0
Points	516	0
Won	131	0
Drawn	123	0
Lost	168	0
For	506	0
Against	582	0
Players Used	132	0

All-Time Record vs Boro

Competition	Played	Won	Drawn	Lost	For	Against
League	12	2	6	4	8	17
FA Cup	0	0	0	0	0	0
League Cup	1	0	0	1	0	1
Other	0	0	0	0	0	0
Total	13	2	6	5	8	18

185

Sheffield United ○

Nickname:	**The Blades**	Telephone:	**0870 787 1960**
Manager:	**Neil Warnock**	Ticket Office:	**0870 787 1799**
Chairman:	**Derek Dooley**	Club Shop:	**0870 442 8705**
Website:	**www.sufc.co.uk**		

Season Review 05/06

Having been in the top-two for most of the season, few could argue that Sheffield United deserved to win promotion. Ten wins from the opening 11 games of the campaign laid the foundations for success.

Manager Neil Warnock continued to court controversy on the touchline, getting into a war of words with Norwich's Nigel Worthington and being sent to the stands against Leeds.

Points / Position

● won ● drawn ● lost H home A away

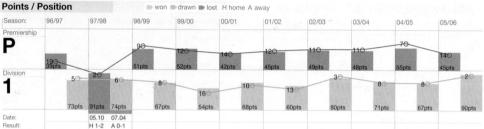

Season:	96/97	97/98	98/99	99/00	00/01	01/02	02/03	03/04	04/05	05/06
Premiership **P**	19○ 39pts		9○ 51pts	12○ 52pts	14○ 42pts	12○ 45pts	11○ 49pts	11○ 48pts	7○ 55pts	14○ 45pts
Division **1**	5○ 73pts	2○ 91pts	6○ 74pts	8○ 67pts	16○ 54pts	10○ 68pts	13○ 60pts	3○ 80pts	8○ 71pts	8○ 67pts	2○ 90pts
Date:		05.10.92	07.04.94							
Result:		H 1-2	A 0-1							

Recent Meetings

05.09.92	09.02.93	05.10.97	07.04.98
○○ 2-0 Attendance: 15,179	**○○ 2-0** Attendance: 15,184	**○○ 1-2** Attendance: 30,000	**○○ 1-0** Attendance: 18,421
Referee: A. Buksh	Referee: T. Ward	Referee: C.R. Wilkes	Referee: E. Lomas
○ 35 Falconer	○ 58 Carr	○ 19 Beck ○ 23 Deane	○ 52 Saunders
○ 83 Wright	○ 60 Deane	○ 59 Whitehouse	

Prem. Head-to-Head

Facts	○ Boro	Sheff Utd ○
Games		
Points	3	3
Won	1	1
Drawn	0	0
Goals		
For	2	2
Clean Sheets	1	1
Shots on Target	11	11
Disciplinary		
Fouls (5 years)	0	0
Yellow Cards	4	3
Red Cards	0	0

Goals by Area
○ Middlesbrough ○ Sheff Utd

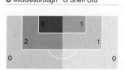

Goals by Position
○ Middlesbrough ○ Sheff Utd

● forward: 2   ● forward: 2
● midfield: 0   ● midfield: 0
● defence: 0   ● defence: 0

Goals Scored by Period

0	0	1	0	0	1
0	15	30	45	60	75	90
0	0	1	1	0	0

Average Attendance

▶ **15,179**

▶ 15,184

All-Time Records

Total Premiership Record	○ Boro	Sheff Utd ○
Played	422	84
Points	516	94
Won	131	22
Drawn	123	28
Lost	168	34
For	506	96
Against	582	113
Players Used	132	34

All-Time Record vs Boro

Competition	Played	Won	Drawn	Lost	For	Against
League	90	38	19	33	131	137
FA Cup	2	1	1	0	4	1
League Cup	0	0	0	0	0	0
Other	0	0	0	0	0	0
Total	92	39	20	33	135	138

Tottenham Hotspur °

Nickname:	Spurs
Manager:	Martin Jol
Chairman:	Daniel Levy
Website:	www.tottenhamhotspur.com

Telephone:	0870 420 5000
Ticket Office:	0870 420 5000
Club Shop:	020 8365 5042

Season Review 05/06

Despite being pipped to Champions League qualification by their great rivals Arsenal on the final day of the season, Spurs could still look back on a campaign in which they made tremendous progress.

Manager Martin Jol was unafraid to put his faith in youth, allowing the likes of Aaron Lennon and Michael Dawson to shine.

Points / Position

won drawn lost H home A away

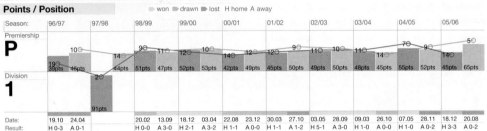

Season:	96/97	97/98	98/99	99/00	00/01	01/02	02/03	03/04	04/05	05/06
Premiership P	19 39pts	46pts 14	9 44pts	11 51pts	12 47pts	10 52pts	14 53pts	12 42pts	12 49pts	9 45pts	11 50pts	10 49pts	11 50pts	14 48pts	7 45pts	9 55pts	14 52pts	45pts	5 65pts
Division 1		2 91pts								

Date:	19.10	24.04		20.02	13.09	18.12	03.04	22.08	23.12	30.03	27.10	03.05	28.09	09.03	26.10	07.05	28.11	18.12	20.08
Result:	H 0-3	A 0-1		H 0-0	A 3-0	H 2-1	A 3-2	H 1-1	A 0-0	H 1-1	A 1-2	H 5-1	A 3-0	H 1-0	A 0-0	H 1-0	A 0-2	H 3-3	A 0-2

Recent Meetings

28.11.04
○○ **2-0** Attendance: 35,772
Referee: P.Dowd
○ 49 Defoe
○ 76 Kanoute

07.05.05
○○ **1-0** Attendance: 34,766
Referee: D.J.Gallagher
○ 11 Boateng

20.08.05
○○ **2-0** Attendance: 35,844
Referee: M.Atkinson
○ 49 Defoe
○ 75 Mido

18.12.05
○○ **3-3** Attendance: 27,614
Referee: H.M.Webb
○ 30 Yakubu ○ 25 Keane
○ 43 Yakubu ○ 63 Jenas
○ 69 Queudrue ○ 83 Mido

Prem. Head-to-Head

Facts	○ Boro	Tottenham ○
Games		
Points	32	26
Won	8	6
Drawn	8	8
Goals		
For	30	23
Clean Sheets	8	8
Shots on Target	133	125
Disciplinary		
Fouls (5 years)	119	124
Yellow Cards	30	46
Red Cards	1	2

Goals by Area
○ Middlesbrough ○ Tottenham

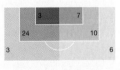

	Middlesbrough	Tottenham
	3	7
	24	10
3		6

Goals by Position
○ Middlesbrough ○ Tottenham

	Middlesbrough	Tottenham
forward:	19	16
midfield:	5	6
defence:	5	1
own goals:	1	

Goals Scored by Period

	4	6	6	4	6	4
0	15	30	45	60	75	90
	1	3	3	4	7	5

Average Attendance

▶ **29,901**

▶ **32,817**

All-Time Records

Total Premiership Record	○ Boro	Tottenham ○
Played	422	544
Points	516	728
Won	131	195
Drawn	123	143
Lost	168	206
For	506	716
Against	582	732
Players Used	132	139

All-Time Record vs Boro

Competition	Played	Won	Drawn	Lost	For	Against
League	74	24	18	32	112	130
FA Cup	4	3	1	0	9	2
League Cup	6	2	3	1	6	8
Other	0	0	0	0	0	0
Total	84	29	22	33	127	140

Watford °

Nickname:	The Hornets	Telephone:	0870 111 1881
Manager:	Adrian Boothroyd	Ticket Office:	0870 111 1881
Chairman:	Graham Simpson	Club Shop:	01923 496 005
Website:	www.watfordfc.co.uk		

Season Review 05/06

Watford were the surprise package of the Championship, finishing third and going on to gain promotion through the Playoffs.

Success was built around a belief instilled in his players by ultra-confident young boss Aidy Boothroyd. The likes of Marlon King and Matthew Spring were given a new lease of life, whilst Ashley Young and Jay DeMerit blossomed into stars.

Points / Position

▶ won ▶ drawn ▶ lost H home A away

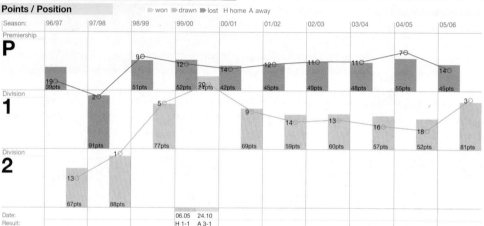

Season:	96/97	97/98	98/99	99/00	00/01	01/02	02/03	03/04	04/05	05/06
Premiership **P**			9○	12○	14○	12○	11○	11○	7○	14○
	19○ 39pts		51pts	52pts	42pts	45pts	49pts	48pts	55pts	45pts
Division **1**		2○	5○	20○ 29pts	9○	14○	13○	16○	18○	3○
		91pts	77pts		69pts	59pts	60pts	57pts	52pts	81pts
Division **2**	13○	1○								
	67pts	88pts								

Date:				06.05	24.10					
Result:				H 1-1	A 3-1					

Prem. Head-to-Head

Facts	○ Boro	Watford ○
Games		
Points	4	1
Won	1	0
Drawn	1	1
Goals		
For	4	2
Clean Sheets	0	0
Shots on Target	15	17
Disciplinary		
Fouls (5 years)	0	0
Yellow Cards	2	2
Red Cards	0	0

Goals by Area
○ Middlesbrough   ○ Watford

1	1	
3		1
0		0

Goals by Position
○ Middlesbrough   ○ Watford

▶ forward:	0	▶ forward:	0
▶ midfield:	2	▶ midfield:	1
▶ defence:	1	▶ defence:	1
▶ own goals:	1		

Goals Scored by Period

1	2	0	0	0	1
0	15	30	45	60	75	90
0	0	0	1	1	0

Average Attendance

▶ **32,930**

▶ 16,081

All-Time Records

Total Premiership Record	○ Boro	Watford ○
Played	422	38
Points	516	24
Won	131	6
Drawn	123	6
Lost	168	26
For	506	35
Against	582	77
Players Used	132	32

All-Time Record vs Boro						
Competition	Played	Won	Drawn	Lost	For	Against
League	20	7	4	9	23	30
FA Cup	1	1	0	0	1	0
League Cup	1	0	0	1	0	1
Other	0	0	0	0	0	0
Total	**22**	**8**	**4**	**10**	**24**	**31**

West Ham United °

Nickname:	The Hammers	Telephone:	020 8548 2748
Manager:	Alan Pardew	Ticket Office:	0870 112 2700
Chairman:	Terence Brown	Club Shop:	020 8548 2730
Website:	www.whufc.com		

Season Review 05/06

West Ham enjoyed a memorable return to the top-flight, finishing ninth and reaching the FA Cup Final. The Hammers came within four minutes of lifting the trophy, but were ultimately undone by some magic from Liverpool's Steven Gerrard.

Manager Alan Pardew won over his many critics with a stylish brand of attacking football firmly in keeping with the traditions of the club.

Points / Position

■ won ■ drawn ■ lost H home A away

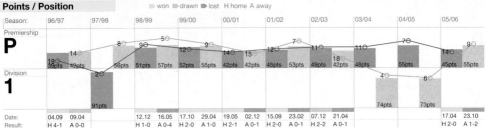

Season:	96/97	97/98	98/99	99/00	00/01	01/02	02/03	03/04	04/05	05/06
Date:	04.09	09.04	12.12	16.05	17.10	29.04	19.05	02.12	15.09	23.02	07.12	21.04			17.04	23.10
Result:	H 4-1	A 0-0	H 1-0	A 0-4	H 2-0	A 1-0	H 2-1	A 0-1	H 2-0	A 0-1	H 2-2	A 0-1			H 2-0	A 1-2

Recent Meetings

07.12.02	21.04.03	23.10.05	17.04.06
OO 2-2 Attendance: 28,283	**OO 1-0** Attendance: 35,019	**OO 2-1** Attendance: 34,612	**OO 2-0** Attendance: 27,658
Referee: G.Poll	Referee: A.G.Wiley	Referee: S.G.Bennett	Referee: M.Atkinson
O 58 Nemeth O 46 Cole J	O 77 Sinclair	O 66 Sheringham O 87 Queudrue	O 41 Hasselbaink
O 88 Ehiogu O 76 Pearce		O 74 Riggott (og)	O 57 Maccarone

Prem. Head-to-Head

Facts	O Boro	West Ham O
Games		
Points	26	20
Won	8	6
Drawn	2	2
Goals		
For	21	17
Clean Sheets	6	6
Shots on Target	99	112
Disciplinary		
Fouls (5 years)	71	86
Yellow Cards	28	28
Red Cards	2	2

Goals by Area
O Middlesbrough   O West Ham

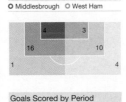

4	3
16	10
1	4

Goals by Position
O Middlesbrough   O West Ham

	Middlesbrough	West Ham
■ forward:	12	7
■ midfield:	5	6
■ defence:	4	3
■ own goals:		1

Goals Scored by Period

	1	5	5	5	0	5	
0	15	30	45	60	75	90	
2	1	2	2	4	6		

Average Attendance

▶ **29,954**

▶ **28,715**

All-Time Records

Total Premiership Record	O Boro	West Ham O
Played	422	426
Points	516	555
Won	131	148
Drawn	123	111
Lost	168	167
For	506	514
Against	582	590
Players Used	132	142

All-Time Record vs Boro

Competition	Played	Won	Drawn	Lost	For	Against
League	50	19	10	21	62	75
FA Cup	4	2	1	1	5	4
League Cup	0	0	0	0	0	0
Other	0	0	0	0	0	0
Total	**54**	**21**	**11**	**22**	**67**	**79**

Wigan Athletic °

Nickname:	The Latics	Telephone:	01942 774 000
Manager:	Paul Jewell	Ticket Office:	0870 112 2552
Chairman:	Dave Whelan	Club Shop:	01942 216 945
Website:	www.wiganlatics.co.uk		

Season Review 05/06

Wigan surprised pundits and supporters alike by finishing in the top half of the table. A trip to Cardiff in the Carling Cup Final also served to highlight just how far the club had come in such a short space of time.

The platform for success was built early in the season, with Paul Jewell's men amassing 25 points from their first 11 Premiership matches.

Points / Position

won drawn lost H home A away

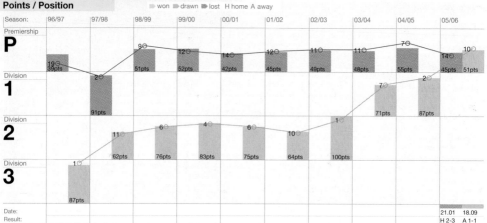

Season:	96/97	97/98	98/99	99/00	00/01	01/02	02/03	03/04	04/05	05/06
Premiership P			9	12	14	12	11	11	7	10
	19 39pts		51pts	52pts	42pts	45pts	49pts	48pts	55pts	14 45pts 51pts
Division 1		2 91pts						7 71pts	2 87pts	
Division 2		11 62pts	6 76pts	4 83pts	6 75pts	10 64pts	1 100pts			
Division 3	1 87pts									

| Date: | | | | | | | | | 21.01 | 18.09 |
| Result: | | | | | | | | | H 2-3 | A 1-1 |

Prem. Head-to-Head

Facts	○ Boro	Wigan ○
Games		
Points	1	4
Won	0	1
Drawn	1	1
Goals		
For	3	4
Clean Sheets	0	0
Shots on Target	7	14
Disciplinary		
Fouls (5 years)	25	22
Yellow Cards	1	2
Red Cards	0	0

Goals by Area
○ Middlesbrough ○ Wigan

	2	1
1		3
0		0

Goals Scored by Period

	1	0	0	1	1	0
	0	15	30	45	60	75	90
	1	1	0	0	1	1

Goals by Position
○ Middlesbrough ○ Wigan

	Middlesbrough	Wigan
forward:	3	3
midfield:	0	1
defence:	0	0

Average Attendance

▶ **27,208**

▶ 16,641

All-Time Records

Total Premiership Record	○ Boro	Wigan ○
Played	422	38
Points	516	51
Won	131	15
Drawn	123	6
Lost	168	17
For	506	45
Against	582	52
Players Used	132	25

All-Time Record vs Boro

Competition	Played	Won	Drawn	Lost	For	Against
League	4	1	2	1	4	5
FA Cup	0	0	0	0	0	0
League Cup	1	0	0	1	1	2
Other	0	0	0	0	0	0
Total	**5**	**1**	**2**	**2**	**5**	**7**

Premiership Results Table 2005/06

Legend:
- ▨ Won
- ▨ Drawn
- ■ Lost
- Yellow Card
- Red Card
- Goal

- **45** Time of 1st Sub
- **45** Time of 2nd Sub
- **45** Time of 3rd Sub
- **45** Time of Goal
- **45** Time of Assist

Match: Players: Substitutes:

Date	H/A	Opponent	H/T	F/T	Pos	First String											Substitutes (1st / 2nd / 3rd)
13-08	H	Liverpool	0-0	0-0	11	Schwarzer	Reiziger	Ehiogu	Southgate	Queudrue	Parlour	Boateng	Downing	Hasselbaink	Yakubu	Nemeth	Viduka · Bates
20-08	A	Tottenham	0-0	0-0	15	Schwarzer	Reiziger	Ehiogu	Southgate	Queudrue	Parlour	Morrison	Downing	Hasselbaink	Yakubu	Morrison	Viduka · Doriva
23-08	A	Birmingham	2-0	3-0	07	Schwarzer	Reiziger	Ehiogu	Southgate	Queudrue71	Parlour	Boateng28	Downing71	Hasselbaink8	Yakubu	Maccarone	Bates · Job
28-08	H	Charlton	0-1	0-3	07	Schwarzer	Reiziger79	Ehiogu	Southgate72	Queudrue	Parlour	Boateng	Downing	Hasselbaink	Viduka 14 45	Maccarone	Mendieta · Morrison
10-09	H	Arsenal	1-0	2-1	07	Schwarzer	Xavier	Ehiogu	Southgate	Queudrue16	Parlour	Boateng15 40	Downing	Hasselbaink73	Yakubu	Pogatetz	Doriva · Maccarone
18-09	A	Wigan	0-1	1-1	08	Schwarzer	Xavier	Ehiogu	Southgate	Queudrue	Morrison	Boateng	Rochemback73	Johnson	Viduka40 59	Pogatetz	Maccarone · Graham
25-09	H	Sunderland	0-1	0-2	11	Jones	Ehiogu	Southgate69	Queudrue	Morrison	Boateng	Rochemback	Johnson	Viduka14	Maccarone	Viduka · Hasselbaink
02-10	A	Aston Villa	1-0	3-2	09	Jones	Xavier	Riggott61	Southgate	Queudrue64	Morrison	Boateng 88	Rochemback	Nemeth	Yakubu	Maccarone1937	Parlour · Hasselbaink
15-10	H	Portsmouth	0-0	1-1	10	Schwarzer	Riggott	Southgate	Queudrue	Mendieta	Rochemback	Doriva	Yakubu	Queudrue	Parnaby · Viduka
23-10	A	West Ham	0-0	1-2	10	Schwarzer	Riggott	Southgate	Pogatetz88	Maccarone	Doriva90	Rochemback64	Viduka	Mendieta	Hasselbaink · Viduka
29-10	H	Man Utd	3-0	4-1	10	Schwarzer	Bates	Southgate	Pogatetz12 18	Doriva77	Rochemback76	Yakubu	Doriva	Nemeth · Viduka
06-11	A	Everton	0-1	0-1	13	Schwarzer	Ehiogu45	Southgate	Queudrue	Pogatetz	Mendieta	Rochemback64	Viduka45 78	Morrison · Doriva
20-11	H	Fulham	0-1	3-2	11	Schwarzer	Parnaby45	Riggott	Southgate	Queudrue	Pogatetz	Morrison64	Hasselbaink25	Yakubu	Doriva · Hasselbaink
27-11	A	West Brom	1-1	2-2	10	Jones	Parnaby	Riggott	Southgate	Queudrue	Pogatetz	Morrison	Mendieta	Hasselbaink76 8	Yakubu17	Nemeth · Doriva
03-12	A	Chelsea	0-0	0-1	10	Schwarzer	Parnaby	Riggott	Southgate	Queudrue	Pogatetz	Boateng	Cattermole45	Hasselbaink	Viduka	Doriva · Hasselbaink
10-12	H	Liverpool	0-0	0-2	10	Schwarzer	Bates66	Riggott	Southgate30	Queudrue	Morrison	Boateng	Cattermole65	Johnson57	Viduka6	Queudrue · Hasselbaink
18-12	A	Tottenham	2-1	3-3	11	Schwarzer	Bates41	Riggott84	Southgate	Doriva	Morrison	Boateng81	Taylor	Johnson	Yakubu18	Ehiogu · Maccarone
26-12	H	Blackburn	0-1	0-2	11	Schwarzer	Riggott45	Ehiogu	Southgate	Queudrue69	Doriva45	Boateng	Cattermole	Johnson31	Viduka	Doriva · Hasselbaink
31-12	A	Man City	0-0	0-1	14	Schwarzer	Riggott	Ehiogu	Southgate62	Pogatetz	Morrison54	Boateng	Cattermole	Rochemback69	Viduka	Nemeth6 · Hasselbaink
02-01	H	Newcastle	1-2	2-2	14	Jones	Parnaby	Ehiogu	Southgate	Pogatetz	Morrison	Doriva	Rochemback	Hasselbaink87	Viduka	Maccarone · Hasselbaink
14-01	A	Arsenal	0-4	0-7	14	Jones	Parnaby	Bates	Southgate	Taylor	Morrison	Cattermole	Mendieta	Viduka87	Bates90 · Maccarone
21-01	H	Wigan	0-2	2-3	17	Jones	Parnaby	Riggott	Southgate86	Pogatetz	Parnaby	Cattermole	Morrison	Viduka66	Hasselbaink · Hasselbaink
31-01	A	Sunderland	2-0	3-0	16	Bates31	Pogatetz19	Taylor	Parnaby	Cattermole	Downing56	Yakubu	Johnson · Cattermole90
04-02	H	Aston Villa	2-0	3-0	17	Schwarzer	Parnaby31	Southgate	Taylor	Mendieta71	Doriva60	Downing19	Viduka1	Davies · Hasselbaink
11-02	A	Chelsea	0-2	0-3	16	Schwarzer	Parnaby	Southgate	Pogatetz	Mendieta87	Cattermole	Downing42	Hasselbaink 7	Yakubu	Eniogu · Johnson
04-03	H	Birmingham	1-0	1-0	16	Schwarzer	Parnaby	Southgate68	Pogatetz	Mendieta	Cattermole	Doriva42	Yakubu32 68	Wheater · Yakubu
12-03	A	Charlton	0-0	0-3	15	Jones	Parnaby	Riggott	Southgate34	Pogatetz	Mendieta	Boateng	Cattermole49	Boateng62	Viduka45	Bates90 · Davies
04-04	H	Chelsea	1-0	1-0	15	Schwarzer	McMahon70	Eniogu	Southgate	Queudrue	Pogatetz	Boateng	Cattermole65	Taylor	Yakubu	Johnson · Maccarone
26-03	A	Blackburn	2-1	4-3	14	Schwarzer	Parnaby60	Riggott	Queudrue86	Boateng41	Maccarone	Taylor	Yakubu40	Pogatetz58 · Doriva
02-04	H	Bolton	1-0	1-1	14	Schwarzer	Davies	Eniogu	Queudrue47	Pogatetz28	Morrison	Boateng	Rochemback	Yakubu	Cattermole · Downing
09-04	A	Man City	1-0	1-1	14	Jones	Riggott	Eniogu	Morrison42	Boateng	Rochemback	Downing72	Yakubu	Davies · Yakubu
15-04	H	Newcastle	0-2	1-2	14	Jones	Davies59	Eniogu	Morrison	Boateng79	Rochemback66	Hasselbaink19 34	Yakubu	Maccarone73-46 · Viduka
17-04	A	Portsmouth	0-2	0-1	15	Schwarzer	Bates41	Riggott	Eniogu	Taylor	Boateng	Rochemback	Downing72	Yakubu	Davies · Maccarone
29-04	H	West Ham	1-0	0-1	15	Schwarzer	McMahon	Riggott	Eniogu	Queudrue	Morrison	Cattermole57	Johnson57 ↔	Yakubu	Cattermole · Doriva
01-05	A	Everton	0-0	1-1	14	Jones	Riggott	Eniogu	Queudrue	Morrison07	Boateng	Johnson43	Maccarone	Taylor · Graham
03-05	A	Bolton	1-1	1-1	13	Turnbull	Jones	Ehiogu	Bates14	Morrison	Cattermole	Parlour43	Maccarone57	Christie19	Johnson 47 ↔	Parlour · Taylor
07-05	A	Fulham	0-0	0-1	14	Turnbull	Davies	Wheater	Taylor	Morrison	Doriva75	Kennedy	Cattermole	Christie51 ↔	Graham51 ↔	Walker · Cooper

Middlesbrough EFL

Barclays Premiership 2006/07 — Premiership history

Date	Team	Home/Away	05-06	Played	History (96-97 → 05-06)	Goals for	Goals against	Scored first	Best result	Worst
19.08.06	Reading	A	N/A	0		0	0	0	N/A	N/A
22.08.06	Chelsea	H	3-0	11		9	7	5	3-0	0-2
28.08.06	Portsmouth	H	1-1	3		2	2	0	1-1	1-1
09.09.06	Arsenal	A	0-7	11		12	30	5	3-0	0-7
16.09.06	Bolton	A	1-1	6		3	7	1	1-1	0-2
23.09.06	Blackburn	H	0-2	9		12	10	4	2-0	1-3
30.09.06	Sheff Utd	A	N/A	1		0	2	0	0-2	0-2
14.10.06	Everton	H	0-1	11		14	14	6	4-2	0-2
21.10.06	Newcastle	H	1-2	10		11	19	5	1-0	1-4
30.10.06	Man City	A	1-0	7		6	2	6	1-0	1-1
04.11.06	Watford	A	N/A	1		3	1	1	3-1	3-1
11.11.06	West Ham	H	2-0	8		19	6	7	4-1	2-2
18.11.06	Liverpool	H	0-0	11		13	11	5	2-0	1-3
25.11.06	Aston Villa	A	3-2	11		8	16	2	2-0	1-5
02.12.06	Man Utd	H	4-1	11		13	19	3	4-1	0-3
05.12.06	Tottenham	A	0-2	11		13	12	4	3-0	0-2
09.12.06	Wigan	H	2-3	1		2	3	0	2-3	2-3
16.12.06	Fulham	A	0-1	5		5	7	3	2-0	2-3
23.12.06	Charlton	H	0-3	7		5	6	1	2-0	0-3
26.12.06	Everton	A	0-1	11		10	21	3	2-0	0-5
30.12.06	Blackburn	A	2-3	9		10	8	2	4-0	2-3
01.01.07	Sheff Utd	H	N/A	1		2	0	1	2-0	2-0
13.01.07	Charlton	A	1-2	7		4	7	1	2-1	1-2
20.01.07	Bolton	H	4-3	6		11	9	3	2-0	1-4
30.01.07	Portsmouth	A	0-1	3		2	8	1	1-5	1-5
03.02.07	Arsenal	H	2-1	11		8	25	3	2-1	1-6
10.02.07	Chelsea	A	0-1	11		4	21	0	2-2	0-5
24.02.07	Reading	H	N/A	0		0	0	0	N/A	N/A
03.03.07	Newcastle	A	2-2	10		8	17	3	2-1	0-3
17.03.07	Man City	H	0-0	7		15	6	4	4-1	1-1
31.03.07	West Ham	A	1-2	8		2	11	1	1-0	0-4
07.04.07	Watford	H	N/A	1		1	1	1	1-1	1-1
09.04.07	Liverpool	A	0-2	11		5	21	2	1-1	1-5
14.04.07	Aston Villa	H	0-4	11		14	24	4	3-0	0-4
21.04.07	Man Utd	A	0-0	11		12	17	6	3-2	0-3
28.04.07	Tottenham	H	3-3	11		17	11	4	5-1	0-3
05.05.07	Wigan	A	1-1	1		1	1	1	1-1	1-1
13.05.07	Fulham	H	3-2	5		10	7	3	3-2	2-2

Legend: ■ won ■ drawn ■ lost □ not played